Forests of Himalaya: Planning and Development

Forests of Himalaya: Planning and Development

Anuraj Diwedi

CYBER TECH PUBLICATIONS
4264/3, Ansari Road, Daryaganj, New Delhi-110002 (India)
Ph.: 011-23244078. Fax: 011-23280028
E-Mail: cyberpublicationsdelhi@yahoo.com

FORESTS OF HIMALAYA: PLANNING AND DEVELOPMENT

Anuraj Diwedi

First Edition 2009

Published by :

G.S. Rawat for **Cyber Tech Publications**
4264/3, Ansari Road, Daryaganj, New Delhi-110002 (India)
Ph.: 011-23244078. Fax: 011-23280028
E-Mail: cyberpublicationsdelhi@yahoo.com

Printed at Asian Offset Printers

Preface

Development objectives reflect planning process, which consistently emphasized the necessity of promoting polices and programmes of economic growth and social welfare. The economic development of a country or region is generally expressed in terms of the growth of its income. The value of the final product excluding the value of inputs used in the process of production is termed as the Gross National Product (GNP). However, these indicators of economic development do not take into account the use and depreciation of the renewable or non-renewable natural resources. As environment being a multi-disciplinary subject involving complex themes like biodiversity, atmosphere, water, land, soil, human settlements, human activities and many others, it is quite difficult to collect, analyze and study relationships among these various components. Hence, there is an urgent need to develop an environmental-economic accounting system to maintain natural resource accounts in totality. Management of natural resources is in the frontline of the struggle for more sustainable and equitable development and environmental degradation is one of the indicators of unsustainable social and economic systems. The information resources management has direct consequences on the quality and quantity of natural resources of any region. The main objective of the information resources management is to promote the understanding, development and practice of managing information resources as key enterprise assets.

The mountain ecosystems are susceptible to accelerated soil erosion, landslides and rapid loss of habitat and genetic diversity. On the human side, there is widespread poverty among mountain inhabitants and loss of indigenous knowledge. In many mountain regions, there is vertical gradient to poverty as about 80% of the people who live there area impoverished. As a result, most of the global mountain areas are experiencing environmental degradation. Hence, proper management of mountain resources and socio-economic development of the people deserves immediate attention.

—Author

CONTENTS

1

Himalaya: An Introduction

In these hills, Nature's hospitality eclipses all men can ever do. The enchanting beauties of the himalayas, their bracing climate and the soothing green that envelope you leaves nothing more to be desired. I wonder whether the scenery of these hills and the climate are to be surpassed, if qualified, by any of the baeuty spots of the world.

Himalayas, also Him+alaya (Sanskrit for "abode of snow"), mountain system in Asia, forming a broad continuous arc for nearly 2600 km (1600 mi) along the northern fringes of the Indian subcontinent, from the bend of the Indus River in the northwest to the Brahmaputra River in the east. The Himalayas range, averaging 320 to 400 km (200 to 250 mi) in width, rises sharply from the Gangetic Plain. North of this mountain belt lies the Tibetan Plateau (Qing Zang Gaoyuan). The Himalayas form the earth's highest mountain region, containing 9 of the 10 highest peaks in the world. Among these peaks are the world's highest mountain, Mount Everest (8848 m/29,028 ft), which is on the Nepal-Tibet border; the second highest peak, K2 or Mount Godwin Austen (8,611 m/28,251 ft), located on the border between China and Jammu and Kashmir, a territory claimed by India and Pakistan; the third highest peak, Kanchenjunga (8,598 m/28,209 ft) on the Nepal-India border; Makalu (8481 m/27,824 ft) on the Nepal-Tibet border; Dhaulagiri (8,172 m/26,811 ft) and Annapurna 1 (8,091 m/26,545 ft) in Nepal; Nanga Parbat (8,125 m/26,657 ft) in the Pakistani-controlled portion of Jammu and Kashmir; and Nanda Devi (7817 m/25,645 ft) in India.

Geologic Formation and Structure

The Himalayan mountain system developed in a series of stages 30 to 50 million years ago. The Himalayan range was created from powerful earth movements that occurred as the Indian plate pressed against the Eurasian continental plate. The earth movements raised the deposits laid down in the ancient, shallow Tethys Sea (on the present site of the mountains) to form the Himalayan ranges from Pakistan eastward across northern India, and from Nepal and Bhutan to the Myanmar (Burmese) border. Even today the mountains continue to develop and change, and earthquakes and tremors are frequent in the area

TOPOGRAPHY

Physically, the Himalayas forms three parallel zones: the Great Himalayas, the Middle Himalayas (also known as the Inner or Lesser Himalayas), and the Sub-Himalayas, which includes the Siwalik Range and foothills and the Tarai and Duars *piedmont* (an area of land formed or lying at the foot of a mountain or mountain range). Each of these lateral divisions exhibit certain similar topographic features. The Great Himalayas, the highest zone, consists of a huge line of snowy peaks with an average height exceeding 6100 m (20,000 ft). The width of this zone, composed largely but not entirely of gneiss and granite, is about 24 km (about 15 mi). Spurs from the Great Himalayas project southwards into the Middle Himalayas in an irregular fashion. The Nepal and Sikkim (a state of northern India) portion of the Great Himalayas contains the greatest number of high peaks. The snow line on the southern slopes of the Great Himalayas varies from 4480 m (14,700 ft) in the eastern and central Himalayas of Nepal and Sikkim to 5180 m (17,000 ft) in the western Himalayas. To the north of the Great Himalayas are several ranges such as the Zaskar, Ladakh, and the Kailas. The Karakoram Range lies on the Tibetan side of the Great Himalayas.

The Great Himalayan region is one of the few remaining isolated and inaccessible areas in the world today. Some high valleys in the Great Himalayas are occupied by small clustered settlements. Extremely cold winters and a short growing season limit the farmers to one crop per year, most commonly potatoes or barley. The formidable mountains have limited the development of large-scale trade and commerce despite the construction of highways across the mountains linking Nepal and Pakistan to China. Older trails, which cross the mountains at high passes, also have limited trade and are open only during the summer months.

The Middle Himalayas range, which has a width of about 80 km (about 50 mi), borders the Great Himalayan range on the south. It consists principally of high ranges both within and outside of the Great Himalayan range. Some of the ranges of the Middle Himalayas are the Nag Tibba, the Dhaola Dhar, the Pir Panjal, and the Mahabharat. The Middle Himalayas possess a remarkable uniformity of height; most are between 1830 and 3050 m (between 6000 and 10,000 ft).

The Middle Himalayas region is a complex mosaic of forest-covered ranges and fertile valleys. While not as forbidding as the Great Himalayas to the north, this range has nonetheless served to isolate the valleys of the Himalayas from the plains of the Indus and Ganges rivers in Pakistan and northern India. Except for the major valley centers such as Srinagar, Kangra, and Kathmandu, and hill towns such as Simla, Mussoorie, and Darjiling (Darjeeling), the region is moderately populated. Within the Middle Himalayas the intervening mountain ranges tend to separate the densely populated valleys. The numerous gorges and rugged mountains make surface travel difficult in any direction. Few roads or transport routes exist between towns, partly because it is expensive to build them over the high, rough terrain. Only major population centers are linked by air and roads with principal cities in India and Pakistan.

The Sub-Himalayas, which is the southernmost and the lowest zone, borders the plains of North India and Pakistan. It comprises the Siwalik Range and foothills as well as the narrow piedmont plain at the base of the mountains. The width of the Sub-Himalayas gradually narrows from about 48 km (about 30 mi) in the west until it nearly disappears in Bhutan and eastern India. A characteristic feature of the Sub-Himalayas is the large number of long, flat-bottomed valleys known as *duns,* which are usually spindle-shaped and filled with gravelly alluvium. South of the foothills lies the Tarai and Duars plains. The southern part of the Tarai and Duars plains is heavily farmed. The northern part was forest inhabited by wild animals until about the 1950s. Most of the forests of this region have been destroyed, and much of the land has been reclaimed for agriculture.

CLIMATE

The Himalayas influences the climate of the Indian subcontinent by sheltering it from the cold air mass of Central Asia. The range also exerts a major influence on monsoon and rainfall patterns. Within the Himalayas climate varies depending on elevation and location. Climate ranges from subtropical in the southern foothills, with average summer temperatures of about 30° C (about 86° F) and average winter temperatures of about 18° C (about 64° F); warm temperate conditions in the Middle Himalayan valleys, with average summer temperatures of about 25° C (about 77° F) and cooler winters; cool temperate conditions in the higher parts of the Middle Himalayas, where average summer temperatures are 15 to 18° C (59 to 64° F) and winters are below freezing; to a cold alpine climate at higher elevations, where summers are cool and winters are severe. At elevations above 4880 m (16,000 ft) the climate is very cold with below freezing temperatures and the area is permanently covered with snow and ice. The eastern part of the Himalayas receives heavy rainfall; the western part is drier.

PLANT AND ANIMAL LIFE

The natural vegetation is influenced by climate and elevation. Tropical, moist deciduous forest at one time covered all of the Sub-Himalayan area. With few exceptions most of this forest has been cut for commercial lumber or agricultural land. In the Middle Himalayas at elevations between 1520 and 3660 m (between 5000 and 12,000 ft) natural vegetation consists of many species of pine, oak, rhododendron, poplar, walnut, and larch. Most of this area has been deforested; forest cover remains only in inaccessible areas and on steep slopes. Below the timber line the Great Himalayas contains valuable forests of spruce, fir, cypress, juniper, and birch. Alpine vegetation occupies higher parts of the Great Himalayas just below the snow line and includes shrubs, rhododendrons, mosses, lichens, and wildflowers such as blue poppies and edelweiss. These areas are used for grazing in summer by the highland people of the Great Himalayas.

Animals such as tigers, leopards, rhinoceroses, and many varieties of deer once inhabited the forested areas of the Sub-Himalayan foothills and the Tarai plain. As a result of deforestation the habitat of most of the wildlife has been destroyed. They are now restricted to special protected areas such as the Jaldapara and Kaziranga sanctuaries in India and the Chitawan preserve in Nepal. There are few animals in the Middle Himalayas because of extensive deforestation. In the Great Himalayas musk deer, wild goats, sheep, wolves, and snow leopards are found. The existence of the Yeti has been reported by highland Sherpas in Nepal but has eluded discovery by several expeditions.

PEOPLE AND ECONOMY

The population, settlement, and economic patterns within the Himalayas have been greatly influenced by the variations in topography and climate, which impose harsh living conditions and tend to restrict movement and communication. People living in remote, isolated valleys have generally preserved their cultural identities. However, improvements in transportation and communication, particularly satellite television programs from Europe and the United States, are bringing access from the outside world to remote valleys. These outside influences are affecting traditional social and cultural structure.

Nearly 40 million people inhabit the Himalayas. Generally, Hindus of Indian heritage are dominant in the Sub-Himalayas and the Middle Himalayan valleys from eastern Kashmir to Nepal. To the north Tibetan Buddhists inhabit the Great Himalayas from Ladakh to northeast India. In central Nepal, in an area between about 1830 and 2440 m (between about 6000 and 8000 ft), the Indian and Tibetan cultures have intermingled, producing a combination of Indian and Tibetan traits. The eastern Himalayas in India and nearby areas of eastern Bhutan are inhabited by animistic people whose culture is similar to those living in northern Myanmar and Yunnan province in China. People of western Kashmir are Muslims and have a culture similar to the inhabitants of Afghanistan and Iran.

The economy of the Himalayas as a whole is poor with low per capita income. Much of the Himalayas area is characterized by a very low economic growth rate combined with a high rate of population growth, which contributes to stagnation in the already low level of per capita gross national product. Most of the population is dependent on agriculture, primarily subsistence agriculture; modern industries are lacking. Mineral resources are limited. The Himalayas has major hydroelectric potential, but the development of hydroelectric resources requires outside capital investment. The skilled labor needed to organize and manage development of natural resources is also limited due to low literacy rates. Most of the Himalayan communities face malnutrition, a shortage of safe drinking water, and poor health services and education systems.

Agricultural land is concentrated in the Tarai plain and in the valleys of the Middle Himalayas. Patches of agricultural land have also been carved out in the mountainous forested areas. Rice is the principal crop in eastern Tarai and the well-watered valleys. Corn is also an important rain-fed crop on the hillsides. Other cereal crops are wheat, millet, barley, and buckwheat. Sugarcane, tea, oilseeds, and potatoes are other major crops. Food production in the Himalayas has not kept up with the population growth.

The major industries include processing food grains, making vegetable oil, refining sugar, and brewing beer. Fruit processing is also important. A wide variety of fruits are grown in each of the major zones of the Himalayas, and making fruit juices is a major industry in Nepal, Bhutan, and in the Indian Himalayas.

Since 1950 tourism has emerged as a major growth industry in the Himalayas. Nearly 1 million visitors come to the Himalayas each year for mountain trekking, wildlife viewing, and pilgrimages to major Hindu and Buddhist sacred places. The number of foreign visitors has increased in recent years, as organized treks to the icy summits of the Great Himalayas have become popular. While tourism is important to the local economy, it has had an adverse impact on regions where tourist numbers exceed the capacity of recreational areas.

Historically, all transport in the Himalayas has been by porters and pack animals. Porters and pack animals are still important, but the construction of major roads and the development of air routes have changed the traditional transportation pattern. Major urban centers such as Kathmandu, Simla, and Srinagar, as well as important tourist destinations, are served by airlines. Railways link Simla and Darjiling, but in most of the Himalayas there are no railroads. The bulk of goods from the Himalayas, as well as goods destined for places within the Himalayas, generally come to Indian railheads, located in the Tarai, by road. The pack animals and porters transport goods from road heads to the interior and back.

ENVIRONMENTAL ISSUES

Economic changes and population increases are threatening the ecology of the Himalayas. In recent years deforestation in the foothills and the Middle Himalayas and overgrazing on the high pastures have led to soil erosion and other environmental problems. Deforestation is a particular concern in the western Himalayas, where increased demand for firewood, extensive tree trimming in order to feed livestock, and construction of roads in the border regions have increased the destruction rate of forests and the number of landslides. Rapid population growth has accelerated pollution, and Himalayan streams that were once clear are now polluted with refuse and sewage. Hill people who use the water for drinking suffer from dysentery; cholera and typhoid epidemics are also common. Large lakes like Dal in Kashmir and Naini Lake (Nainital) have also become polluted.

Regional variations in environmental degradation exist in the Himalayas. Conditions range from a critical situation in the Himalayas of Nepal, Sikkim, Uttarakhand, and Kashmir to a moderately serious situation in Bhutan and the eastern Himalayas. If rapid development continues in Bhutan and the eastern Himalayas without due regard for conservation, the problems there may assume critical proportions in the near future. The governments of India, Nepal, and Bhutan are aware of the dangers of environmental degradation in the Himalayas, and environmental management concerns are being integrated in development projects in this region.

HISTORY OF HIMALAYAS

The Himalayas are not merely a geographical feature, a range of mountains; they epitomise a people's civilisational identity that goes back to the dawn of history. If these majestic mountains were not there, the rain clouds sweeping up from the Indian Ocean would have passed over the Indian subcontinent into central Asia leaving it a burning desert.

Archaeological evidence reveals that urban civilisation first emerged in the valleys of the rivers coursing down from the Himalayan mountains. When man elsewhere was cautiously emerging from his cave shelters, spectacular cities flourished at Mohenjodaro and Harappa in the Indus valley.

Climate of Himalayas

Himalayan Coverage Area:	2,250-km
Average Width:	200-km
Himalayan Forests:	Pine, Deodar, Fir, Oak, Rhododendron, Birch
Monsoon Season:	Mid-June Till The End Of September

Saga of Mountains, Forests, Pastures

The Himalayas with dazzling pinnacles of snow-covered ranges extend for 2,250-km from the Namcha Barwa on the bend of the Tsang-po (Brahmaputra) to Nanga Parbat on the Indus. The range runs east to west up to central-Nepal and then takes a southeast to northwest direction. The average width of the Himalayas is about 200-km. The compositions of the forests on this mighty range are effected by the combined effect of altitude, rainfall and latitude. The rainfall, mainly from the monsoons, decreases from the east to the west. Comparatively, in winter, due to the influence of tropical west wind drift, the northwest areas have more precipitation in the form of rain and snow. From these snow covered ranges with big glaciers, flow the great rivers that have made the Indo-Gangetic plain one of the most fertile in the world and the heart Land of India.

Climatic Variation in the Himalayas

The Himalayan Alpine climate varies according to the elevation. It gets colder as the elevation increases and gets wetter as the elevation drops. As a result the temeparture and climatic changes in the Himalayan regions change very quickly. All of a sudden there can be occurances of monsoons, floods, high winds, snowstorms and other types of precipitation, which makes the climate over here quiet an unpredictable and dangerous one.

The two major seasons of the Himalayan region are winter and summer. During the winter the region recieves the maximum snow with very icy temperatures. Summer are quiet mild over here, making the places overe here quiet good summer holiday hideouts. Usually throughout the year te Alpine Himalayan region recieves Snow.

Beyond the Monsoon

The regions such as Ladakh & Zanskar that lie to the North of the main Himalayan range and escape the full impact of the monsoon. Humidity is always low in these regions, and receives only a few centimeters of rainfall a year. These regions also experience some of the coldest temperatures anywhere in the world, and it doesn't get any warmer till the spring season in late April or early May.

In June, daytime temperatures frequently rise to the mid 200Cs, the snow on the passes melts and most of the treks can be undertaken from then on until the middle of October. Heavy rainstorms can occasionally be experienced in July and August, and River crossing should be undertaken with great care at this time. By September the conditions are ideal, and they normally remain so until late October even though nigh-time temperatures may fall below freezing. By November, the early winter snows fall on the passes closest to the Himalayas. In winter the villagers still travel, enduring the intense cold, to follow the valley floors where River crossings are no longer a problem.

After October the daytime temperatures drop, but the weather is generally settled until the middle of November when the first of the heavy winter snows fall on the high mountain passes. Winter months from December to March are often bleak. April and May are characterised by heavy precipitation, which falls as snow in the mountains, precluding trekking over the passes until the spring snows melt in June.

Most of the hill states of the West Himalayas including Kangra and Chamba, the Kullu valley, Shimla in Himachal and most regions of the Garhwal and Kumaon in Uttaranchal come under the influence of the Indian monsoon. Both Darjeeling and Sikkim are subject to the Indian monsoon that sweeps up from the Bay of Bengal, bringing heavy rainfall from early June until the end of September. The post-monsoon months of October and November provide settled conditions, with clear views of the mountains, although nighttime temperatures above 3,500m frequently fall below freezing.

Forest Cover-The Glory of the Himalayas

Because of the constant most of the Himalayan regions have a harsh environment therefore few animals and plants can survive over here. The few plants that do inhabit the Alpine consist of rhododendrons, the tea plant and shrub type plants. They have to adapt to the freezing temperatures, high winds and to a short growing season. That is why most of the plants grow low to the ground.

The Hindustan-Tibet road now called National Highway No. 22 takes one right across the Himalayas from the plains over forested mountain ranges, along the Sutlej through the gorge in the great Himalayan range near Shipkila on the Indo-Tibet border. One of the most interesting and accessible areas are the forests on the ridge line that form the Indo Gangetic watershed on which lie Shimla, Narkanda and the most beautiful forests of silver Fir starting from Narkanda. Part of the Hindustan-Tibet road run along this watershed ridge.

From the plains to the snow clothed mountains, one goes through fine forests of Pine, Deodar, Fir, Oak, Rhododendron, Birch and finally between the tree line and the snows, rich alpine pastures. Inhabited areas, on cultivated terraced fields, can be seen women in their customary colourful clothes decorating the hillside like alpine blossoms.

The mountain fauna that are found in the Himalayan Alpine are similar to the mountain animals found in the surrounding areas of the Himalalayas. Some animals that have adapted the Himalayan climate include the mountain goat, which has a thick coat for warmth and strong hooves for running up the rocky slopes.

The Awesome Himalayan Panorama

To know the mountains one has to be amongst them. In the evening as one begin settling down so do the mountains, valleys and clouds. It is a wonderful sight to see a sea of clouds sinks in repose in the deep valleys. At the same time the setting sun converts the surrounding peaks into molten gold which gradually fade away into pale pink and steel grey.

At night, the moon lends a peculiar charm to the snow transferring the rugged peaks and ridges into soft contours. The hamlets in the valleys, surrounded by fields, are in deep slumber. The silence of the mountains is complete. The only sound one can hear is of the campfire.

In the morning, the rising glow of the sun reflects from peak to peak and then descends to the lower slopes awakening all. The sun's warmth rouses the clouds to gradually climb the mountains, hugging the valley sides as they rise and engulf the peaks with their crowns of snow. This is an experience so vivid and revitalizing that it can never be forgotten.

Natural Warning

In recent years, there has been great emphasis on saving the trees but the actual progress has been insignificant. Day by day, the trees are being destroyed and being cut down without replacement and without a thought for our children's future. Overgrazing and ruthless assault on herbs is destroying the meadows and pastures.

In the absence of forests, there will be less precipitation in the form of rain and snow-leaving the grand peaks without their white mantle. This ecological damage, if not redeemed, will lead to catastrophes in the form of extreme floods, droughts, forests fires and disappearance of wildlife.

The diversity of the plants, herbs, flowers, landscapes is truly stunning and reflects Nature's brilliant ecological plan. The lines taken from Devistotra, a Hindu Shastra, (500 BC) presents quite a clear picture of the Himalayan lands:

THE PEOPLE & TRIBES

Ethnic Himalayan People: Negroids, Mongoloids and Aryans

The Inhabitants and the Migrants

The Hindu epics and Puranas refer to the original inhabitants of the Himalayas-the Kulinds, Kiratas and Kilinds, Kiratas and Kinnars and later texts mention the Khasas and the Darads. Today three ethnic types constitute the Himalayan population: Negroids, Mongoloids and Aryans.

From very early times there have been migrations into the Himalayas and within it. Spiritual quest motivated a few to migrate there, and a small minority responded to the call of these mountains to test their own endurance and will power. Pursuit of profit propelled others. Reasons of state dictated the posting of garrisons even in remote, desolate areas. All these factors combined over a period of time to change significantly the complexion of the local populace. There have been waves of migration from Nepal to Sikkim and Kumaon, for instance, and from Tibet. At present it is extremely difficult to separate the different racial strains.

Bhutiyas of Bhutan

The Bhutanese are Bhutiyas of Mongolian origin who refer to themselves as Drukpa-inhabitants of Druk Yul or the 'Land of the Thunder Dragon'. Apart from a few obscure areas of Nepal and Ladakh, and Spiti in India, the Bhutanese are the only large group to follow traditional Buddhism and, despite the building of roads and controlled introduction of tourism, have maintained many aspects of the culture.

People of Sikkim

The Sikkimese consist of three different groups-the Lepchas, the Bhutiyas and the Nepalis. The Lepchas are the original inhabitants but are now in a minority. Not much is known of their history before their conversion to Buddhism and the enthronement of Phuntsok Namgyal as the first historic ruler of Sikkim.

Nepali People

The people of Nepal are a complex mix of racial patterns. The dominant Hindu castes of Brahmin, Thakur and Chetri, along with several others speak Nepali. The Gurungs, Magars, Tamaings, Rais and Limbus form the Gurkha regiments of the British and Indian armies. These are part of the mongoloid, tribally organized groups of hill farmers who dominate the middle hills. The Sherpas of the Solo Khumbu region in the northeast of the country are amoung the many Bhutiya groups who speak dialects of Tibetan.

People of Himachal Pradesh

In Kumaon and Garhwal, in the central Himalayas, Khasas and Doms were the original inhabitants. The Khasas, historians surmise, were a west Central Asian nomadic tribe who entered through the northwest and spread from Kashmir to Assam.

People of Uttaranchal

In Himachal Pradesh, the descendants of these Khasas are known as "Kanets" and now claim Rajput status. The majority of the population in the present-day central Himalayas has Khasa ancestry. Immigrant Brahmins and Kshatriyas from the plains brought caste division with them and introduced new forms of social organization rooted in Hindu orthodoxy.

The Ladakhis

The Ladakhis are of ethnic stock different from that of the people of Kumaon and Garhwal. According to folklore, Ladakh was once totally populated by Darads. The latest archaeological finds give credence to this popular belief. The Mons belonging to the Mongoloid stock, and who are now far more numerous there, seem to have migrated at a much later date.

Most people in the Himalayas sustain themselves by a combination of agriculture and animal husbandry. Until very recently, those inhabiting the higher reaches migrated to lower altitudes during the winter months. Trade played an important role in the lives of the frontier villages in Ladakh, Himachal, Kumaon and Garhwal. Before the advent of the British, the contacts of Sikkim and Bhutan with Tibet were closer and more frequent.

2

Ecotourism in Himalayas

Nature worship and the conservation ethic have been an integral part of Indian thought and traditions and its also followed by India's Himalayan neighbours. For centuries, the country has nurtured the philosophy of the oneness of life, the tradition that humankind is a part of nature and one should look upon all creation with the eyes of a friend.

It is tragic that in recent years, the mad pursuit for material ends has created in India and elsewhere a situation in which progress has become synonymous with exploitation of nature in all its manifestations. Today the entire Himalayan range, with its rich and unique biological diversity, is facing a deep crisis and is in the danger being destroyed. It is being relentlessly denuded of its rich forest cover. Fortunately, this has been led to some realisation, and now the beginnings of a new awakening about human responsibility towards nature are discernible.

CROWING GLORY OF TOURISM IN HIMACHAL PRADESH

States Comprising The Himalayan Range: Arunachal Pradesh, Nagaland, Tripura, Manipur, Meghalaya, Mizoram, Sikkim, Himachal Pradesh, Jammu And Kashmir, Uttranchal And Darjeeling District Of West Bengal

"The Himalayas": The Skanda Puranas have held Himalayas and Himachal Pradesh in high esteem and reverence.

"As the due is dried up by the morning sun, so are the sins of mankind by the site of Himachal". The Himalayas, the youngest, loftiest of all the mountains in the world and embracing seven out of the ten highest peaks, sprawl approximately 2,560-kms from North western to the south eastern along with its extension in North eastern India and has breadth from 250-km to 400-km. States of India namely Arunachal Pradesh, Nagaland, Tripura, Manipur, Meghalaya, Mizoram, Sikkim, Himachal Pradesh, Jammu and Kashmir, Uttranchal and Darjeeling district of West Bengal are located in Himalayas.

The Himalayan Landscapes

The undulating Himalayas welcome with bottle green shrubbery in the foothills of Shivalik Ranges, crescent shaped, snow clad Dhauladhar over shadowed by the Pir Panjal and the Great Himalayan Ranges. The land is dotted by beautiful lakes and valleys located between an altitude of 350 metres and approximately 6,810 metres, intercepted by rivers and sprawling valleys.

The forests, flora and fauna, wild life and natural scenic beauty with salubrious climate is a haven for the visitors. The alpine land, spread over Lahaul and Spiti to Pangi valley, is an ardent destination for Aplinists and a feast of hedonic nature's bounty.

In Himalayas, medicinal herbs have been growing throughout nature kindness from the times immemorial. Adventure sport is another area of tourism activities, which yields greater scope for trekking, camping, mountaineering and skiing, etc.

Visiting the Land of Gods

The fairs and festivals, customs and gatherings attended by the locals represent the unconceited simple disposition and hospitable populace. To visit Himachal, by itself, is an experience of heritage. Himachal is popularly described as "Dev Bhumi". The temples, churches, Gurdwaras, monasteries besides bearing testimony to the typical pieces of architecture and woodcarving enjoy the international fame.

With several spurs and sub system, the Himalayas are a strong spine for the state of Himachal Pradesh in Northern India. They have also given the area an enormous geographical spectrum-and one that is unparalleled in the world. To sum up, it is truly said,

"A sweeter and a lovelier land,

framed in the prodigality of nature.

The spacious world cannot afford to have again."

GREEN TOURISM FOR HIMACHAL'S COLD DESERT

Location: Lahaul & Spiti, Himalchal Pradesh

Coverage Area: 12.000-sq-kms

Vales of Barren Splendour

Landlocked behind formidable mountain barriers in the western Himalayas, sheltered from the rain-bearing monsoon winds, the remote and desolate district of Lahaul-Spiti in Himachal is renowned not only for some of the wild, untamed and enchanting mountain scapes but also for its unique Buddhist culture.

Covering a total area of over 12,000-sq-kms, Lahaul-Spiti is the largest district of Himachal Pradesh. It shares a common border with Tibet in the east. A lofty offshoot of the great Himalayan range in the southeast separates it from Kinnaur. In the north, the Baralacha range separates it from the cold desert of Ladakh, while the Chamba and Kullu district lie to the west respectively.

Lahaul's only link to the outside world is by a road, which runs over the 3,980 m high Rohtang Pass. Lahaul is separated from Spiti by a high mountain range running towards the north from the great Himalayan range. A treacherous road over the Kunzam Pass connects the two valleys. Another road from Kinnaur links Spiti to the Hindustan-Tibet road.

Withstanding the Harsh Environ

Enmeshed in the folds of the great Himalayas, the climate is cold and arid, with very little rainfall. The topography, therefore, consists of dry, dusty desolate mountains, virtually devoid of vegetation spread endlessly in all directions like a moonscape, resembling Ladakh and Tibet. The monotony of this stark, haunting russet landscape is broken only by shades of green along the cultivated river valley.

Sculpted by the wind and moulded alternately by freezing cold and searing heat, the landscape of this frontier district has evolved a distinctive profile. Steep towering cliffs of hard rocks rise up into the perpetual azure sky all around, their slopes covered with heaps of weathered rocks. At the centre, the rivers have played their part, cutting deeper and deeper creating fertile banks. Few parts of the Himalayas can compare with Lahaul Spiti for sheer grandeur. And splendour of the mountains, for here nature holds sway in its wildest and grandest manner.

Bearers of a Historic Cultural Heritage

Marked by high mountains, bleak rugged topography and a harsh climate, the cultural landscape of this Himalayan borderland is characterised by a unique blend of two adjacent cultures. The Sino-Tibetan in the north and the Indian culture in the 7th century AD and with the passage of time it became the major religion of Lahaul-Spiti

Today the district is studded with numerous Buddhist temples and monasteries including Labarang, Gondhala, Dalung, Keylong, Guru-Ganthal, Darcha, Markula in Lahul and Dhankar, Mud, Lidang, Rangrik, Ki (also spelt as Kye), Losar and Tabo in Spiti. A millennium old Tabo is one of the area's most revered monasteries. Often called the "Ajanta of the Himalaya" because of its breathtaking murals and stucco images, tabo's sanctity in trans-himalayan buddhism is next only to tibet's tholing gompa.

Apart from their religious influence the monasteries are also strongholds of tradition and treasuries of the region's art and manuscripts. Gompas, forts and chorten scattered all over the vastness of this cold desert provide an unending feast for the sightseer and for scholars, some authentic foot-notes and references to the local history and culture.

The Lahaul district of Himachal is one rare pocket in the Indian Himalayas where one may trace a continuous course of development of Trans-Himalayan Buddhism and it is probably one of the last remaining areas in which the original Tibetan-Buddhist culture remains untouched either by communism as in tibet, or by the dissolving influence of tourism to which ladakh has been exposed.

Traditions Blending with Modernisation

The traditional economy of this tribal belt was based on agriculture, sheep rearing and trade. The subsistence economy and culture evolved in response to the hostile environment. However with massive developmental works such as road construction, modern agriculture and horticulture, Government services alongwith the presence of a large number of "outsiders", armed forces, traders, government servants and road workers has altered the traditional way of life.

Changes have occurred in dress patterns, food habits; traditional occupations like sheep rearing and even in the religious life. Although change is inevitable and no community wishes to preserve itself as a museum of backwardness, it is the rapid pace of change and a lack of understanding of the nature of change, which a society is unable to control, or direct that touches a cord of concern. The development of tourism accelerates this process of change and rapidly pushes traditional societies into the global economy totally ill-equipped.

Promoting Tourism

Ladakh was opened to tourism in the early 1970s without making any adequate preparation and ensuring safeguards. Since then, uncontrolled tourism has transformed Ladakh from a traditional to a typical tourist destination and many see western culture swamping the Ladakhi way of life. Today, the self-sufficient Ladakhi economy has undergone a massive and dramatic shift to one, which is dependent on the outside.

However, unlike Ladakh where uncontrolled tourism has disturbed the delicate ecological balance and brought drastic socio-cultural changes, Lahaul-Spiti is yet to face the full force of tourism. Tourism, if successfully managed, can contribute to the ability of the tribal people of this district to control and direct the change they are undergoing. Tourism development, poverty alleviation, awareness generation and strengthen the self-sufficient economy. This is the key to turning tourism's impacts from a burden into lasting sources of benefit. Isolated for centuries due to the inaccessible terrain and inhospitable climate this region is fragile, hence adequate safeguards need to be taken to protect this tribal belt from the adverse influence of tourism.

Such fragile areas should be open only to a very limited number of high spending tourists with proper regulatory control as is being done by Bhutan. Inspite of the large foreign exchange earnings that tourism brings, the Bhutanese government has been far-sighted enough to consider the hidden cost of tourism to its environment and culture by strictly controlling the number and the movement of tourists in the country. With only two entry points into the district, the government can easily restrict the number of tourists to the carrying capacity of the fragile environment. This, of course, is not a very fashionable decision to take but it does place the interest of the local people and their environment before short-term and cost-laden profits.

Tourism is only commencing in Lahaul-Spiti. The government therefore needs to finely tune the tourism industry to the local culture and the environment. The vulnerable nature of tourism to unstable political, social and economic conditions and seasonal nature of tourism dominant in the mountains should be overcome by efficiently planning the tourism infrastructure to make it multifunctional.

In fact tourism development must be integrated with the overall development of the region and the local people should be invited to participate in tourism right from the planning stage. It is also necessary to ensure some incentives to the locals from tourism. Environmental considerations must be integral in development of tourism in this region. Great care needs to be exercised to conserve the local culture, which is its greatest asset.

By planning and promoting a healthy, sustainable, tourism industry in this cold desert district, the government will have fulfilled its share of responsibility but in the end, it may not be the number of tourists but their sensitivity towards the local culture and environment that will determine the complexion of tourism and the future of this unique heritage.

THE LAST AWAKENING CALL

Mountains, forests and pastures are the mothers of rivers that sustain life. Their catchment areas are the water basins for hydel projects and dams. Destroy the forests and one will find dams silting and going dry; hydel projects will remain a dream and drought a common occurrence. Scarcity of water will affect food production and there will be no answer to the frantic cries of the cities and villages for water between individuals, states and nations, and progress adversely affected due to lack of power.

Things Effecting Nature

In recent years trees have so badly lopped that they are left only with a crown of green top; herbal collections on massive scales by agents of drug plant owners; uncontrolled grazing by animals; forests set on fire by villagers to get better growth for grazing with no thought for wild animals and birds; fish being electrocuted in mountain streams; large forest areas encroached upon by farmers and tourism developers; forest rest houses demolished by 'timber looters'; barren, hollowed out hillsides due to mining; murder of the majestic deodars by cutting a hollow at the base of the trunk and then setting it on fire. Land, water and forests resources are being degraded and depleted at a galloping speed. With over-exploitation for agricultural purposes and to meet the ever-increasing demands of the cities, the sub-soil water is receding at an alarming rate. If the rivers too go dry, the holocaust can well be imagined. Deforestation will lead to desertification as is happening in parts of China where the desert sand dunes are spreading at the rate of 200-sq-kms per month.

Deforestation

Forests are critical for preserving the green covering on mountain soils. Extensive deforestation and grazing results in barren surface, soil erosion and porosity. The porous soil, during the monsoons and cloud bursts, soaks in water gets loosened and whole mountain sides slide down taking with them trees, farm lands, villages and finally damming the rivers-leaving behind barren scars on the mountains which will further increase erosion.

Most vulnerable to this kind of nature's fury are the run-of-the-river schemes Hydel projects and big gravity dams especially when their catchment areas have been deforested. "Among mountains, I am the Himalaya" (Bhagvat Gita)-this was the pride with which our ancestors and sages looked up to the most beautiful, majestic and mighty snow-capped mountains. Today, however, the same Himalayas are the most degraded mountains in the world-a eco-disaster in the making.

Wisdom is required not to plunder but to preserve. It is time to wake up to this "last awakening call", otherwise we are heading for the Himalayan eco-disaster and with it the "Last Bugle Call".

WILDLIFE RESERVES & CONSERVATION AREAS

Introduction

Nepal is a land of extreme contrasts in climate and geography. It has a unique topography ranging from lowlands with sub-tropical jungles to arctic conditions in the Himalayan highlands. Within a mere 150-kms, the land rises from near sea level in the south to over 8,000m in the North. This together with the monsoon rainfall along the south facing slopes, has resulted in compacting virtually all climate zones found on planet earth. As a result, Nepal has been endowed with a great diversity of life-zones providing a home for a large variety of plants, birds and animals.

The Terai Region

The Terai lowland are defined by a belt of well-watered floodplains streching from the Indian border northward to the first slopes of the Bhabhar and the Shiwalik range. This is the richest habitat in the land with tall grasslands interspersed with riverine and hardwood sal forest. Here one can see wildlife such as the Swamp Deer, Musk Deer, Black Buck, Blue Bull, the Royal Bengal Tiger, Gharial and Mugger Crocodiles and the last of a breed of Asiatic Wild Buffalo. This area is also rich in birdlife with variety of Babblers and Orioles, Koels and Drongos, Peacocks and Floricans, and a multitude of wintering Wildfowl.

The Protected Areas in Terai Region

There are five protected areas in Nepal-Koshi Tappu and Parsa in the east, Sukla Phanta and Dhorpatan for hunting in the west and Shivapuri in the mid-mountain region. The churia, also known as the siwalik, is the southern most range of the himalaya. No where do there rise above 1,220 meters. This range is famous for fossil deposits of pleistocene mammals, among them 10 species of Elephants, 6 Rhinoceros, Hippopotamus, Sabre-Toothed Cats, various Antelopes and Primates such as the Orangutan, long extinct in the Subcontinent.

Doons and the Royal Chitwan National Park

Situated north of the Churia are broad, low valleys of the Inner Terai known as the Doons. These valleys are not unlike the outer plains with Tall Elephant Grass, swamps and Ox-bow lakes where the last of the one horned Rhinoceros survive. Royal Chitwan National Park in the Inner Terai of central Nepal is the first and best protected area in the kingdom. Once one if the most famous big game hunting areas in Asia. Chitwan now offers protection to a large array of mammals such as the One-Horned Rhinoceros, Tiger, Leopard, Sloth Bear and the Gaur (Wild Bison) as well as more than 400 species of birds.

Mahabharat Range

Higher in the north between 2,000 and 3,500m lies the Mahabharat Range with its Oak crowned crests. The hills of this mildland are covered by a moist temperate forest of Deodar, Oak, Maple and Birch in which are found Deer, Ghoral, Serow, Leopard and Monkey. The gorgeous multicolored Impeyan Pheasant (Nepal's National Bird) is also found here with other endangered birds like the Koklas and Cheer Pleasants.

PROTECTED AREAS IN THE MAHABHARAT RANGE

Protected areas in this zone include Khaptad National Park in the far-west, Dhorpatan Hunting Reserve, northwest of Pokhara and Shivapuri Wildlife Sanctuary near Kathmandu valley higher still, nearer the snowline, are the alpine mountain flanks which are the haunt of Snow Leopard, which preys on blue wheep and the Himalayan Tahr. Rarely seen are the Wolf, Black and Brown Bears and Lynx. The Sherpas, Managba, and Dolpa-Bas are some of those who farm and graze their livestock on the high mountain pastures. Langtang, Sagarmatha (Everest), Shey-Phoksundo and Rara National Parks are the protected high altitude areas of Nepal.

Seasons

Nepal's climate range from tropical in the lowlands to arctic in the higher altitudes. Above 90% of the rain falls during the monsoon June to September. Vegetation is at its lushes during this season. The best time is October and November to visit the high altitude Himalayan parks.

The winter months, between December and February, attract large number of visitors to the lowland parks. Koshi Tappu, Parsa, Chitwan, Bardia and Sukla Phanta are best visit during this time. This is also good time to observe wintering birds, including Wildfowl and Waders. From March to May, it is warm at lower altitudes and cool above 3,000m. This is an ideal time to visit high altitude nature sanctuaries of Everest, Annapurna, Langtang, Rara, Khaptad, Shivapuri, Makalu-Barun and Dhorpatan. This is when the Rhododendron and alpine flowers burst into bloom.

TEMPERATE FORESTS

Temperate forests are mainly found in the middle altitudes of the Himalayas. They are found both along the main Himalayas and on the transition zone between itself and the barren cold desert areas. Dry temperate forests are also found in the drier parts of the Himalayas and the barren Transhimalayan region. The forests are usually found in areas experiencing temperate climate. Their altitude varies from 1800m to 3000m depending on local conditions. Mixed Temperate Coniferous forests, also known as the western mixed coniferous forests, are an attractive forest typical of the moister regions of the western Himalaya, having a mixture of temperate zone conifers like the deodar, blue pine, fir and spruce. There may occur broad-leaved species mixed with the conifers in small proportions particularly in moist shady depressions.

Individual trees attain a height of more than 40 m though the height attained by the trees of this forest type is relatively lesser than those found in the very moist zone of the western Himalaya. This is probably due to the harsh climatic conditions prevailing in the drier parts.

This forest type is found in the main Himalayas and the transition zone between itself and the cold desert regions, generally between an elevation of 1800 and 3000 m. It is well developed in the upper Ganga valley and Kali valley of Uttarakhand, India, and in the Satluj valley of Kinnaur.

As the name suggests, it grows in areas of typical temperate climate. Summers are mild and warm with the average maximum temperature rarely exceeding 32 C. There is a short autumn season after which winter sets in. The first snowfall of the season may occur as early as in mid-November. Snow accounts for a considerable part of the total annual precipitation. In winter the temperature remains below the freezing point for fairly long period.

During the past few decades these have come under an enormous strain due to due to large scale deforestation for fodder, fuelwood and constructional purposes.

In the wetter parts of the same region exist the Temperate moist mixed deciduous forests have broad-leaved species which thrive in the wetter climate. In the drier regions within these forests, conifers, and even patches of grasslands can be found. Individual trees may attain a height of about 20 m. These forests range from 1800m to 3000m in the relatively wetter regions. it usually develops in moist shady depressions and along streams and rivers. The forests are found all along the main HImalayas as well as in the transition zone to the cold desert regions. Other temperate forests include forests of oak at an altitude of 2500m-3500m. They are dense forests with individual trees rising upto 20m and more in height. In drier patches, these forests are intermixed with deodar and blue pine. The oak forests are mainly found in regions experiencing climatic conditions from temperate to sub-arctic. Snow forms the majority of the annual precipitation, with hailstorms occurring in April and May. These forests have also undergone degradation due to felling of trees for fuelwood, fodder, and timber. Along with the oak forests lie the fir forests. They usually occur slightly higher-between an altitude of 2600m-3600m.

Other forests in the middle altitudes include the cypress forests between the altitude of 1800m and 2800m, in regions of temperate to sub-arctic climate. These occur in relatively drier conditions and hence are open forests.

Forests of blue pine are found between an elevation of about 2100m and 2600m in areas of temperate to sub-arctic conditions. They can be found in areas of relatively poor and shallow soil. In these regions grasses and other species thrive during the rainy seasons and die out later on. A thick layer of pine needles covers the forest floor under these forests. These forests can even grow on poorer soils like the highly sandy soils near rivers. This forest is a pioneering vegetation and can grow on very rocky soils, fresh landslides and even recently burnt areas.

Forests of chilgoza or neoza pine occur in the drier cold desert regions. Tree growth is sparse due to the harsh climatic conditions which may even result in stunted or malformed trees. These trees gain a height of upto 18m. The soil in the region is generally fragile, poor in nutrients and very rocky at places. Chilgoza forests occur commonly in the Kinnaur Himalayas of India, extending from the banks of the Satluj river up to the middle elevations in the valley.

Dry temperate forests, as the mane suggests are found in drier areas of the region having temperate to sub-arctic conditions. They occur between an elevation of 2000 and 2500m.

These forests include both broad-leaved and coniferous species. Open patches of grasslands are found with these forests. The trees, however, are relatively short and do not grow to more than about 18 m. These forests occur in areas of poor shallow soils which otherwise get eroded quite fast. The regions usually receive little rainfall and a large amount of snowfall throughout winter.

Dry forests of Deodar occur in dry tracts between 1800-3000m with trees becoming stunted at higher elevations. The soil quality is generally very poor and prone to erosion. At higher elevations, between 2700m and 4300m, juniper forests are found. These are open evergreen forests consisting of dwarfed and stunted individual trees. The climatic conditions here are even more severe-varying from sub-arctic to arctic. Summer temperatures usually do not exceed 28°C while winters are bitterly cold.

THE EFFECT OF DISTURBANCE LEVELS

Taxus baccata L. subsp. wallichiana (Zucc.) Pilger has come into prominence in recent years because of its over exploitation from the Himalayan forests for pharmaceutical drugs. Despite wide elevational distribution (1770-3400 m elevation), it never forms exten-sive stretches and commonly occurs as undercanopy species. Further, it is an extremely slow-growing tree with poor seed germination. Along the disturbance gradient Taxus shows different population patterns. Least disturbed mixed broadleaf forest association shows stable population. The number of seedlings was related to crown cover and soil pH. The size class distribution of T. baccata population indicates that this species is on its way out at the study site. The threat is not only because of excessive harvesting but also due to degradation of forest sites for other reasons.

TAXUS BACCATA

(a small evergreen tree, family Taxaceae) is distributed between 1700 and 3400 m altitude, along west to east from Afghanistan to north-eastern Himalayan states in India. This tree commonly occurs in patches as under canopy associate of either conifers (Abies pindrow and Cedrus deodara) or broadleaf tree species (Quercus semecarpifolia, Aesculus indica and Juglans regia). Excessive harvesting to meet pharmaceutical requirements for taxol (ref. 1) has caused severe threat to the survival of the species due to its slow-growing nature and poor seed germination. The possible threat to T. baccata due to over exploitation was recognized at the beginning of this century, because of the multiple traditional uses. Consumption of seeds along with the aril (a sweet, fleshy cup-like structure surrounding the seed) by birds, monkeys and humans causes regeneration failure, as observed in a few areas. Further, the species is unlikely to reproduce in cleared forest areas or under large canopy gaps, as young plants require deep shade. In recent years, information has been generated on T. baccata, but very little is known about the regeneration of this species in comparison to other tree species of the region. This study has been addressed to elucidate: (i) population structure of T. baccata in different forests and disturbance levels, (ii) regeneration status in different forests, and (iii) identification of associated factors that favour seedling recruitment.

The study area (Jageshwar) lies between 29°35-29°39 N and 79°59-79°53 E in the Kumaun Himalayan region of central Himalaya and occupies about 120 ha. The different forest associations sampled occur between 1810 and 2050 m altitude. T. baccata occurs in small groups of 5-10 individuals, in two associations: (i) Cedar forest (dominance of Cedrus deodara in canopy and a low occurrence of undercanopy tree associates, e.g. Neolitsea pallens), and (ii) mixed broadleaf forest (co-dominance of various tree species, e.g. Juglans regia, Aesculus indica, Quercus leucotrichophora and Q. floribunda). In these forests disturbance level was identified as least, moderate and heavy in terms of biomass removal, tree cutting and livestock grazing for circumference at breast height (CBH) in 7-14 randomly distributed 100 m^2 quadrates. Individuals up to 30 cm height were counted as seedlings, > 30 cm height but < 10 cm CBH as saplings and > 10.1 cm CBH as trees. Soil samples (40 cm depth) were collected from each forest site. The samples were analysed for moisture, pH, organic carbon, total nitrogen and available phosphorus. Along the disturbance gradient Taxus population shows different patterns. Least disturbed mixed broadleaf forest association shows stable population of Taxus as evident by greater number of small individuals than large individuals, termed as Type I population (Figure 1). In contrast, saplings and some of the subsequent size classes of this species were not found in moderately disturbed sites of the same forest. Presence of greater number of plants in the older age classes (higher CBH class) indicates failure in conversion of seedlings to saplings during the recent past. This may be due to alteration in micro-site conditions by biotic disturbances.

A similar pattern was observed in the Cedar forest. At highly disturbed sites only the oldest tree category was present with more individuals in higher than in lower size classes, indicating failure of regeneration in the past (termed as Type III population). Susceptibility of Taxus to biotic disturbances (as apparent from the absence of regeneration and lower girth class trees at highly disturbed site) is similar to its high altitude tree associate, brown oak, of the Central Himalaya. At moderately disturbed sites, Taxus population structure with peaks and troughs was observed which indicates irregular seedling establishment along the time scale (termed as Type II population). In the cedar forest seedlings are abundant but their conversion into saplings is poor.

Distribution of Type II population is common among late secondary species that depend on conspicuous canopy gap for regeneration. A Type II population is characteristic of a light demanding, early pioneer species having a pool of dormant seeds in soil, while this pattern for a primary or late successional species, such as T. baccata, reflects no recruitment of seedlings to saplings. The three types of populations (as described earlier) occur in a single sequence through which the population passes on its way to extinction (from Type I to Type III), and T. baccata populations in the study area appear to be under such a transition.

Occurrence of only few seedlings and saplings in moderately and heavily disturbed forest sites suggests that Taxus requires shaded environment. Regression analysis also indicates that crown cover was positively related to seedlings and saplings number ($P < 0.05$). The undisturbed shaded environment has also a nutrient-rich soil with high moisture content, and the nutrient concentrations (C, N and P) declined with increasing levels of disturbance. Nutrient-rich shaded forest stands may constitute natural habitat for regeneration of this species; however, soil carbon and N individually explain only 34% and 56% of the variation in the presence of seed-lings, respectively. Soil pH has a reverse trend compared to the nutrients. Further, soil pH of a site was negatively related to the presence of Taxus seedlings ($P < 0.05$).

The combined impact of all the nutrients along with pH describes 95% of the variation in seedling population. It seems that in the current chronic form of disturbances, gaps formed are too small but they have severe impact on regeneration of the species. The failure of regeneration of a species would not be realized as long as old trees of Taxus will provide the raw material. Resulting from recent global awareness about this genus, a management plan has been suggested at the ecosystem level, which recommends protecting Taxus habitat to meet the genetic, population and ecosystem level objectives. Further, it has been emphasized that this practice should be at a scale large enough to buffer the disturbances because the undercanopy plants of old growth forests (like Cedar) require a considerably long disturbance-free period (as in the case of Taxus). It can be concluded that the Himalayan Taxus is under threat not only because of excessive harvesting but also due to degradation of forest sites due to other reasons. Biotic disturbances are apparent at the present study site but other factors like chilling temperatures, direct sunlight, warm and dry summer may also contribute to poor regeneration and subsequent recruitment processes.

In vitro antibiotic susceptibilities of Yersinia enterocolitica and Yersinia intermedia isolated from sewage effluents Yersinia enterocolitica, an important food-and water-borne enteric pathogen, causes acute gastroenteritis, entero-colitis and mesenteric lymphadenitis as well as a variety of extraintestinal disorders. Y. enterocolitica has been isolated from a variety of zoonotic and environmental sources. However, pigs and water have generally been regarded as the most important reservoirs of this organism. Y. enterocolitica is highly adaptable to aquatic environment and is capable of surviving in water for longer periods. Many water-borne outbreaks of yersiniosis have been documented. A number of studies have reported the antimicrobial susceptibilities of Yersinia strains isolated from humans, animals and food. There is paucity of information about the antibiotic susceptibilities of Y. enterocolitica of aquatic origin. Hausnerova et al. studied 64 strains of Y. enterocolitica isolated from river water and fish, and found these to be sensitive to chloramphenicol, tetracycline, neomycin and colistin. Recently, Tzelepi et al. reported antibiotic susceptibilities of seven Y. enterocolitica and thirty Y. intermedia strains isolated from river and drinking water, and mussels harvested from sea water; these strains were found to be resistant tolactam antibiotics, viz. ampicillin, carbenicillin, ticarcillin, cephalothin, amoxycillin/clavulanate and cefoxitin.

All strains, however, were sensitive to non-lactam antibiotics such as amikacin, tetracycline, chloramphenicol, gentamycin, tobramycin and cotrimoxazole. Further studies on isolates obtained from other aquatic sources and from different parts of the world would help in judiciously assessing the over-all susceptibilities of these isolates. Among the various aquatic sources, sewage and sewage effluents constitute an important source of Y. enterocolitica and other related species like Y. intermedia. Their discharge in surface waters may play a significant role in the transmission of human yersiniosis. To the best of our knowledge, there is no report on the antibiotic susceptibilities of Y. enterocolitica and Y. intermedia isolated from the Indian subcontinent. Here we present the results of a study concerning in vitro antibiotic susceptibilities of Y. enterocolitica (19 isolates) and Y. intermedia (12 isolates) isolated from sewage effluents in New Delhi.

Yersinia strains were isolated from sewage effluents as follows. Effluent samples were collected from five sewage-treatment plants located at different sites covering the entire metropolitan area of Delhi. Effluent samples of 25-30 ml collected from the final settling tank was inoculated to 10-fold volume of phosphate-buffered saline containing sorbitol and bile salts and kept at 4°C for 3 weeks. After this period, a loopful (0.04 ml) of the sample was treated with 0.1 ml of 0.5% KOH in 0.5% sodium chloride for 30 s (ref. 14). Cold-enriched and KOH-treated samples were plated on CIN (Cefsulodin-Irgasan-Novobiocin) and MacConkey agar medium (Himedia Laboratories, India). The plates were incubated at 25-26°C for 24-48 h. Colonies, which had combined features of characteristic bull's eye morphology on CIN agar and flat NLF (non-lactose fermenting) growth on MacConkey agar, were subjected to detailed biochemical characterization. Isolates identi-fied as belonging to genus Yersinia were biotyped and serotyped at Institut Pasteur, Paris or Central Public Health Laboratory Service (CPHL), Colindale (London) and have been provided with accession numbers of the respective laboratories.

Antibiotic susceptibility testing of bacterial strains was performed at 35°C by the agar diffusion method accord-ing to the procedure of Bauer et al.. The antibiotic concentrations were chosen according to the recommen-dations of the National Committee for Clinical Laboratory Standards (NCCLS) and manufacturers of disks. The zone of inhibition was measured with slipping calipers. NCCLS susceptibility criteria were used to interpret the strains as resistant, sensitive or intermediate. The anti-biotic-impregnated disks and Mueller-Hinton medium were obtained from Himedia Laboratories, India. A total of 31 strains of Yersinia spp. were isolated from June 1997 to November 1998. These were identified as Y. enterocolitica biotype 1A (19 isolates) and Y. intermedia biotypes 1, 2 and 4 (12 isolates). When analysed sepa-rately, no difference in antibiotic susceptibilities of Y. enterocolitica and Y. intermedia was observed.

This study shows antibiotic susceptibilities of Y. entero-colitica and Y. intermedia isolated from sewage effluents in India. Barring a few differences such as those seen with ceftazidime, piperacillin and cefuroxime, the findings are similar to those reported from other parts of the world. Nevertheless, it would be of interest to understand the reasons for the observed resistance of our isolates to cef-tazidime, a third generation cephalosporin and also to cefuroxime and piperacillin. It may highlight the effect of the nature of the aquatic environment (sewage vs surface waters) or the geographical origin of the isolates on the antibiotic susceptibilities of yersiniae.

The occurrence of resistance to antibiotics in aquatic isolates that represent environmental reservoirs may have direct consequences for the treatment of disease in humans

BIODIVERSITY

Bounded to the East by the Himalayan Mountains, the Great Himalayan National Park (GHNP) forms part of the boundary between four ecological zones:

(1) the dry deserts of interior Asia and the well-watered lowlands of the Indian plains,

(2) the Oriental and Palearctic faunal realms,

(3) the high plateau of Tibet and the jumbled Himalayan peaks, and

(4) the catchments of the Beas and Sutlej Rivers, both mighty tributaries of the Indus.

Because of its complex geography and its great variations in altitude, the limited area of the Park encompasses an enormous range of species, which span the subtropical to the alpine and include those characteristic of the south-east Asian forests as well as those found across Siberia and the Asian steppes. Few ecological sanctuaries present such a variety of wildlife habitat and biological diversity in such a small area.

The Park is the foremost priority for conservation in the North-West Himalayas. Its remote location has thus far spared the Park many of the problems that have affected natural ecosystems elsewhere in India. The occurrence of temperate and alpine ecosystems in a geographically compact area make GHNP the most significant and biggest conservation unit in the Western Himalayas. This status further protects the relatively inaccessible rugged terrain which represents the ecology, geology, and biota characteristic of the North-West Himalayas.

The boundaries of GHNP are contiguous with the Pin Valley National Park in Trans-Himalaya, the Rupi-Bhawa Wildlife

Sanctuary in Sutlej watershed, and the Kanawar Wildlife Sanctuary. Together the varied wildlife habitats of these protected areas support the full range of Western Himalayan biodiversity, from tropical to alpine and Tibetan. Thus, the Park is a crucial protected area because it connects other islands of biodiversity. This increases the availability of migration routes between protected areas which is essential for the survival of many animals.

From the roadhead at Gushaini or Neuli, the trails leading to the Park pass through subtropical pine forests. They rise towards the dense coniferous and mixed deciduous woods of the temperate zone, which is entered at about 1800 m. In summer, the spreading canopy of green and silver oaks and horse chestnuts provide welcome relief from the sun. Above this zone, at about 2500 m, cool-temperate forests of fir and spruce occur on northerly slopes, with brown oaks on southerly aspects. Above 3000 m, these forests grade gently into a sub-alpine zone of birches and rhododendrons, diminishing in size as the tree line is approached. Above 3000-3200 m, we find alpine meadows, splashed with a great variety of flowers and higher again is the realm of rock and ice that rules the high peaks and ridges.

Among the large mammals that visitors may encounter, there are several species of herbivores that are characteristic of the Park. The Goral (Naemorhedus goral), a small goat-antelope is found in the lower forests; the Himalayan Tahr (Hemitragus jemlahicus) in the higher forests, and above the tree-line the Bharal, or Blue Sheep (Pseudois nayaur). These mammals are the prey for Leopards (in the forest zone) and Snow Leopards (above tree-line). Himalayan Black Bears inhabit the forests, while Asiatic brown Bears occur on the alpine meadows.

Among birds, the Park is well known as the most important locality in India for the endangered Western Tragopan. Four other species of pheasant occur in or adjacent to the Park, the one most likely to be seen by visitors is the Himalayan Monal, an abundant bird in the higher forests, although rather shy. Raptors are also a prominent feature of the Park, with Lammergeiers, Himalayan Griffon Vultures, and Golden Eagles being seen regularly. A great variety of other birds occurs, some of which reach their western limit in the Park.

The flora of GHNP shows affinities with Mediterranean, Tibetan, and the Peninsular Indian region. For example, species of Valerians, Dactylorhiza, Yew, and Leycesteria are typical taxa which extend to Afghanistan and west China. Other affinities that are met with here are in form of buckthorn (Hippophae) of palaearctic region; Cedar trees, herbaceous Violets, and grasses such as Poa of Mediterranean region; and spurge (Euphorbia) shrubs of Peninsular India. In addition, GHNP has a number of endemic species of Himalayas, for example several species of balsams (Impatiens), species of Androsace, Hedysarum, Draba (Whitlow grass),etc.

Many visitors are drawn to the mountains and the wildlife of the Park. The indigenous culture of the mountain villages, adjacent to the Park, also offer unique experiences for the traveler. Isolated for centuries from the large urban centers, these remote hamlets developed a highly distinctive culture, based on the worship of local deities (devta) which are celebrated in numerous local, regional and national festivals. From the characteristic architecture of the houses and temples, and the folk wood carvings that decorate them, to the silver jewelry and woven wool shawls and blankets, there is a great range of local crafts to see.

Nor should the visitor ignore the clear interdependence of people and environment that is characteristic of traditional lifestyles. Although the high valleys of the Park are remote and support a varied flora and fauna, the signs of traditional use are everywhere. They form an intimate part of the Park's ecology. An understanding of the role that traditional practices (e.g., grazing, burning, and medicinal plant collection) have had on the Park's biota is important before we can fully appreciate the forces that have contributed to development of the ecosystems we see today.

3

Sustainable Development of the Himalayan Region

The Indian Himalayan region occupies a special place in the mountain ecosystems of the world. These geodynamically young mountains are not only important from the standpoint of climate and as a provider of life, giving water to a large part of the Indian subcontinent, but they also harbour a rich variety of flora, fauna, human communities and cultural diversity. Despite the abundance of natural resources, most of its people are marginalized and still live on subsistence level. The unscientific exploitation of natural resources is leading to increasing environmental degradation and ag-gravating the impact of natural hazards. There is a need to evolve new paradigm to restore balance between economic interest and ecological imperatives with due regards to socio-cultural principles.

With the increasing realization that the natural resources of mountain areas are vital for both upland and downland people, the Global Agenda for sustainable development has brought mountains to sharp focus. Development needs addressing local aspirations and national compulsions have to be met if economic upliftment is to be achieved. However, development interventions also imply a demand on re-sources as well as modifications of existing natural sys-tems. Development in the mountains, therefore, has to have a different approach, given the fragility and vulnerability of the Himalayan ecosystems due to the uniqueness of mountain specificities. Development interventions ignor-ing the imperatives of mountain specificities will invaria-bly result in resource misuse and subsequent accelerated environmental degradation, which would be disastrous not only for the local populace, but also for downstream inhabitants. Such negative impacts of unplanned develop-ment, insensitive to mountain specificities, are already becoming common, the most frequent being the regular incidences of landslides, river obstructions and flash floods in the mountain and recurrent floods in the plains. In addition to the negative impacts of localized develop-ment activities, the effect of climate-induced changes, an outcome of unsustainable practices and waste generation, on the mountain systems is frightening. Global warming and its effects on glacier recession have far-reaching implications both in time and space. The intense vulnerability of mountain ecosystems and their elements to the human as well as climate-induced changes, therefore, is of great con-cern. Not surprising, therefore, that the complexity of such issues continues to receive considerable attention at the global fora like the WSSD (World Summit on Sustainable Development, Johannesburg, August 2002) and Bishkek Global Mountain Summit (October 2002). These events have arrived at a consensus that mountains would require specific approaches and resources for sustaining livelihood needs and improving the quality of life. This would require an integrated approach, which gives due consideration to closely intertwined aspects of human socio-cultural/socio-economic systems and natural ecosystem components/processes.

UNIQUENESS

Among the global mountain system, the Himalaya is the most complex and diversified, and separates the northern part of the Asian continent from South Asia. The region being a discrete geographical and ecological entity, figures prominently in major biophysical settings of the planet earth. This vast mountain range (over 2500 km in length, between 80 and 300 km wide and rising from low-lying plains to over 8000 m asl) produced a distinctive climate of its own and influences the climate of much of Asia. The great variation in topographical features causes immense diversity in climate and habitat conditions within the region. Tem-poral and spatial variations caused by diversity in geological orogeny have resulted into a marked difference in climate and physiography and consequently in the distribution pattern of biotic elements.

This spatial position and heterogeneous dispersion of biodiversity elements have led to complexity in biogeographical patterns of the region. The eastern Himalaya (including northeast India) that harbours about 8000 species of flowering plants is considered a cradle of flowering plants, whereas the western Himalaya supports over 5000 species of flowering plants. The Indian Himalayan region (IHR) as a whole, supports nearly 50% of the total flowering plants in India of which 30% flora is endemic to the region.

There are over 816 tree species, 675 edibles and nearly 1743 species of medicinal value found in the IHR. In view of growing threat to biological diversity, conservation and rational use of biodiversity in the Himala-yan region could bring enormous economic benefits to the local populations and can indeed contribute to sustainable development.

The region is known as a 'water tower of the earth'. Approximately 10-20% of the area is covered by glaciers, while 30-40% remains under seasonal snow cover varying from 0.48 0.43 to 2.20 1.25 million km^2. Despite the vast water resources (1,200,000 million m^3 annual flow of Himalayan rivers) trends such as diminishing regulatory effects of glaciers, streams and rivers are gradually occurring in the region. This region has a total geographical area of about 530,795 km^2 inhabited by 31,593,100 people, representing 16.16% of the total area and 3.73% of the total population of India. The literacy rate (7 years and above) of IHR (about 67%) is marginally higher than the national average (65.4%) recorded in the 2001 census. Its forests display phenomenal biodiversity that is used to meet diverse needs

of the people. The forest biomass value in some oak forest stands of Central Himalaya, 545-782 t ha^{-1} yr^{-1}, is typical for the region. The Himalaya with its vast green cover acts as 'sink' for carbon dioxide. Estimates of annual carbon sequestration by the forests of western and northeastern Himalaya are computed to 6.49 mt, that values to 843 million US$ (A. K.

Tewari, unpublished data). This is one of the important ecosystem services being performed by the Himalayan forests. The beautiful landscapes, numerous rivers and streams cascading down the mountain slopes, diversity of cultures and religions, and colourful festivals of indigenous/ethnic communities present strong attractions for people from all over the globe, be they nature-lovers, tourists, or seekers of peace and truth.

ENVIRONMENTAL SECURITY AND PEOPLES' ASPIRATIONS

The people of the IHR, like elsewhere in other mountain ecosystems, are heavily dependent for their livelihood on their immediate natural resources and production from primary sectors such as agriculture, forestry, livestock, etc. The dependency of the continually growing population on finite resources, lack of viable technologies to mitigate the mountain specificities and enhanced production to meet the demands are depleting the resources along with increasing marginality of farmers, ultimately promoting poverty.

Despite its rich biological and cultural resources, the region is under-developed. Present trends of environ-mental health suggest that existing interventions are un-sustainable. Economic indicators also do not reflect the desired effects on economic upliftment.

In addition, the inherent fragility of the mountains as well as the increased vulnerability of the Himalaya to human-induced environ-mental impacts make people live in the shadow of fears of natural hazards. Large number of studies carried out in the region focusing on development interventions/initia-tives reflect the unscientific exploitation of resources lead-ing to increasing environmental degradations. Reduced dense forest cover, accelerated soil erosion and increased silting of water bodies, drying-up of springs, re-placement and disappearance of species and increased ratio of energy expended in fodder, fuel collection, and agricultural activity that increase drudgery of the womenfolk are some of the tell-tale symptoms of environmental ill-health.

ENVIRONMENT AS A HOLOCOENOTIC RESOURCE SYSTEM

Ecology is the science that elicits the functional inter-relationships among the different components of environ-ment on the one hand, and between the organisms and environment on the other. A major ecological principle states that the environment is holocoenotic in nature, and therefore any change in one component is bound to change the states of all other components.

For example, deforestation leads to increased run-off (hence floods), increased soil erosion (hence siltation of water bodies), disappearance of species (hence gene erosion), and atmospheric loading of CO^2 (hence global warming).

Thus the demand for timber and firewood across the country has had an impact on the forests of the Himalaya and deforestation in the Himalaya affects the flood situation in the Gangetic Plains. This ex-plains how the scale of deforestation effects ranges from local to regional to global.

Thus environment not only com-prises the life-support system for biological organisms, but is also a system of interacting resource subsystems. The term resource implies management. Proper manage-ment will not disrupt a system because a dynamic equilibrium will be maintained among its subsystems and components. Therefore, environmental degradation is the outcome of mismanagement leading to imbalance and over-exploitation of resources.

Interdependence of ecological and socio-economic activities The problems in the Himalaya are complex, having intri-cate linkages between social, economic and ecological concerns.

The solutions, therefore, cannot be addressed in isolation. To cite an example, the agro-and forest ecosystems are so intricately inter-related and inter-dependent that it is futile to talk of forest management in isolation without considering the cropland. In the Central Himalayan region, it is estimated that the cost of subsistence agriculture on the forest ecosystem is high. For example, for each unit of en-ergy obtained in agronomic production, seven units of energy are expended from the forest through the use of firewood, fodder and vegetal manure. A greater ratio of forest to cropland (5.18: 1) is needed for sustenance of agriculture against the present ratio of 1.66: 1. Problems have appeared because of the reduction in this ratio, im-plying that the carrying capacity of forests has already been exceeded.

Similarly, pasture development or revege-tation of wasteland without solving the problems of animal husbandry, fodder and fuel is not possible. The traditional agri-silvi-pastoral mode of subsistence living of the inhabi-tants of the region is no more sustainable, both ecologi-cally and economically.

It is apparent that sectoral practices of management (or development) will not work, and therefore, the only approach which will work is a holistic one consistent with ecologi-cal and social principles.

This approach also implies that the hill and adjoining plains must be taken as the macro-planning unit, with smaller structurally and functionally definable units for micro-level planning. The various eco-systems should be categorized into protective, productive and waste-dissipative systems and should be managed accord-ing to their roles.

Therefore, the basis of any planning for sustainable development in mountain areas has to be centred around man's relationship with nature. The rela-tionship is desired to be governed by a sense of justice and equity. Each culture is the result of the people trying to survive within their environment and indeed of an at-tempt to optimize the use of its resources.

Lifestyle and production systems develop steadily by experimentation and observations over centuries, till they become so cul-turally incorporated that they are like genetic knowledge.

This has been inherent in many tribal societies, but in the modern acquisitive society 'economy' gets priority over 'ecology'. There is need to evolve a new paradigm to re-store balance between economic interests and ecological imperatives. Although the ecological and economic sys-tems have a myriad of inter-connections, the most simple and most obvious is this: ecological system provides raw materials to the economic system and absorbs the waste generated by the economic system.

Therefore, the system will be constrained by the productive and waste-absorption capacities of the ecological system. When one or both these capacities are exceeded, ecological backlashes are bound to occur.

Once the waste-dissipative capacity of the Ganga was exceeded, severe pollution problem emerged which is now costing the government a huge sum of money, with still doubtful level of final out-come. Similar is the case for water bodies in the hills. When timber extraction or biomass extraction exceeded the limit of harvestable productivity of the forest, the lat-ter began to diminish.

The ecological and economic considerations are there-fore to be combined to attain ecologically sustainable deve-lopment. Both ecological and economic values can be served individually in a variety of ways, but combining ecological and economic considerations adds geometri-cally to the complexity of development programmes.

When socio-cultural systems are added onto the ecological-economic relationships, the situation becomes further complicated. However, development driven solely by economic considerations has changed the aspirations, value systems and management priorities. Demographic and legal factors further complicate the application of ecological considerations to development of goals and processes.

ACHIEVING SUSTAINABLE DEVELOPMENT

Simply stated, sustainable development implies the use of ecological system in a manner that satisfies current needs without compromising the needs or options of future generations. Strategies for sustainable development must be based on reliable and comprehensive data on natural, socio-cultural and socio-economic resources, as well as on the environmental set-up.

These strategies should incorporate traditional knowledge and established production systems after they have been carefully evaluated. The aim of sustain-able development should be to maximize human well-being or quality of life without jeopardizing the life-support environment. Although there is no unique defini-tion of quality of life, the following groups of variables together might be considered its indicators:

(i) economic variables: per capita income, employment stability, income distribution;

(ii) ecological variables: ecological degradation, environmental quality, use of renewable and non-renewable resources, human-initiated energy consumption;

(iii) social variables: social security, emotional support, intellectual growth and mental satisfaction;

(iv) cultural heterogeneity, and

(v) political variables: scope and use of government services, political participation, political power advantage and policies.

Solutions to the ecological and economic problems in the IHR are to be sought within the permissibility of mountain specificities and adaptability of people, which is governed by socio-cultural principles.

Identifying sustainable landuse practices, promotion of on-farm activities, value addition to all resources and adoption of environment-friendly technologies, restoration of degraded ecosystems, biodiversity conservation, water resource and hydro-power development, promoting community-based management, upgrading in-frastructure, improving quality education and capacity building to ensure benefits, are but a few priority activities to improve livelihoods, income and environment of the IHR.

CONCLUSION

The unique majestic Himalaya has provided immense ecosystem goods and services in the past and, with proper planning and management will be able to provide the same in the future also. However, we must acknowledge the fact that the whole IHR is facing anthropogenic pressure leading to overall degradation of its environment. Once symptoms of environmental deterioration become apparent, most often the only option left is to react to the situation and try to cure the problems by costly corrective measures.

It is much better however, to be able to anticipate the problem and take up preventive measures in the beginning. Proper education at various levels, long-range database and a holistic approach would bring us nearer to sustainable development ensuring better quality of life, improved eco-nomic status, and minimized adverse effect on life-support environment. There is also a need to experiment and devise ways and means to ensure that the development does not destroy its bio-cultural diversity and social fabric. The Himalayan region should not be burdened with back-ward-dragging heritage of the past, nor be constrained by the mistakes that bigger states have committed.

4

Himalayan Subtropical Pine Forests

The Himalayan subtropical pine forests are a subtropical coniferous forest ecoregion covering portions of Bhutan, India, Nepal, and Pakistan.

The ecoregion extends across the lower elevations of the great Himalaya range, from Pakistan's Punjab Province in the west through Pakistan administered Azad Kashmir, the Indian states of Jammu and Kashmir, Himachal Pradesh, and Uttarakhand, Nepal, the Indian state of Sikkim, to Bhutan in the east.

The predominant tree in the ecoregion is the drought-resistant Chir Pine (Pinus roxburghii).

HOW DEGRADED ARE HIMALAYAN FORESTS?

An IRS-1D multispectral image is used to measure the extent to which central Himalayan forests are degraded. The study area covers most of the eastern half of Uttaranchal state in the Indian Himalayas. Accuracy assessment was performed on a sample taken from an Ikonos 1-meter resolution image. We estimate that 61% (48-73%) of the forested area has less than 40% crown cover, with numbers in brackets denoting the 90% confidence interval. The calculation of confidence intervals is a novel feature of the study that is important in view of the fact that satellite image interpretation is never free of error. The results show that the Forest Survey of India's widely cited figures considerably understate the extent of degradation.

Over the past few decades there has been a great deal of concern about ecological degradation and deforestation in the Himalayas. The main aim of this paper is to provide estimates of the area of forest degraded in two Himalayan districts with 90% confidence intervals by using satellite imagery. Since all interpretation of satellite images is subject to error, it is important to provide not just point estimates, but also confidence intervals around those estimates. To the best of our knowledge, this has not been done for estimates of forest degradation in the Himalayas or elsewhere.

Degradation is measured in terms of crown cover. An IRS-1D multispectral LISS-III satellite image from May 1998 that covers an area of 20,000 square km in the Indian central Himalayas northwest of Nepal, is analysed. We present a vegetation map and estimates of the percentage of the area under forest or scrub, and the percentage of the forested area that is degraded. These figures are presented along with 90% confidence intervals, derived from crown cover counts done on a sample from an Ikonos 1-m resolution panchromatic image from April 2000.

The Forest Survey of India's biennial State of Forest Reports1, based on interpretations of IRS imagery, have been the main source of district-wise data on the state of forests in India. However, their estimates are presented without confidence limits or error matrices, and no information about the interpretation method is given. This study finds that a greater proportion of the forest area in two districts of Uttaranchal is degraded than the Forest Survey of India estimates would suggest.

DESCRIPTION OF THE AREA

The study area lies in the Kumaun and Garhwal regions in the state of Uttaranchal, and includes a small area in western Nepal. It lies between 79°E; 30.5°N and 80.75°E; 29°N, and ranges from 300 to over 7000 m in altitude. Terraced agriculture is found up to a height of about 1800 m on the gentler slopes.

The lower elevations from the plains at 300 m up to about 1000 m contain Submontane Seasonal Broadleaf forest with sal

(Shorea robusta) as the dominant species. The submontane zone has little human settlement. From 1000 to 1800 m there are chir pine (Pinus roxburghii) forests. From 1500 to 3000 m, overlapping the range of the pines, is a broadleaf forest consisting mainly of oaks, banj (Quercus leucotrichophora) and other Quercus species. Finally, there are the Mid-montane Needle-leaf Evergreen Forests from 1700 to 3000 m and higher, consisting of deodar (Cedrus deodara), firs, spruces and other species. Singh and Singh also identify some less common formations not described here. In some areas, grasslands occur naturally. While these forests intergrade into each other and there are mixed stands, there is, nevertheless, a strong tendency towards exclusive stands, particularly for the first three types of forest described above.

Forest degradation has resulted from a number of human uses. Overgrazing, lopping for firewood and fodder, resin tapping in the presence of fire, and commercial felling have all contributed to degradation. Degradation reduces crown cover and can proceed to the point when only scrub is left. Since, except for small areas of juniper above the treeline, scrub does not occur naturally in the area, we treat scrub as degraded forest.

The degradation of the forests has been a major blow to rural residents of the area who have suffered from the lack of firewood (the main source of energy for cooking and heating), fodder and grazing, and the adverse effects on springs which are the main water sources for villages on the slopes. Degradation may also affect areas in the plains since it may increase the runoff during the monsoon, leading to increased flooding during the monsoon months and reduced water supplies at other times of the year. Finally, of course, forests play a role in carbon fixation.

Methods

The aim was to obtain estimates of the area under forest or scrub and the percentage of the forest area degraded, together with confidence intervals for these estimates. A two-stage classification process was applied to the IRS image. In the first stage, training sites acquired during two years of fieldwork in 1997-99 were used to separate pine from broadleaf forests and forests from other classes.

This was done using a supervised maximum likelihood classification into 11 classes which were subsequently concatenated. In the second stage, quantitative estimates of canopy cover from the Ikonos imagery were used to separate the two forest types into dense and degraded classes. The Ikonos data were used to obtain sample error matrices for the classifications. These were used to compute producers' accuracies, that is the probabilities of classifying pixels from a given true class in the various classes. Point estimates of the true class proportions were obtained by inverting the producer's accuracy matrix and multiplying it by the vector of class proportions from the classified map. Confidence bounds for these point estimates were obtained by bootstrapping the sample error matrices and associated estimated true class proportions. The details are discussed below.

Classification and Accuracy Assessment

An IRS-1D LISS-III scene of 31 May 1998 (Path 98, Row 50) was used. We obtained an almost cloud-free image on a date that was close to the summer solstice. This was done so as to get an image with a sun elevation that was as high as possible (74) in order to minimize the shadowing that occurs in steep mountain terrain at a latitude of 30°N.

The LISS-III sensor on an Indian Remote Sensing satellite collects reflectance in four spectral bands with wavelengths 0.52-0.59 m (band 2, green), 0.62-0.68 m (band 3, red), 0.77-0.86 m (band 4, near infrared), and 1.55-1.70 m (band 5, near infrared). (Band 1 is a panchromatic band that we did not use. The spatial resolution (pixel size) of bands 2, 3, and 4 is about 23.5 23.5 m, as compared to the Landsat Thematic Mapper's 28.5 28.5 m. When the spatial distribution of land types is highly fragmented, as is the case in mountainous subtropical landscapes5, a relatively small pixel size is desirable to reduce the likelihood of mixed pixels, that is, pixels with more than one land cover class in them. Band 5 has a pixel size of about

70.5 m, resampled to the same resolution as bands 2, 3 and 4. As mentioned above, the vegetation map was generated in two stages. During several visits to the field from October 1997 to September 1999, potential training sites were identified by visual inspection. These sites were chosen in contiguous patches of vegetation that were at least 100 m across and which could be accurately located on a 1: 25000 Survey of India topographic map.

Ground features, compass, altimeter, and a GPS was used to locate the training site on a map. Each site was marked as a polygon leaving a 30-m buffer of the same vegetation around the polygon to eliminate errors in the signatures arising from edge effects and registration error. After eliminating sites that were in shadow or had positional errors, 169 sites, each consisting of one of eight classes, were selected for training. These were:

(1) dense broad-leaved forest,
(2) open broad-leaved forest,
(3) broad-leaved scrub
(4) dense pine forest,
(5) open pine forest,
(6) grassland,
(7) agriculture, and
(8) bare land.

The broad-leaved forest with a basically closed canopy was classified as dense. Conifers, mainly pine, were classified as dense if it was not possible to see the ground when the forest was looked at from the outside, and if the trees were close enough to leave no gaps between them. Signatures for the classes

(9) water bodies,
(10) snow, and
(11) cloud, were taken directly from the image.

Since the registration error from attempting to georeference the whole IRS image was high, those parts of the satellite image containing the training sites were georeferenced with root mean square registration errors ranging from 0.45 to 1.03 pixels.

The image was classified using the method of maximum likelihood assuming that the four bands were jointly normally distributed with different parameters for each class, and with each class given a prior probability of being equally likely. The entire procedure was implemented with Erdas Imagine 8.4 software. Classes (1)-(3) of those mentioned above, were merged to form a class called broadleaved forest (BL), (4) and (5) were merged to form Pine forest, (6) and (7) were merged into a category called Grasses, and the others were merged to form a category called Other.

After this study was underway, Ikonos 1-m resolution imagery became available. This offered an opportunity to improve the measurement of forest degradation since aerial photographs of this region are not in the public domain and were not available to us. An image from 24 April 2000, covering a transect 30 km in length from north to south and 2.5 km wide was procured from among the few images available for the area (Figure 1). This was intended to span the altitudinal zones corresponding to different vegetation types in the region. The Ikonos image was registered to the IRS image with a root mean square error of 0.7 IRS pixels.

After a field visit to prepare a key for visual interpretation, a random sample of 1024 points was taken from the transect. 75 75 m windows around these points were visually interpreted to correspond with the classes described above. The purpose of the 75 75 m windows (roughly equivalent to 3 3 IRS pixels) was to ensure that the true class of an IRS pixel at a point was correctly determined.

A smaller window might have led to true classes being incorrectly determined due to registration error. An additional sample of 256 points was randomly taken from areas rich in vegetation types under-represented in the original sample. These areas were determined visually from the Ikonos image, so that the additional points were selected on the basis of the reference or true class, and not the map class.

Six hundred and eight points for which the entire 75 75 m window fell in a single class, were retained for analysis. If the 75 75 m window contained more than one class, then we could not confidently assign the true class of the IRS pixel containing the random point, since registration error might lead to a shift in the location of the IRS pixel on the Ikonos image.

A producer error matrix for this sample, P = [pjk], where pjk is the percentage of points in class k that were classified by the maximum likelihood procedure as class j. Here the true class k refers to the 75 75 m window about the point, while the map class j refers to the class of the IRS pixel containing the point. This error matrix presents only three classes, broad-leaved forest, pine forest, and grassland and agriculture.

The Other class is not presented since its confusion with forest classes is negligible. Table 1 shows that separation of the three vegetation types is good, with over 80% producer accuracy being achieved for all three.

It was found that the first stage classification done above, while differentiating quite well between different forest types and grasslands and agriculture, performed poorly in distinguishing between dense and open classes in the same type of forest. We resorted to the second stage procedure described below to separate dense and open classes. A 10-m grid was laid on the Ikonos image and a 7 7 segment of this grid centred on each random point in the forest classes was used to measure crown cover.

The proportion of the 49 squares in each segment of the grid that were covered by tree crowns was the measure of crown cover. Of the 608 points, 553 points for which reliable crown cover counts were possible were retained.

Crown cover was used as the indicator of degradation. Any cutoff level for classifying an area as dense or open, is, of course, arbitrary. Two cutoffs were used: 40 and 80%. Eighty per cent was thought to be appropriate since an undisturbed broad-leaved forest in this region would have a closed canopy2. The 40% cutoff was used for comparison with the data generated by the Forest Survey of India, which uses a 40% cutoff.

The data were topographically normalized by using the ratios of band 5 to bands 2, 3 and 4. Classification into dense and degraded classes for both cutoffs for both broad-leaved and pine types was done using the maximum likelihood classifier applied to the three band ratios and aspect. Aspect is defined as a continuous variable taking all values from 0 for south-facing pixels to 1 for north-facing pixels.

The aspect variable was created in ArcMap 8 software using freely downloadable elevation data with a 90 m resolution from the SRTM (Shuttle Radar Topography Mission). (We are grateful to a referee for suggesting the use of aspect data for improving the classification accuracy which resulted in narrower confidence intervals.) The prior probabilities were chosen to roughly maximize the sum of classification accuracies of dense and degraded types while not allowing any of them to fall below 50% in the assessment sample.

Notice that there is still considerable misclassification of open or degraded categories as dense and vice versa, even after the use of the second-stage procedure.

The fact that the different forest types are classified with a fairly high degree of accuracy, but separation of degraded from dense forest is subject to considerable error is only to be expected.

There is not much difference between forests with crown cover slightly less than 40% and slightly more than 40%. There is no natural sharp distinguishing feature and so considerable misclassification is unavoidable in the latter case. For the purpose of estimating areas in the various classes, however, this need not matter as long as the producer error matrices are estimated with sufficient accuracy.

For this purpose, classification accuracy matters only insofar as it helps to reduce the variance in the estimate of the inverse of the producer error matrix. What is important is that a large enough sample of points be taken from each true class. Sample sizes for the different classes in our study were fairly large, ranging from 70 to 145. We elaborate on these points below.

Point Estimates of Degradation

The producer error matrix is defined by P = [pjk], where pjk is the probability that a pixel that is truly in class k gets classified in class j. From the vegetation map, the shares of land s = (s1,..., s5) under five classes (dense and degraded broad-leaved and pine forests, and grassland and agriculture) in the IRS image were obtained. The other classes either represented tiny fractions of the area like bare land, or (like snow) had negligible confusion with other classes, and so were excluded from the error matrix. Now,

s = Ps*,

where s* is the unknown vector of true shares of land in each class. Therefore, the vector of true shares of land in each class is given by

s* = P-1s.

Let P ^ = [p^ jk], where p^ jk is the proportion of sample pixels really in class k that were classified as class j. Replacing P by P ^ yields the following estimate, due to ref. (6), of the true shares of land in each class:

s^ * = P ^-1s.

s^

* is a consistent (roughly speaking, unbiased in large samples) estimate of s* if P^ is a consistent estimate of P. P is a consistent (in fact, unbiased) estimate of P, provided the misclassification probabilities in the Ikonos image area from which the sample was drawn are the same as the misclassification probabilities for the area as a whole, and for the subregions of interest.

This is our assumption. Since the vegetation types are the same and the Ikonos image covers a transect of the area, this assumption is thought to be reasonable, although, of course, it is unlikely to be wholly accurate. The more narrowly each class is defined, the more likely it is that the assumption will hold. On the other hand, expanding the number of classes raises the cost of getting a sample of a given size for each class, and also raises the probability of infeasible estimates (class shares that are less than zero or greater than one). With these considerations in mind we chose to use five classes.

The consistency of P does not require a simple random sample. It is sufficient that each subsample from a given true class be random. This is important since we would not have been able to obtain enough points in the rarer classes with a simple random sample. Note that it is certainly not true that the actual shares of land in each class are the same for the sampled area and the areas of interest.

This is why it is not possible to use the alternative adjustment procedures for estimating s* proposed by Tenenbein and Card. Those methods rely on consistent estimates of user accuracies ujk, that is, the probability that a pixel mapped as class j was really from class k. To get consistent estimates of user accuracies, the sample must be taken from an area with representative true class shares. This can be difficult for the following reasons.

Reference data usually come from either field observations or high-resolution imagery. Field samples are expensive. A randomly chosen point may prove to lie on the boundary of different true classes when visited in the field. This is especially likely to be the case in tropical or subtropical montane areas with high variability in landuse.

Using such a point is likely to result in the confusion of registration error with classification error. Dropping such points raises the cost of getting a sample of given size. Highresolution images (as in our study) are often available only for portions of the area of interest, and, therefore, are not representative of the shares of land use classes in the area of interest. Finally, if there is more than one area of interest, as in our study, methods utilizing the user error matrix would require a sample from each of these areas, thus multiplying the cost of the study.

The drawback of the method used here, which uses the producer error matrix, is that it requires a matrix inversion. This means that s^

* could have elements that are less than zero or greater than one. This problem is unlikely to occur if the diagonal elements of P (the probabilities that classes are correctly classified) are sufficiently close to l, and if the class proportions are not too unequal.

Matrices with diagonal elements too close to zero are illconditioned, meaning that small changes in the elements of such a matrix can lead to large changes in its inverse. Since it is P ^-1 that is used in the calculation of the true class proportions, if it is ill-conditioned, then the estimated true class proportions will have a large variance. A simulation study found that if the producer accuracies (that is, the diagonal elements) were at least 0.7, then this problem did not occur. This is why obtaining a classification accuracy of 70% in each class is desirable but higher accuracies are not necessary, provided the assessment sample size in each class is large enough.

Some of the diagonal elements in the error matrix are less than 70%, resulting in considerable variation in the inverse matrix. However, as we shall see below, we can still conclude that degradation has been overestimated by the Forest Survey of India. Thus, despite the low classification accuracies in some classes, we can still reach useful conclusions because the confidence intervals inform us about the limits of the likely errors.

Confidence bounds for the degradation estimates

We now come to the main contribution of this paper: computing confidence intervals for our estimated proportions of the areas in the different classes. s^

* is a useful estimate only if we know how much error it is likely to contain. The 90% confidence intervals on the elements of s^

* were computed as follows. One thousand random 'bootstrap' samples with replacement were drawn from the sample of 553 points used for accuracy assessment above, each being of the same size as the original. (See ref. 12 for a discussion

of bootstrap methods in the context of estimating error rates in classification problems.) Each bootstrap sample is thus a random draw from the original sample and results in a different distribution of band ratios in each true class. Then s^

* was calculated for each bootstrap sample by re-calculating P ^-1 and multiplying it by the original map proportions vector s. The 5th and 95th percentiles of the frequency distribution of s^

* thus generated give us the 90% confidence intervals on s^

*. The most straightforward way to narrow the confidence intervals and increase the precision of the estimates is to use a larger sample for those classes for which the sample size is small. This will reduce the sampling variability between bootstrap samples and thus narrow the confidence intervals on the error matrix, and therefore, on the proportions of the area in different classes. An increased sample size may also improve classification by allowing better estimates of the parameters although this effect is likely to be small except when starting from a very small sample size. Of course, increasing the sample size is costly in terms of increased field visits, or acquisition, geo-registration, and visual interpretation of high-resolution images.

Results

Referring to Table 3, we see that 72% (68-77%) (throughout the paper the ranges refer to the 90% confidence interval) of the old Almora district, subsequently split into Almora and Bageshwar, was under forest or scrub in 1998.

The Forest Survey of India (FSI) estimated the area under forest or scrub to be much lower: only 48%. As mentioned in the introduction, the FSI estimates are presented without any information on the interpretation methods used and without confidence bounds.

In fact, the FSI estimated the area under scrub in Almora district to be only about 1% of the total area, an unbelievably low number. This probably accounts for much of the wide discrepancy between their estimates and ours. Of the forest (including scrub) area, we find that 78% (68-86%) was degraded, i.e. had a crown cover of less than 40%. The FSI estimates the forest degraded to be just 19%. Again, a good part of the discrepancy is probably due to their misclassification of scrub and other degraded forests as non-forest.

A caveat that needs to be made at once is that our IRS image does not cover the whole of both districts (Figure 1). Nevertheless, this cannot account for such huge discrepancies. The part of Almora district not in our image is very small. The part of Pithoragarh left out is larger, but most of this is under permanent snow.

The FSI's underestimation of the forest and scrub area and related underestimation of the proportion of forested area that is degraded is repeated in the Pithoragarh district (subsequently split into Pithoragarh and Champawat). We estimate the forest or scrub area in the Pithoragarh district to be 71% (67-75%) while the FSI figure is only 36%. Again, their figure for the per cent of the total area of the district under scrub is rather low: just 4%. We find that 58% (45-70%) of the forested area has a crown cover below 40% while the FSI estimate is 31%.

While there is one other large-scale study that uses visual interpretation of 1972 Landsat MSS data and aerial photographs for ground truths13, it is unfortunately not directly comparable with ours, since they used different crown cover cutoffs and made no attempt to distinguish between scrub and grasslands. There are also a number of studies of much smaller areas in the region 14-17. They are all based on aerial photographs from the early 1970s and they generally found smaller proportions of forest with high crown cover than we do. Tiwari and Singh17 also included a time-change analysis using recent IRS imagery and found a decline in the extent of forests with high crown cover.

CONCLUSION

The results presented here suggest that the extent of forest loss in the Central Himalayas has been considerably understated in the widely cited estimates by the Forest Survey of India, partly because the extent of forest land that has been degraded has not been adequately counted. This paper has demonstrated a method for finding confidence intervals for the estimated areas under different classes. While the estimated confidence intervals for the proportion of the area forested in the two districts studied are closer, those for the proportion of forest with less than 40% crown cover are wider, a natural consequence of the fact that crown cover is a continuous variable. Despite the wide confidence intervals for degradation, the official figures lie below the lower limits of our confidence intervals in both districts. This illustrates the importance of giving confidence intervals for estimates of areas. Larger assessment samples, while more expensive, would narrow the confidence intervals, thus improving the precision of the estimates.

5

Patterns of Water Potential among Forest Types of the Central Himalaya

Water potential (y) of soil and trees was measured in 16 forests from 450 to 2310 m elevation in the Kumaun Himalaya, during a two-year period. Predawn y, averaged across all species at a site was high (i.e. not stressful) at low elevations and variable at higher elevations. The incidence of low y at high elevations was opposite the usual pattern elsewhere. Midday y varied similarly. Patterns of plant and soil y differed. y values, especially in summer and winter, were severe enough to affect tree growth adversely. A major factor controlling vegetation development and species distribution is water availability.

Central Himalayan forests grow in a strongly seasonal climate with several dry months. Indirect evidence and initial measurements indicate that this long dry period does limit tree species distribution and forest development. Himalayan forests extend from the lowest mountain slopes with nearly tropical temperatures to timberline. The low elevations appear likely to be drier than above; although precipitation varies inconsistently with elevation, lower temperatures and greater cloudiness at higher elevations should increase the effectiveness of precipitation.

The status of water availability is assessed using 'water potential', for which the highest value normal is zero; a high water potential (near zero) means that water is easily available to plants and a low value means that it is not easily available, inducing water stress. This report addresses one hypothesis of Zobel and Singh that water potentials become low enough to determine the distribution of Himalayan trees and vary among forest types, with lowest potentials during winter at high elevations and during the pre-monsoon heat at low elevations. This is a description of landscape-level patterns of tree moisture status in monsoon climate forests of Asia and in forests dominated by evergreen trees with leaf longevity of one year. It helps to test further our contention that Himalayan forests differ significantly from those in other regions.

Sixteen stands at nine locations from 450 to 2310 m elevation were selected to represent major forest types near Nainital, Kumaun region. Rainfall in Kumaun varies substantially; the Nainital basin is particularly wet. Weather during the years of the study included a very warm, dry pre-monsoon season in 1995 and a wet one in 1996; winters also differed in precipitation. Soils at the sites varied, including 60 to 75% sand, 6-29% silt and 8-24% clay. Coarse fragments were high within pine and cypress forests, and sand was highest beneath forests of cypress and sal. pH varied from 6.4 to 7.1.

Stands were classified subjectively into five forest types based on the estimated potential late seral dominant tree species. Types were named by the shortest appropriate common name of the dominant tree: sal, Shorea robusta; pine, Pinus roxburghii; oak Quercus leucotrichophora (banj), Q. floribunda (tilonj) or both; cypress, Cupressus torulosa; and mixed, which included at least 2 oaks and at least 2 deciduous species per stand.

The number of stands and the species sampled for each type was: sal (3), sal and pine; pine (2), pine; oak (6), banj, tilonj, Rhododendron arboreum; and pine; cypress (2), cypress, banj, tilonj and Cornus macrophylla; and mixed (3), banj, tilonj, Q. lanuginosa, R. arboreum, Carpinus viminea, Machilus duthiei, Fraxinus micrantha and C. macrophylla. For 13 sites in and near the Nainital basin, sites were grouped to determine whether physiographic location (basin, lower ridges, higher ridges) produced any consistent patterns in water potential.

At each stand, 3-5 trees of each major species were selected within 1 ha or less. Sample trees were 2-19 m tall; heights were usually similar among species at a given site.

Water relation attributes were sampled during six seasons per year for two years (October 1994-December 1996): fall-after monsoon rains with high soil moisture, but clear, dry and cooling weather; winter-after the dry fall months, with effects of extended freezing weather at higher elevations; spring-with warming temperatures, but before most new leaf production begins; early summer-with warm weather, supporting most production of new leaves; summer-the hottest season at the end of the dry months before the monsoon rains begin, while some leaves are continuing to expand; and, rainy season-hot, but wet, with generally very high soil moisture (sampled only in 1995).

Water potential (y) was measured as described by Zobel and Singh, before dawn when tree y should be maximal and at equilibrium with soil moisture, and at midday, when y should be minimal. Measurements of plant y were made on twigs with leaves, using a pressure chamber (Model 1000, PMS Instrument Co, Corvallis, OR, USA); during winter and spring, leafless twigs of deciduous species were measured. Soil y was measured once per sample date at 60-cm depth for three representative locations per stand using a thermocouple psychrometer (SC-10A, Decagon Devices, Pullman, WA, USA, with a NT3 microvoltmeter). For statistical analysis, variables were tested for normality using the Kolmogorov statistics. Those significantly departing from normality were transformed to produce a normal distribution. Overall the sites mean soil water potential (y) at 60-cm depth varied from-0.48 MPa during the rainy season to-2.60 MPa during summer, with an extreme low for the oak type of-3.51 MPa in summer. Such soils are dry enough to reduce growth and metabolic processes for mesophytes.

Soil y did not change significantly with elevation, both overall and in individual seasons. Physiographic position, after considering the effects of elevation, did not significantly affect soil y overall ($P = 0.312$), but influenced it significantly during the dry summer of 1995 (P = 0.020) and the dry winter of 1995-1996 (P = 0.033); the Nainital basin had higher soil y than the adjacent ridges, by at least 2.6 MPa in summer and by 0.7 MPa in winter. Despite substantial differences among means for individual forest types, there was much variability in soil y within types and the differences among them were not significant overall or in any season. The two study years differed significantly (P <0.0001) in soil moisture during both summer (1995,-3.43 MPa, 1996,-1.27 MPa, P = 0.0001) and winter (1994-1995,-0.36 MPa, 1995-1996,-1.59 MPa, P < 0.0001), considering only sites sampled during both years. This allowed us to contrast plant y between a wet and a dry year for summer and winter.

Predawn plant y varied significantly among sites at all sampling times except early summer 1995. Predawn y was significantly and negatively related to elevation overall and in all individual seasons, with low elevations having high y, and high elevations having a wide range of y. The correlation of predawn y with elevation was strongest in fall and winter (r^2 = 0.521 and 0.489, respectively) and weakest in spring and the rainy season (r2 = 0.158 for both). Predawn y varied with physiographic position differently than did soil y, being significant only in the drier winter when the lower elevation ridge sites had predawn y 0.4 MPa higher than the Nainital basin and the higher ridge (P = 0.002). Forest types, based on dominant late-seral tree species, differed significantly (P < 0.0001), and the relative values of types changed with season. Within individual seasons, types varied in all seasons, except the rainy season.

The sal type was most consistently high and the mixed type, most consistently low. All other seasons were significantly drier than the rainy season; summer was driest and summer, winter and early summer were all drier than fall. The contrast between dry and wet summers seen in soil y was reflected also in predawn plant y, but the difference was much less (1995,-1.22 MPa; 1996,-0.70 MPa; P < 0.0001). In winter, however, despite a strong differential in soil y, predawn plant y values were similar between years (1994-1995,-0.75 MPa; 1995-1996,-0.82 MPa; P = 0.433).

Water potential during midday declined significantly as elevation increased ($r^2 = 0.147$, $P < 0.0001$), considering data from all seasons. Variation with elevation was significant during all individual seasons, except the rainy season and strongest in winter and fall ($r^2 = 0.502$ and 0.402, respectively). Physiographic position was significantly related to midday plant y only during the dry winter 1995-1996, when sites on lower ridges were 0.5 MPa lower than those in the basin and higher ridges. Midday y varied significantly among seasons ($P < 0.0001$) and among forest types ($P < 0.0001$). Averaged across types, values were highest during the rainy season, lower and similar from fall through spring, and lowest in early summer and summer. Values varied significantly among forest types in most seasons, most strongly in fall and winter.

The sal types had the highest midday y in all seasons; cypress and mixed types were each lowest in two seasons. The contrast between the dry and wet summers seen in soil and predawn y also occurred in midday (1995,-2.07 MPa; 1996,-1.29 MPa; $P < 0.0001$). In winter, however, the dry and wet years were similar (1994-1995,-1.05 MPa; 1995-1996,-1.13 MPa) as they were for predawn y. Extreme values of midday y were most frequent in summer, with 62% of site species means below-1.5 MPa, in contrast to none during the rainy season and 14% during fall; however, means of midday y <-2 MPa occurred in all seasons, except the rainy season.

Plant y was less severe than that of the soil, but was low enough to limit growth and physiological processes of forest trees. Almost half the species site means of predawn y measured in summer were below-1 MPa, with a secondary concentration of low values in winter; winter predawn y below-1 MPa occurred at all sites above 2000 m elevation.

Reduction in osmotic potential associated with cold-hardiness, may contribute to low winter y; likewise, cold-induced xylem cavitation may also reduce winter y values. y values lower than ours have been measured for these species. For only two species, however, and then rarely, were our y values below the turgor loss point, determined using pressure-volume analysis.

Extreme predawn y values for each site (the average for all species at the time of measurement with the lowest average) were compared with three studies in the summer-dry climate of western Oregon, USA. Two studies used data from a single year, and third one11 used the minimal value for each site from 2 to 4 years of sampling. At higher elevations, Himalayan tree y values were within the range of those from the forests in Oregon, but below 1600 m they were higher than most y values from Oregon. Oregon forests were sampled by measuring conifer saplings 1-2 m tall, whereas Himalayan trees were all larger. In both regions, y during drought becomes more extreme as tree size declines. The fall predawn y in the Himalaya would be 0.4-1.3 MPa lower if 1-2 m tall trees had been used, based on samples of two oaks at one site. Thus, at higher elevations, drought appears to affect our sampled trees to an equivalent or greater degree as in the summer-dry situation in conifer forests of western Oregon. At lower elevations, however, the Oregon forests would have had more severe y even if 1-2 m tall trees had been sampled in our study.

Low elevation forests of sal and pine with sal at or below 1320 m, did not suffer low plant y, despite several circumstances that might have caused them: a longer and more severe dry season at low elevations, midday temperatures of 40-42°C during summer sampling, and occasional dry soil. At high elevations, y in some sites was as high as for the sal type, but in some situations all the higher elevation types reached lower potentials than forests including sal. The gradient of decreasing y with increasing elevation in the Himalaya is opposite that described for other forest gradients. In those areas, the lower elevational limit of forest appears to be set by drought. In the western coastal United States, for example, where drought coincides with the warm season, the lowest elevation forests exhibit the lowest y. Higher elevation forest types are differentiated by temperature, but not by their growing season y and even small trees in higher elevation communities may show little evidence of moisture stress. Three studies in western Oregon, USA illustrate this difference: extreme predawn y is positively and significantly correlated with elevation for the combined Oregon data set (r^2 = 0.128, n = 70, P = 0.0014), whereas our extreme Himalayan predawn y values are negatively and significantly correlated with elevation (r^2 = 0.437, n = 16, P = 0.0053). Similar to our situation, y in evergreen Mediterranean oak forest declined from 400 to 1145 m elevation, although the decline exceeded 0.7 MPa only in winter. The reversed gradient in the Himalaya may result from several factors:

(1) The sal forests we measured are still far up a rainfall gradient from any climatically-determined ecotone to non-forest vegetation.

(2) There is ample subsurface water movement down the lower slopes of the study area, which outcrops in the terai marshlands south of our study area, paralleling the base of the Himalaya.

(3) Sal trees are deeply rooted.

(4) Other forest types, not yet studied by ecologists, may occupy the drier sites of the lower slopes in the study area.

These forests, distributed amongst the sal types we measured on the mountain slopes, include drought-deciduous, tropically-derived taxa among the dominant trees. The difference between predawn and midday plant y(y) varied significantly among forest types, considering all seasons and in fall and early summer. y was high in cypress and oak types, and low in sal and mixed types. It was least in the rainy season (0.16 MPa), and greatest in early summer and summer (0.70 MPa in both). y did not vary significantly with elevation in any season or overall. Similarly to predawn and midday y values, y differed significantly between summers with dry and wet soil, but not between the contrasting winter seasons.

Predawn plant y was positively and significantly correlated with soil y. Correlation was strongest during the rainy season (r2 = 0.55) and significant in all other seasons, except spring. Despite this correlation, plant y varied in patterns different from those of soil y. Contrasts in soil y between wet and dry summers and winters were large and significant. Although predawn plant y differed similarly between summers (albeit less) as did soil, predawn plant y did not differ between winters, despite a difference in mean soil y of > 1.2 MPa. In contrast, midday plant y differed between years only in winter. The decline in plant y with elevation occurred despite no significant gradient in soil moisture. Plant predawn y was higher (i.e. moister) than that of soil over all seasons for both years and in all individual seasons except fall of both years (plant was y no different from soil) and in winter and spring of 1994-1995 (plants drier than soil). Among 96 site season combinations, 43 showed predawn plant y moister than soil; 11 combinations had plants drier than soil; and the remaining 42 showed no significant difference between plant and soil. Of the 11 situations in which plant predawn y was drier than soil, six were during the rainy season. Tree species that we measured produce 58-99 % of their fine roots in the top 60 cm of soil (S. P. Singh and G. C. Pathak, unpublished data), but apparently come into y equilibrium with moister soil layers than we measured on most sites, especially during the drier seasons.

These results represent the collective behaviour of the most important tree species in the most important forest communities along a 1900 m gradient, from tropical to cool-temperate forests. The patterns of y that we report suggest that water availability exerts substantial control over Himalayan forest distribution and composition. Rikhari et al. reported a similar conclusion based on measurements of soil moisture in oak forests in the same area.

Even in its broad scope, as presented here, some aspects of water availability in the central Himalaya occur in patterns contrary to those reported from other forest regions. As for other characteristics of central Himalayan trees and forest ecosystems, these forests are distinctive in important aspects of their water relations.

They cannot be accurately represented or understood only by reference to forests studied elsewhere. To summarize, our data confirm the hypotheses of Zobel and Singh2 that Himalayan trees suffer significant water stress and that forest types differ in their degree of water stress; the pattern of plant y among types, however, differed from that proposed. Low elevation sal and pine forests retained high water potentials the year round, whereas trees in some high elevation types became significantly dry in both summer and winter. Also, soil y at 60-cm depth could not be used to predict patterns of plant y.

A HIGHLY MOSQUITOCIDAL BACILLUS THURINGIENSIS VAR. THOMPSONI

A strain of Bacillus thuringiensis isolated from a soil sample in Pondicherry was examined for its flagellar antigenicity, mosquito larvicidal activity and protein composition. This strain was found to agglutinate with the antisera belonging to B. t. thompsoni and exhibit high toxicity towards the larvae of the species of Culex quinquefasciatus, C. tritaeniorhynchus, C. sitiens, Anopheles stephensi and Aedes aegypti, respectively. The 28 kDa protein which has been reported to be predominantly present in the mosquitocidal strains of B. thuringiensis was found to be present in a higher amount in this strain. Also, the mosquito larvicidal activity and electrophoretic profile were comparable to that of a strain of B. t. var. israelensis which is known to be highly toxic to mosquitoes. THE use of bacterial agents for mosquito control, especially Bacillus thuringiensis var. israelensis (Bti) is gaining widespread importance. Among various species of B. thuringiensis, serotypes B. t. israelensis, B. t. darmstadensis, B. t. kyushuensis7, B. t. morrisoni, B. t. fukuokaensis, B. t. medellin, B. t. canadensis, B. t. shandongiensis, B. t. amagiensis, B. t. jegathesan and B. t. higo are reported to be toxic to mosquitoes However, among all these varieties, Bti holds its place as the highly toxic mosquitocidal serotype. At the Vector Control Research Centre, Pondicherry a survey for the isolation of mosquito larvicidal bacterial agents was undertaken and during this programme several strains of B. thuringiensis were isolated from various sources, i.e. soil, water, larvae and roots of aquatic weeds representing diverse habitats. Among these, one strain of B. thuringiensis belonging to the serotype B. t. thompsoni (H-12) was found to be highly toxic to different species of mosquitoes.

This strain (VCRC Accession No. B175) was isolated from a soil sample collected near Pondicherry15. Water dispersible powder (WDP) was prepared from sporecrystal complex (SCC) of this strain and mosquito larvicidal activity determined as described by Manonmani et al. For comparison, a strain of Bti (VCRC Accession No. B17) was included in all the studies. The B. t. thompsoni strain was found to be toxic to 5 species of mosquitoes tested, namely Culex quinquefasciatus, C. tritaeniorhynchus, C. sitiens, Anopheles stephensi and Aedes aegypti and the LC50 values of this strain for these mosquito species were 250, 220, 300, 790 and 600 ng/ml, respectively. The corresponding values for Bti strain were almost similar to those of B. t. thompsoni.

As per this, the relative susceptibility of the different mosquito species to the two B. thuringiensis strains, can be arranged as C. tritaeniorhynchus < C. quinquefasciatus < C. sitiens < A. aegypti < A. stephensi. Thus, the LC50 values were lower for culicines than for anophelines (Table 1). This is in agreement with the findings of several other workers16-19. The protein profiles of the SCC of the two subspecies of B. thuringiensis were compared. Proteins were extracted as per the procedure of Yamamoto et al. and SDS electrophoresed on 10% polyacrylamide gel21. The proteins of both strains were found to resolve into 9 bands. However, 6 were present in major amounts in Bti (MW: 12, 24, 28, 40, 53 and 65 kDa), whereas only 4 were seen in B. t. thompsoni (MW: 12, 24, 28 and 40 kDa). Although solubilization of the crystalline parasporal inclusions from final whole culture of the 2 strains gave a complex profile of proteins, a 28 kDa protein reported

6

Thinking Beyond Dominants

Understanding the dynamics of mountain ecosystems, especially in relation to global climate change, requires strengthening of ecological databases. This calls for recognizing both the strengths as well as weaknesses of existing data sets. The existing ecological data sets on the Himalayan forests are considered appropriate for inclusion in any predictive model. However, to address issues of regional and global concerns, these databases need further strengthening. We attempt to highlight some of the weaknesses of Himalayan forest database and provide evidences from a case study of Myrica esculenta-a dioecious tree, to establish that hitherto neglected nondominant species have the potential to reflect changes. Such species also need to be taken into consideration while formulating forest conservation plans in the region.

The extent and diversity of Himalayan forests is well known and evidences indicate that these forests differ significantly from both tropical and temperate forests of the world. Such interpretations call for in-depth investigations, especially to understand the significance of variations in patterns within and among forests. This will facilitate the compatibility (and inclusion) of available Himalayan forest data sets with global databases. Until this happens, Zobel and Singh believe ecological generalizations at a global scale and the conclusions drawn about critical global/regional questions may prove erroneous and invalid.

While, on the one hand, recognition of Himalayan database among ecologists at a global level is needed, on the other, and perhaps more importantly, initiatives are required to further strengthen Himalayan forest database so as to enhance our ecological understanding at a local level. This understanding would be effective in addressing issues of conservation and management at local and/or regional level. A critical assessment of available information makes it amply clear that the Himalayan forest database:

(i) often exaggerate the ecological value of selected prominent (dominant/co-dominant) taxa and grossly underestimate the role of other associates. As a result, the management and conservation prescriptions largely focus on issues related to dominant taxa;

(ii) largely remain silent on possible effect of habitat/spatial heterogeneity on demographic processes (e.g., dispersal, recruitment, survival, etc.) of individual species (including the widely known dominants). As a consequence, potential predictive values associated with a species remains masked, and questions on inter and intra-specific interactions of plants remain unanswered;

(iii) mostly appear biased in favour of hermaphrodite or monoecious group of species. Therefore, many significant dioecy dependent effects on structure and function of forest stands are not accounted for. Among others, these aspects highlight the gaps in Himalayan database. These gaps can be filled only if studies are designed to collect data on individual species in representative forest stands.

Although creation of database on all associates in a forest appears to be a daunting task, studies on selected species, with frequent presence in regional forests and proven sensitivity towards ecological and socio-economic systems, improve applicability and effectiveness of Himalayan forest database. In particular, the species (or their assemblages) with narrow ecological amplitude might emerge as surrogate to reflect changes in forest ecosystem pattern or processes and could provide a basis for effective management. In this context, an attempt was made to generate evidences from a detailed case study of Myrica esculenta Buch.-Ham. ex D. Don (vern.-Kaiphal)- an ecologically and economically important tree, which frequently forms distinctive stands in Himalayan temperate forests. The species, a dioecious moderate-sized evergreen tree, also offers an opportunity to address hitherto neglected aspects of dioecy-dependent heterogeneity in these forests. The study explores the role of M. esculenta in determining the structure of forest communities (Kumaun, west Himalaya, India), and the results are discussed for their wider ecological implications in the region.

CONTRIBUTION TO COMMUNITY COMPOSITION

In the region (central Himalaya sensu Singh and Singh) chir pine (Pinus roxburghii), banj oak (Quercus trichophora) and mixed broad leaf forests are the most widely distributed community types between 1000 and 2200 m elevation range. M. esculenta is a common associate of these forests. Considering tree density and basal area as major attributes of stand structure, M. esculenta-containing stands in these forests showed an overall similarity with the other forest stands (without or with diffused M. esculenta individuals) in the region. Therefore, from a self-thinning perspective, Myrica stands revealed age (growth) similarity of tree individuals with the rest of the regional forests. However, higher density of saplings suggested that the competition among trees for space is not severe in M. esculenta stands. This would imply that these stands have scope for further increase in density of smaller trees until a substantial crown overlap develops. Considerably high densities of young (seedling and sapling) individuals in Myrica stands need additional explanation. Presumably, these stands provide a better niche for recruitment of dominant species and M. esculenta itself6. The precise details from local habitat features (i.e. microhabitats) are not available to explain these processes. One important factor could be the nitrogen fixing ability of Myrica, which has been reported to change the fertility status of stand elsewhere7.

FAVOURABLENESS OF SITES AND HABITATS

M. esculenta stands, in all conditions (habitat and canopy conditions), maintain significantly higher male tree density and in most cases, males showed larger mean tree size. Studies elsewhere reveal occurrence of differential growth and/or reproductive effort among dioecious plants and that higher proportion of males indicate extremes of species range and resource-poor habitats. Therefore, male biased sex ratio of M. esculenta could be indicative of its peripheral geographic range of distribution and also an overall resource-poor condition of habitats in the region. However, in order to establish these assumptions, investigations on ecological aspects of the sex ratio, especially from other climatic extremes, like eastern Himalaya, are needed. Analysis and documentation of such information over a range of spatial extent will prove immensely useful in indicating climate/habitat changes, if any, in the region.

Moreover, in view of sex segregation on a narrow spatial scale (i.e. Kumaun Himalaya), increased femaleness coupled with greater seedling recruitment and establishment of rich sapling banks in high altitude sites, is indicative of overall suitability of these sites. Considering the upper distribution limit of M. esculenta around 2200 m asl, the present findings suggest likely expansion of this species towards upper distribution limits. The observation of better germination potential of seed6 from high altitude provenance further strengthens these possibilities.

IMPLICATIONS FOR COMPOSITIONAL CHANGES

Overall higher density of young individuals in forest stands with reasonable Myrica dominance has significant implications on composition of regional forests. Apparently, the presence of M. esculenta in these forest stands facilitates higher recruitment (seedling) and stocking of young (sapling) individuals. The increase was recorded in both the dominant species and in M. esculenta also. These observations assume greater significance when a low seedling/sapling density is being reported frequently from the forest stands in the region. M. esculenta shows habitat/ source specific variations in natural recruitment and seed germinability6. The relative high contribution of Myrica seedlings and saplings in chir pine forests is indicative that this habitat provides a satisfactory regeneration niche. Also, seeds obtained from this habitat showed higher germination response.

All these evidences tend to make one presume a likely future increase of M. esculenta density in these forests. Since the fruits of Myrica are edible and its seeds are dispersed widely by animals, especially by the rhesus macaque (Macaca mulata), common langur (Presbytis entellus) and birds, this increase may be expected even in sites away from Myrica-prevalent stands.

The experiments on seeds obtained from sources located at different altitudes showed significant variation in germination. Seeds from high altitude source revealed significantly high germinability. The findings of laboratory germination more or less followed the pattern of natural regeneration6. Such results of altitudinal variation are interesting and merit consideration while describing the future trends of forest vegetation in the region. In general, the marked alterations in regeneration patterns (individually and/or collectively) are to affect the composition of all three Myrica habitats (i.e. Pinus roxburghii forest, Quercus leucotrichophora forest and mixed broad-leaf forest). The intensity of changes may be more prevalent in stands located at upper limits of Myrica distribution (i.e. 2000-2200 m asl). On a wider perspective, when upward migration of life zones (species and forest boundaries) is expected in mountains as a widespread consequence of global warming, the trends of frequent Myrica recruitment at its upper distribution limit accompanied by the results of differential responses of seed germination and recruitment in forest habitats may provide an insight as to how the composition of regional forests may tend to change in future. This, however, needs to be authenticated through the evidences of future experimental research.

Implications for Management and Conservation of Regional Forests

Preceding discussion leads us to consider fresh management options in forests in the region. For instance, the implications of male-biased sex ratio of M. esculenta can be viewed as an overall resource-poor situation of these forest habitats. On the other hand, the increased femaleness of M. esculenta accompanied by markedly high recruitment in Myrica stands at higher altitudes may be considered as an evidence of possible upward shift in species/forest boundaries in the region. Such considerations need due attention in management/conservation plans concerning regional forests.

Moreover, the trends of better Myrica recruitment (natural regeneration and experimental responses of seed germination) in chir pine forests (Figure 1) have significant implications. These forests, usually forming stands of their own with very few associates in tree and shrub layer, have prevailed and expanded in the region1. Despite the proven value for conserving nutrients efficiently on steep hill slopes16, on account of their invading nature and poor species richness1,17, chir-pine forests are not viewed positively by the conservation biologists and environmentalists18. The present investigation has, however, established that these habitats if used properly, can prove beneficial for promotion of M. esculenta-an ecologically and economically important species for the region.

CONCLUSIONS

Intensive ecological researches on Himalayan forests have highlighted the significance of voluminous data sets at a global scale. However, overemphasis on dominant and co-dominant taxa has led to biases in ecological interpretations. There is an urgent need to reduce these biases, particularly when the responses of Himalayan ecosystems, as in case of other mountain systems, are being considered as early warning indicators of global climate change. The present ecological study on hitherto little-known tree species (M. esculenta) draws reasonably sound conclusions on predictive value of such ecological database. For instance, the data sets provide important clues for:

(i) predicting possible changes in composition and boundaries of major forest types in the region,

(ii) understanding implications of such changes for addressing issues of forest management especially in the event of climate/habitat change, and

(iii) recognizing the importance of dioecy-dependent variations for strengthening the ecological database on Himalayan forests.

PLANT DIVERSITY IN SIX FOREST TYPES OF CENTRAL HIMALAYA

Quercus spp. (oaks) and Pinus roxburghii Sarg. (chirpine) are the major forest-forming tree species in the Central Himalayan region. P. roxburghii forest is generally pure with low total species richness of shrubs and herbs, while mixed-broadleaved forest has high total species richness. Shrubs and herbs show high species richness in P. roxburghii mixed-broadleaved forest and low species richness in Quercus semecarpifolia Sm. forest. Quercus leucotrichophora A. Camus forest has high tree diversity, while shrub and herb diversity is highest in Cupressus-Quercus mixed forest.

Anthropogenic disturbances are changing the species richness and diversity, which influence the soil and environmental conditions. Thus, the conservation and management of these forests will be important for the sustainability of human and land in the region.

The most striking feature of the earth is the existence of life, and the most striking feature of life is its diversity. Topography, soil, climate and geographical location of a region influence the vegetation diversity of the forest ecosystem.

The Himalayan forest vegetation ranges from tropical dry deciduous forests in the foothills to alpine meadows above timberline. Forest diversity is the main source of livelihood of the people living in Uttaranchal, Central Himalaya. India is among the important megabiodiversity centres of the world, with a lot of contribution from the Himalayan ecosystem. Biodiversity is used variously for fodder, fuel wood, timber, leaf litter for manuring crop fields, construction, industrial raw material and several non-timber forest produce.

Forests of this region are mainly dominated by Pinus roxburghii Sarg. (Chir Pine) and Quercus leucotrichophora A. Camus. (Banj oak). Chir pine often forms a pure crop in this area, but sometimes it also mixes with certain broadleaved species like Q. leucotrichophora, Quercus glauca Thumb, Pyrus pashia Ham., Myrica esculanta Linn. and Rhododendron arborium Sm. Q. leucotrichophora prefers cooler aspects below

1900 m asl and is found in either pure or mixed with other broadleaved species.

The increasing population trend over the last few decades and consequent dependence on plant products has led to the vast exploitation of natural flora and fauna of this region. The accelerating effects of human activities on biodiversity might impact ecosystem functioning. This has renewed interest in the effect of diversity on ecosystem and on ecosystem services essential to society6.

Several studies documented that the changes in the landuse, habitat fragmentation, nutrient enrichment and environmental stress often led to reduced plant biodiversity in natural ecosystem. Forest biodiversity of Uttaranchal has been studied by different workers. In the wake of efficient socio-economic development and for the betterment of soil, livestock and human, the conservation of biodiversity in the Himalaya is assumed to be of great significance.

The present study deals with species richness and plant diversity in relation to anthropogenic disturbance in different forest types of Uttaranchal. The study area (Uttranchal, Central Himalaya) is located between 79 23 and 79 42°E, and 29 20 and 29 30°N. The altitude ranges between 1300 and 2600 m asl. The climate is influenced by monsoon pattern of rainfall. Generally, the average annual rainfall ranges between 200 and 250 cm; three-fourth of this occurs in the rainy season (mid-June to mid-September).

The mean monthly minimum temperature ranges between 2.0 (January) and 15.0°C (July) and mean maximum temperature ranges between 4.0 (January) and 28.0°C (May). The rocks of the study area are a complex mixture of mainly sedimentary, low-grade metamorphosed and igneous.

The study was conducted in six forest types of Uttaranchal Himalaya. Each forest type is named after the dominant tree species12. The size and number of the samples were determined15. Species composition for trees, shrubs and herbs was prepared after a thorough survey of different forests. Within each forest type, all the vegetation layers, i.e. trees, shrubs and herbs were analysed for species richness and diversity. The tree canopy cover was measured by randomly placing ten transects of 400 m^2 in each forest. Herbaceous cover was determined by line intercept method.

Trees were analysed in ten 100 m^2, shrubs in 25 m^2 and herbs in 1 m^2 plots randomly in each forest. Herbs were analysed during peak growing season.

Plants and the flora were identified with the help of plant taxonomists. Species richness was determined as the number of species per unit area. Species diversity was calculated by using Shannon-Wiener information index. Data were analysed for single factors by analysis of variance (ANOVA). Linear correlation was developed for tree cover and species richness. Correlation coefficient was also determined for various richness and diversity parameters. A total of 132 species was recorded from the study area, out of which 22 were trees, 43 shrubs and 67 herbs.

Highest tree diversity was found in the P. roxburghiimixed-broadleaf forest. Maximum shrub and herb richness was 27 and 47, respectively, in P. roxburghii-mixed broadleaf forest and minimum in Q. semecarpifolia forest (9 shrubs and 13 herbs). Among tree species, Q. leucotrichophora was widely distributed and present in all the forest types, except in Q. semecarpifolia forest. Similarly, Pyracantha crenulata M. Roemer, a shrub, was present in all the forests except in Q. semecarpifolia forest. Anaphalis contorta Hook. f, an erect herb, and Chrysopogon serrulatus, a grass, showed their presence in all the forest types.

Maximum mean tree species richness per 100 m2 was found in Q. leucotrichophora forest, whereas the highest mean shrub richness (25 m^2) was found in P. roxburghii mixed-broadleaf forest. Maximum herb species richness (1 m2) was in P. roxburghii mixed-broadleaf forest and Cupressus-Quercus forest. ANOVA indicated that the mean tree richness was significantly higher ($P < 0.01$) in P. roxburghii mixed-broadleaf forests and Q. leucotrichophora forest compared to Q. floribunda and Q. semecarpifolia forests. Mean shrub richness was significantly higher ($P < 0.05$) in P. roxburghii mixed-broadleaf forest and Cupressus-Quercus forest compared to other forest types. Mean herb richness was significantly lower ($P < 0.01$) in Q. semecarpifolia forest. The overall total and mean species richness were lowest in Q. semecarpifolia forest. The total tree species richness was positively correlated ($P < 0.01$) with shrubs and herbs. Similarly, the total shrub richness was positively related ($P < 0.01$) with herb richness.

Q. floribunda and Q. semecarpifolia forests had the highest tree crown cover, while P. roxburghii mixed-broadleaf forest had the lowest. Forests around human habitation are lopped frequently for fodder and fuel wood. This may be one of the reasons for low crown cover. Total shrubs and herbs richness significantly decreased ($P < 0.01$) with increasing tree cover. Shrub cover significantly decreased ($r = -0.73$, $P < 0.01$) with increasing tree cover. Tree species diversity was positively correlated with shrub diversity ($r = 0.81$, $P < 0.01$) and herb diversity ($r = 0.67$, $P < 0.05$).

Forest biodiversity is the main source of livelihood of the people of Uttaranchal. Agriculture is the main occupation around which all human activities are centred and is mainly managed at the cost of the surrounding natural forests. The forests present around the crop fields are highly degraded due to continuous anthropogenic disturbances.

Thus, the biodiversity of these forests is under great anthropogenic pressure. P. roxburghii mixedbroadleaf forest is present around the crop fields in midelevation and has the highest anthropogenic disturbances. Q. semecarpifolia forest is situated on the higher elevations and has the least anthropogenic disturbances.

High richness and diversity was reported in P. roxburghii mixed-broad leaf forest, while lower values were reported in pure P. roxburghii and high altitude forests. Disturbances promote undergrowth species diversity, possibly by allowing several species to maintain their population in open canopy. More penetration of light in open-canopied forest may enable each species to develop large populations that may be less vulnerable to local extinction. The frequent anthropogenic disturbances in P. roxburghii mixed-broadleaf forest were responsible for the low crown cover, while Q. floribunda and Q. semecarpifolia situated away from the human habitation were characterized by high crown cover. Canopy disturbance frequently enhances plant biodiversity. This enhanced biodiversity could be related to environmental heterogeneity in the form of patchy light availability, spatial heterogeneity in soil resources and local deposition of fallen trees.

Alternatively, the increased diversity could be caused by addition of colonizing species to a disturbed community, regardless of environmental heterogeneity-as long as the number of colonizing species exceeds the number of species lost to the disturbance. The forest will be less protective if the canopy is concentrated only at the top. However, if the top-layer trees are supported by deep and dense canopies in lower strata, the vegetation will be more protective.

Thus, the anthropogenic disturbances play an important role in change, loss or maintenance of plant diversity of a region. Trees are lopped for fuel wood, fodder for the domestic animals, timber for house construction and industrial raw materials. Various produces like removal of forest floor biomass, edible fruits, fibre, gum, resin, dyes, tannin, spices and more importantly, medicines are exploited from these forests.

These anthropogenic disturbances not only influence the soil, nutrient and water conditions, but also influence climatic conditions. The conservation and management of biodiversity of these forests will be important for the sustainability and improvement of soil nutrient and water conditions of the region.

CHARACTERIZATION AND SCREENING OF BACTERIA FROM RHIZOSPHERE OF RICE GROWN IN ACIDIC SOILS OF ASSAM

Three groups of rhizobacteria were isolated using three selective culture media from the rhizosphere of rice grown at fifteen locations in Assam. Four bacteria in each group were selected for taxonomic identification, characterization and also for screening the superior isolates to promote rice growth. The isolates of phosphate-solubilizing and fluorescent bacterial groups were found to be eight different species. The three isolates of azospirilla group were identified as Azospirillum brasilense and the fourth isolate was identified as Azospirillum amazonense.

RAPD analysis of the Azospirillum isolates indicated that azospirilla were four distinct genotypes. These bacterial strains showed differences in growth pattern, IAA production level (2.0-21.6 g/ml of culture supernatant), antibiotic resistance profile and nitrogenase activity (0.33-0.75 nmol C2H4 h-1 100-cc root volume) in the inoculated roots. A. amazonense A10 (MTCC 4716), Bacillus pantothenticus P4 (MTCC 4695) and Pseudomonas pieketti Psd6 (MTCC 4715) increased rice grain yield by 55.5, 12.2

7

Conservation Issues in the Himalayan Region

INTRODUCTION

The Himalayan region is bestowed with varied landscape features that provide multitude of habitats to a diverse array of faunal communities including several species of wild ungulates (Prater 1980, Section 1 of this issue). The region covers nearly 11% of India's geographical area and range from sub-tropical to alpine zones. The region is well known for extensive alpine biome, temperate conifer and broadleaf forests, sub-tropical (foot-hill) forests, temperate grassy slopes, and various other habitats. Despite tremendous potential, most of the areas in this region exhibit low abundance of wild ungulates. It is an irony that there are more Himalayan Tahr (Hemitragus jemlahicus) in New Zealand in comparison to the Himalayan region (Caughley 1967, 1970). This fact generally speaks of the status of wild ungulates in the region. Most of the ungulates are found in small isolated pockets and largely restricted to Protected Areas (PAs). Even within the PAs, especially in the eastern Himalaya and adjacent hill states, wildlife and ungulate densities are very low (Katti et al., 1990). It is not surprising that a naturalist, having conducted large mammal surveys in the eastern Himalaya, is known to have commented, "the stage is beautiful but many of the actors are missing".

Questions on mountain ungulate conservation in the Greater Himalaya range from 'What are the reasons for low ungulate abundance in the Himalayan region' to 'What are the major issues pertaining to their conservation' and 'What are the ways and means to achieve better conservation status for mammals in general and the ungulates in particular'. We address these issues and strategies for conservation for mountain ungulates in the Greater Himalaya in this article.

Major Conservation Issues

Several factors have led to low abundance and poor conservation status of ungulates in the Himalayan region. Firstly, the Himalayan ecosystem is relatively young, fragile and low in primary productivity. With the increase in human population the area has undergone rapid degradation, fragmentation and loss of wildlife habitat. Poaching and trade of animal parts, competitive exclusion by the domestic livestock, faulty land use practices, and human-wildlife conflicts are other factors affecting wild ungulates and other faunal communities (Gaston et al., 1983, Green 1985, Sathyakumar 1994, Sathyakumar et al. 1993, Vinod & Sathyakumar 1999). Some of the issues related to conservation of wildlife ungulates are discussed below.

Habitat Degradation and Fragmentation

(i) Alpine Habitats of the Greater Himalaya: The region above natural tree line (ca. 3300-3600 m above mean sea level in the western and north-western and ca. 3600-3800 m in the central and eastern Himalaya) represent alpine habitats which are characterized by treeless vegetation, alpine scrub and meadows. The ungulates frequently inhabiting this zone are Blue sheep (Pseudois nayaur), Himalayan musk deer (Moschus chrysogaster), and Himalayan tahr. The major causes leading to degradation and fragmentation of alpine habitats include overgrazing by livestock (Kala and Rawat 1999), commercial harvest of wild medicinal herbs, uncontrolled tourism and mountaineering in certain areas (Sathyakumar 1993a). The area is very prone to soil erosion, avalanches and landslides owing to steep and fragile terrain. Very few PAs in the region give complete protection to alpine habitats except a few (e.g., Valley of Flowers NP and Nanda Devi National Park [NP] in Uttaranchal). However, a majority of the PAs remain neglected in terms of management even though they represent important habitats for typical faunal communities (Kothari 1995, Rawal & Dhar 2001).

(ii) Sub-alpine Forests: The area between ca. 3000 m and natural 'tree line' represents an important ecological belt throughout the Himalaya. Besides Himalayan musk deer and serow (Nemorhaedus sumatraensis), it forms summer habitat for two important ungulates viz., Hangul (Cervus elaphus hanglu) in the west (Kashmir Valley) and Takin (Budorcas taxicolor) in the east (Mishmi hills, Arunachal Pradesh). Of all the habitats in the Himalayan region, the sub-alpine forests have undergone maximum degradation and fragmentation owing to anthropogenic activities such as collection of non-timber forest produce (including montane bamboo, mushroom, medicinal and aromatic plants), poaching, livestock grazing and camping by the herders (Awasthi et. al. communicated). Sathyakumar et al. (1993) have reported that increased livestock grazing and associated impacts have led to low musk deer densities in many areas in Kedarnath Wildlife Sanctuary. The subalpine forests, 'tree line' and the alpine scrub interspersed with alpine meadows is the optimal habitat for musk deer but this habitat, particularly the 'tree line' has degraded in many parts of the Himalaya due to cumulative impacts of livestock grazing. Most graziers prefer to camp and graze their livestock in and around 'tree line' due to availability of fuel wood, water, food and cover for livestock.

(iii) Montane forests of North-Western and Western Himalaya: The forested habitats in middle elevation rages (1500-3000 m) in the western and north-western Himalaya exhibit a great diversity of flora and fauna. The major vegetation types include Himalayan Dry Temperate (conifer), Himalayan Moist Temperate (broadleaf), and several other categories (Champion &

Seth 1967, Singh and Singh 1987). In many areas (especially on south facing gentle slopes) the forests have been transformed into the scrub jungle and cultivation. The common ungulates of the forested habitat include Himalayan musk deer, serow, goral, sambar (Cervus unicolor), barking deer (Munitacus muntjac) and wild pig (Sus scrofa). Much of the forested habitats in the region are affected by encroachment for habitation and cultivation, livestock grazing, lopping of trees for fodder. These activities have led to failure of regeneration and resultant change in the structure and composition of forests. Rawat et al. (1999) have reported that plant species diversity have changed with an increase in unpalatable plant species in the fringes of Kedarnath Wildlife Sanctuary as a result of human use. The forests of Western Himalaya are rich in wild mushrooms including highly prized morel (Morchella esculenta). Local people, in large groups, visit several parts of such PAs in order to collect this mushroom thereby causing heavy disturbances and affecting the threatened and sensitive species of fauna such as Himalayan musk deer and pheasants (Vinod and Sathyakumar 1999, Ramesh et al. 1999).

(iv) Central and East Himalayan Montane Forests: Major forest types in the middle elevation (1500-3000 m) ranges of Sikkim (Central Himalaya) and Arunachal Pradesh include Temperate Broadleaf Forests, Conifer forests and bamboo brakes. These forests support Himalayan musk deer, serow, takin, several other ungulates such as Asian elephant (Elephas maximus), gaur (Bos gaurus), sambar, wild pig and various other mammals including primates, and carnivores. But for the occasional fire (localized in certain areas) and slash and burn agriculture in some parts of Arunachal Pradesh, much of the forested habitats in the central and eastern Himalaya are intact (IIRS 2002).

(v) The Shivaliks and sub-Himalayan Forests: This zone (<1500 m) represents the sub-tropical climate, varied topography, rich alluvial soils and intermingling of taxa from the Indo-malayan and Palaearctic regions. The major forest formations, according Champion & Seth (1968) include Sub-tropical Dry Evergreen Forests, Sub-tropical Pine Forests, Northern Dry Mixed Deciduous Forest, Dry Shivalik Sal Forest, Moist Mixed Deciduous Forest, Sub-tropical Broadleaf Wet Hill Forest, Northern Tropical Semi-evergreen Forest, and Northern Tropical Wet-evergreen Forest. The Shivalik hills are best represented between the Ganges and Yamuna rivers in Uttaranchal. The entire belt all along covers an area of ca. 40,000 km^2 of which only <2100 km^2 area falls under PAs represented by Simbalbara WS, Rajaji and Corbett NPs. Ecologically, entire Shivalik belt is considered as highly sensitive zone. This region suffers heavy fragmentation and degradation of habitat due to human encroachment and proliferation of exotic weeds such as Lantana camara, Parthenium hysterophorus, Cassia tora, and Sida spp. Hajra (2002), based on the analysis of remote sensing data of Shivalik zone in Uttaranchal found that even though south facing slopes appear to be suitable for goral, but only about 13% area was moderately suitable and less than 1% area is highly suitable for this species. Rest of the area is either forested or very steep and not available for goral.

(vi) The North-Eastern Hills: The natural landscapes and habitats in this region have been extensively modified due to shifting cultivation or slash and burn (Jhum) agriculture. Besides, pressure on the land due to exploitation of forest for timber and lack of a scientific forest management has led to proliferation of exotic weeds and degradation of forests. With tremendous increase in human population during recent decades the jhum cycle has come down from 20-30 years to about 5 years and even up to 3 years in many areas. Reduction in jhum cycle due to increase in pressure on land has accelerated the process of habitat degradation and fragmentation which has affected ungulates and other faunal groups in the region (Mishra et al., 1994).

(vii) Temperate Grassy Slopes: The temperate belt in the western and north-western Himalaya support an extensive grassland habitat which is largely anthropogenic in nature. These grassy slopes have developed largely on the south facing, steeper slopes which cannot be cultivated and are burned during winter to promote grass growth. Such slopes are grazed and maintained as hay slopes or 'Ghasnis' in many sectors of Western Himalaya. The steeper and inaccessible areas are occupied by Himalayan tahr and goral (Schaller 1973, Cavallini 1990, Johnsingh 1992, Lovari & Apollonio 1993, Sathyakumar 1994, Mishra & Johnsingh 1997). Goral is one of the prominent species of mountain ungulates that has evolved in this habitat in the region (Mishra 1993, Pendharkar 1993). The gentler slopes close to human habitation have degraded over the years and goral habitat has been reduced considerably. The temperate grassy slopes and adjacent woodlands of Dachigam NP, Kashmir valley support a highly threatened subspecies, the Hangul or Kashmir stag. The grassy slopes of Dachigam are also reported to have degraded considerably over the years (Khursheed Ahmed, personal communication).

Habitat Loss

Excessive degradation and fragmentation eventually leads to habitat loss. Systematic studies documenting loss of ungulate habitats in the Himalayan region are lacking. Hence, it is difficult to point out clear cases of this phenomenon. However, in most of the sectors, there are plenty of evidences indicating the shrinkage of wildlife / ungulate habitat. Green (1986) reported that over 70% of potential musk deer habitat has already been lost due to habitat loss and habitat degradation in the southern side of the Greater Himalaya. Based on the spatial time-series analysis of remote sensing data, Awasthi (2001) has pointed out that in upper regions of Bhagirathi Valley, Garhwal Himalaya there has been a considerable increase in the area of human inhabitation and cultivation during last 30 years. This study also indicates that much of the sub-alpine and temperate broadleaf forests have converted into scrub vegetation. Conversion of forested habitat into scrub, is in a way loss of habitat especially for the sensitive ungulates such as Himalayan musk deer. Displacement of human populations for the developmental projects, construction of roads along the sensitive habitats, encroachment of forests for agriculture and heavy infestation of exotic weeds are other causes of habitat loss in the region.

Competition with Domestic Livestock

Owing to high seasonality and low primary productivity, the Himalayan region supports relatively low ungulate / herbivore biomass. It is therefore, obvious that with the increase in the biomass of domestic livestock in many areas, wild ungulates have suffered competitive exclusion. Rawat (1998) has pointed out that several areas in the Himalaya there is an overstocking of livestock leading to decreased productivity and degradation of pastures. Sathyakumar et al. (1993) have reported that increased livestock grazing and associated impacts have led to low musk deer densities in many areas in Kedarnath Wildlife Sanctuary. Although animal husbandry is one of the main stay of livelihood in the Himalayan region, the management of livestock especially disease surveillance, rotational grazing and pasture management have been neglected leading to conflicts with wildlife as well as PA managers.

Poaching: All mountain ungulates of the Greater Himalaya are seriously threatened due to poaching for meat, skin/hide, and for products such as the 'musk' from Musk deer.

Poaching for meat (bush meat hunting) is common in many parts of the Greater Himalaya, particularly in the Eastern Himalaya (See Section II-Arunachal Pradesh State Report). Species such as the goral, tahr, serow, takin are poached for meat/hide by local villagers and indigenous people throughout their distribution range. There are instances of wild mountain ungulate meat served in local restaurants in towns or villages adjoining wilderness areas. Although, the extent of poaching by local villagers or indigenous people is not known, there are evidences of the consequences of high poaching levels in many areas where mountain ungulates have become either locally extinct or occur in very low densities. Poaching for sport and meat by the personnel of the security forces in the international border areas, also have led to serious impacts on mountain ungulate populations.

Poaching of musk deer for 'musk' is rampant through out the Greater Himalaya for its high commercial value (about US $ 65,000/kg in 1985) in the international markets (Green 1986, Sathyakumar 1993b). This has led to local extinctions of this species in many parts of the Greater Himalaya. As a result, the once continuous distribution of musk deer is now confined to some isolated pockets and in most of these areas they occur in very low densities. Similarly, poaching of Himalayan tahr and goral have either resulted in local extinctions or very low densities in many areas.

General Strategies for Conservation

1. Most of the protected areas in the Himalayan region lack adequate man power and funds for proper management. In addition, several PAs have ill defined boundaries leading to conflicts between the local communities and PA management. There is an urgent need to strengthen the management of most of the PAs allocating more well trained and motivated staff, budget and infra-structure.
2. Several PAs and Reserved Forests in the Himalayan region need to be brought under community reserves where local people could be made partners in conservation and management. Through various programmes such as community based eco-tourism and participatory management of natural resources the illegal activities such as trade of animal parts and poaching could be gradually brought down.
3. There is an urgent need to increase trans-boundary co-operation between India-Nepal, India-China and India-Myanmar to control the illegal trade of wildlife products. Measures should be taken to register all the arms (licensed guns, etc) with the Wildlife warden or the Divisional Forest/Wildlife Officer.

4. Currently, there is no organised system of harvesting wild medicinal and aromatic plants and uncontrolled harvest often results in the degradation of habitat. There is a need to evolve policies related to rotational harvest of medicinal plants for the benefit of communities and there is a need to control excessive pressure on the land. As part of eco-development measure cultivation of medicinal plants needs to be promoted in the buffer zones of various PAs where human pressure for these commodities is excessive.

THE MOUNTAIN UNGULATES OF THE GREATER AND TRANS-HIMALAYA

Mountains are widely acknowledged as the 'water towers' of the world in addition to being rich repositories of, often, unique biodiversity. Recognizing these values of the mountains, the UN had declared the year 2002 as the 'International Year of the Mountains' to generate awareness about the conservation and sustainable development of the mountains.

The Himalaya are the most prominent mountains in India and the region covers ca. 12% of the country's 3.3 million km2 geographical area. The present issue is dedicated to a fascinating, yet little known part of its fauna-the mountain ungulates inhabiting the cold, rugged mountains of the higher Himalaya-the ridaks or the Mountain Monarchs, as some mountain people call them.

In this chapter, we give a brief overview of the Himalayan region, its wildlife values and the reasons for choosing the present theme for the Bulletin.

The Himalaya and Associated Mountains

The Himalaya are the youngest of world's mountain chains and have among the highest peaks in the world. These mountains form the watershed for most of the rivers flowing in northern India, which sustain millions of humans who inhabit the Indo-Gangetic plains. The high ranges of the Himalaya stop the northward flow of the monsoon clouds and thus responsible for the climate and prosperity of the people living in the northern region of the Indian subcontinent. The Himalaya trace an arc of over 2,500km, from the Nanga Parbat in the west, to the Namche Barwa in the east in a roughly NW-SE orientation. In Jammu & Kashmir, the mountains and valleys of the Pamirs and the Hindu Kush spread further west, the Karakorum, east and the Kunlun mountains towards the NE, this forming one of the most formidable mountain complexes of the world. Further north, the Altai and Tien Shan ranges lead into the heart of Cenral Asia. There are a range of low mountains further that emerge from the western fringes in Pakistan, and align in a NE-SW orientation towards the deserts of Baluchistan as the Salt and the Kirthar ranges. In the east, the mountains take a sharp southward turn from Namche Barwa into the mountains of Myanmar and Bangladesh, moving further into south east Asia. The Himalaya, are thus a part of the largest mountain complex of the world and bridges its major realms, the oriental in the east and south, the Palarctic along the north and the Ethiopian along the west.

The vast spread of the Himalaya has a width varying from 200km in parts to over 500km in others. This expanse has a great variation in topography as well as biodiversity along the south to north, and the east to west axis. Humidity in general declines from east to west and from south to north, along the Himalaya.

The foothills, or the Siwalik mountains are uplifted glacial debris, at places extending to ca. 1,000m above mean sea level. Higher on are the 'Middle Himalaya' extending up to ca. 3,000m as undulating hills, at places cut steeply by flowing torrents and rivers. Beyond the Middle Himalaya, is the towering Greater Himalayan range consisting primarily of igneous formations with patches of sedimentary rocks. Bulk of this area is covered with huge glaciers and peaks, with relatively arid, cold valleys in their fold. Across this great barrier, is the vast arid expanse of the Tibetan Marginal Mountains and the Tibetan Plateau, often referred to as the Trans-Himalaya. The Trans Himalaya are categorized as the Zone 1 (with two provinces) as per the biogeographically classification by Rodgers & Panwar (1988) and roughly covers 5.6% of the country's geographical area.

The rest of the Himalaya are categorized as the Zone 2 (with four provinces) and covers roughly 6.4% of the country.

More interesting facts about the Himalaya such as the orogeny of the Himalaya, ecological zonation, and flora and fauna can be found in Schaller (1977) and Polunin & Stainton (1992), apart from numerous other publications.

The Mountain Ungulates of the Himalaya and Trans-Himalaya

The ungulate fauna of the Himalaya include species such as the chital, sambar, wild pig, Asian elephant, species that are found in other parts of the country too. There are however various cervids, moschids, bovids and equuids unique to the Himalaya or limited to the high mountain chains of Central Asia. Most of these species evolved to inhabit the niches produced by spectacular mountain building during the Cretaceous and Tertiary that created new, usually cold and bleak landscapes, and are well adapted to these harsh environments. This little known fauna comprising of 15 species/subspecies have been selected for the present ENVIS Bulletin (Table 1). The taxonomy of this group of animals is greatly debated and we have mostly limited our listing to classification by Schaller (1977), Schaller (1998) or Shackleton (1997). We have not included the Wild Goat (Capra aegagrus) and the Shou or Sikkim stag (Cervus elaphus wallichi), since its occurrence in the country are not confirmed.

It is noteworthy that this assemblage of species/subspecies constitutes ca. 50% of India's ungulate fauna. Many of these species are wild relatives of sheep, goat, horse/donkey and yak, thus adding value to this assemblage as an important genetic pool.

The ungulates of the high mountains are prey to charismatic predators such as the snow leopard, Tibetan wolf and common leopard. An understanding of their ecology can thus help in better management of the entire region.

Most of WII's ENVIS Bulletins so far have been taxa based (elephants, small cats, crocodilians, non-human primates) or on the PA network in the country. The issues on taxa usually provide exhaustive articles from experts with either a species or a regional focus. As alluded to earlier, in this volume we have confined ourselves to the Himalayan region among all the mountain chains in the country due to its unique value as the highest, significant ecological entity, grand and fragile, yet harbouring some of the most pristine habitats for wildlife left in the country. Within the Himalaya, we have chosen accounts on those ungulate species that are either unique to the Himalaya or are confined to the mountain ranges alone.

Layout of the Issue

The issue is divided into five Sections in order to cover various facets of mountain ungulates and their conservation. Section One gives species accounts of the fifteen species/ subspecies present in the country. The two chapters in this section give brief accounts of the species in the Himalayan and the Trans-Himalayan regions in a 'field guide' format. This, we believe, should be useful for the lay user as well as the serious reader to easily acquaint with the species, its distribution, status, habitat, behavioural traits, morphology and key biological facts. We have tried to give clear photographs of all species, but where not available, we have given sketches.

There is a wealth of information available with the State Forest/Wildlife Departments on animal distribution and status, their vision for wildlife conservation, and management actions being taken. Often, these efforts are little known and appreciated. The Section Two on ' Protected Area Network and State Reports on Status and Management of Mountain Ungulates' is meant to bridge this gap to some extent. The Himalaya are spread over six Indian states. We were able to receive articles from five of them which are presented in this section.

The fragile Himalayan region is faced with numerous conservation issues. Some of them such as livestock grazing in Protected Areas and human-wildlife conflicts are common with the rest of the country, but there are unique socio-economic peculiarities that make dealing with them more challenging.

These issues and possible solutions for them are detailed for the Himalayan and the Trans-Himalayan regions in Section Three of this Bulletin.

The Himalaya have fascinated naturalists since time immemorial. A few decades ago however some scientists and naturalists have painstakingly documented the region's wildlife, often under very harsh conditions and with few facilities. We have tried to bring this perspective on what was their driving force, their trials and tribulations in initiating these studies, in Section Four-'Semi-Scientific Accounts by Veterans on Research and Conservation Experiences on Mountain Ungulates'.

Although there have been few quantitative studies and assessments on the mountain ungulates in the Himalaya, there is a wealth of information as anecdotal accounts that reveal a lot about the species. We have developed and included an exhaustive bibliography on the useful references for mountain ungulates and about conservation of the region in general as the last section of this volume.

The Wildlife Institute of India has pioneered research on wildlife in the Himalayan region since its inception, the very first research project being an extensive survey on the snow leopard and its prey species in the Western Himalaya. Through the twenty years of its existence, WII researchers and scientists have worked hard under daunting conditions to conduct over 30 critical studies and 20 surveys documenting the varied facets of the region's biodiversity and conservation issues. Through this Bulletin we wish to add an important and useful compilation on the conservation of the magnificent mountains crowning the country.

8

Species of the Greater Himalaya

GORAL

Two subspecies of goral occur in India, viz., the Grey goral (N.g.goral) distributed in the Western Himalaya (upto 3,300m) and Shiwaliks in the states of Jammu & Kashmir, Himachal Pradesh, Uttaranchal and Haryana; and the Brown goral (N.g.hodgsni) in the Eastern Himalayas and the hills of N.E. India in the states of Sikkim, northern West Bengal, Arunachal Pradesh, Nagaland, Meghalaya and Mizoram. Another species, the Red goral (Nemorhaedus baileyi) is reported to occur in a small region in Arunachal Pradesh at the junction of Tibet, Yunnan and Myanmar. Inhabits sparsely wooded slopes with open grassy patches in a wide range of habitats that includes alpine meadows, subalpine forests, temperate forests, subtropical pine forests, tropical moist deciduous forests of Shiwaliks, and montane wet temperate and evergreen forests in N.E. India.

A monomorphic mountain goat as body size, horn size and colouration are same in both sexes. However, adult males could be distinguished from females based on the body size and horn size, if observed at close quarters. The general body colour of Grey goral is yellowish grey suffused with black and the hair on the pale area is not tinged with rufous or brown. The chin, upper lip, undersides of jaws and throat patch are white. The dark spinal stripe, if present, does not pass beyond the withers. There is no stripe down the middle of the tail and none up the back of the thighs. The body colour of Brown goral is golden or rufous brown specked with black. The black spinal stripe reaches to the root of the tail. A dark ill-defined stripe runds up the back of the thighs from the hocks. Both males and females have short insignificant sharp horns black in colour which diverge slightly, curve backwards, marked with rings or ridges.

A cliff-dwelling mountain goat occurs singly or in pairs or in small parties of 3-5 individuals. Aggregations of >5 individuals (largest reported 13 individuals) may occur during feeding depending upon the food resource availability and distribution. Predators are the Common leopard and the Himalayan yellow-throated Marten. When approached by a predator or human, goral makes an alarm call "Hiss" runs for escape cover or escape terrain, and may stop to look back. Actively feeds during early mornings and late afternoons resting under cover during noon. Goral are primarily grazers, although they feed upon tender shoots of certain shrubs and leaves of trees when available.

MAINLAND SEROW

Nemorhaedus sumatraensis Bechstein 1799

Vernacular/other Names: sarao, thar (nepali), ramu (Kashmiri), gya (Sikkim)

Taxonomy

Family: Bovidae

Sub Family: Caprinae

Tribe: Rupicaprini

Conservation Status

IUCN: Vulnerable

CAMP: Not evaluated

IWPA· Schedule I

CITES: Appendix-I

U.S. ESA: Endangered

In the southern side of the Greater Himalaya (2,000-3,300m); and in the hills of N.E. India (>200 m). Occurs in the states of Himachal Pradesh, Uttaranchal, Sikkim, Arunachal Pradesh, Mizoram and Manipur. Temperate and subalpine forests in the Greater Himalaya and montane wet temperate and evergreen forests of N.E. India. Two subspecies of serow are reported to occur in India, the Black Serow (N.s.edwardsi) distributed in the western and eastern Himalaya and the Red Serow (N.s.rubidus) distributed in eastern Himalaya.

An elusive mountain goat, with a large head, donkey-like ears, thick neck and short legs. The coat is coarse and rather thin; it colour varies from grizzled black or blackish grey-roan to red.

In the darker males, the head, neck, and the mane that covers the nape and withers are grizzled black. The black passes into rusty red on the shoulders, flanks and lower thighs, and turns a dirty grey on the inside of the limbs and belly. The muzzle, throat and chest have varying amounts of white. Both sexes have horns which are black, conical and closely wrinkled for three quarters of their length

A solitary and shy mountain goat inhabiting steep, rugged, inaccessible densely forested habitats that includes thickly wooded-gorges with boulder-strewn slopes and shallow caves or overhangs. Although solitary in nature, serow is also found in pairs and in groups of three or four. Serow is a territorial species and appears to be nocturnal or crepuscular. Predators are the Common leopard and possibly Red fox and Himalayan yellow-throated Marten on the young. When disturbed, gives an alarm call that is a loud whistle. It feeds on a variety of food items including oak leaves, shrubs, grasses, montane bamboo, ferns, mosses and lichen.

TAKIN

Budorcas taxicolor Hodgson 1850

Vernacular/other Names: Not known

Taxonomy

Family: Bovidae

Sub Family: Caprinae

Conservation Status

IUCN: Endangered

CAMP: Not evaluated

IWPA: Schedule I

CITES: Appendix-II

U.S. ESA: Not listed

Arunachal Pradesh. Tropical forests (900-1,200m), dense bamboo and rhododendron forests (2,000-3,000m). Recently reported from Kyongnosla Alpine and Pangolkha Wildlife Sanctuaries in Sikkim.

A clumsy heavy animal, having a convex face, heavy mouth, and tremendously thick neck. The muzzle, except for a base spot at the extremity is covered with hair. Withers are slightly raised and its narrow back arches in the center and slope downwards to the root of the tail. Body colour ranges from dark brown to golden yellow. Withers are conspicuously lighter in tone. Adult males are golden yellow merging into dark brown or black on the flanks and quarters. There is a dark dorsal stripe. Young males are reddish brown in front merging into black. Calves all black. Females are grayer than males with no yellow. The dark dorsal stripe is inconspicuous in females and young males. Horns of young Takin grow straight up from the head with an outward tendency. Later they grow outwards and then downwards. In final stages, the horns grow forward and bend downwards and outwards with the points growing up.

Inhabits the steepest and most thickly wooded habitats in the mountains. In summer, found in large herds of even up to 300 individuals, and break up into small parties in winter. Generally active during early morning and late afternoon, while resting in cover during mid day.

HIMALAYAN TAHR

Hemitragus jemlahicus H.Smith 1826

Vernacular/other Names: jungli bakri (Hindi), thar, karth (male), tanne, bakri (female) jharal, jharal-thar, (local names) kras, jagla (Kashmiri) yang, reiwo (nepali)

Taxonomy

Family: Bovidae

Subfamily: Caprinae

Conservation Status

IUCN: Vulnerable

CAMP: Low Risk

IWPA: Schedule I

CITES: Not listed

U.S. ESA: Not listed

Inhabits a narrow strip along the southern side of the Greater Himalaya between 2,000 and 4,400m in the states of Jammu & Kashmir, Himachal Pradesh, Uttaranchal & Sikkim. Temperate and Subalpine forests interspersed with open steep slopes, temperate and subalpine scattered tree and scrub habitats, alpine scrub and meadow habitats.

A mountain goat with finely formed head, narrow erect ears, a heavy body, and long robust limbs. The body is covered with tangled masses of coarse, flowing hair, particularly well developed in adult males and forms a prominent ruff and mane that may attain a length of 25 to 30 cm, up to the knees in males. They also have a long mantle of hair that drapes from the side and rump. The fur is deep reddish brown, and there is dark mid dorsal streak, not always distinct. Old males are darker, particularly on the back and quarters. Females and young males are lighter brown and the kids much paler. Both male and female have massive horns almost of equal size. The horns are close-set, stout at the base, keeled in front and wrinkled except towards the tips. They curve backwards, and in old males continue downwards.

Group-living mountain goat that inhabits the most inaccessible terrain characterized by open steep slopes, scattered trees, scrub and grassy blanks, cliffs and rocks. Tahr live in mixed herds (1-77) for most of the year excepting for a brief period in spring when many adult males segregrate after rut to higher altitudes. Adult females and juveniles have fairly fixed home ranges and move considerably between altitudes. Predators are snow and common leopards and Himalayan yellow-throated marten. Poaching for meat by man is common. They seldom stray far away from cliffs and precipitous terrain that serves as escape terrain. Tahr are good climbers and traverse ledges and rock faces with great agility to reach scattered patches of vegetation. Tahr is a grazer feeding mainly on grasses, sedges, herbs, ferns and mosses. Prefers to feed actively during early mornings and late afternoons, and resting during mid day.

HIMALAYAN MUSK DEER

Moschus chrysogaster Hodgson 1839

Vernacular/other Names: kasturi mrig, kastura, bina, (local Names), roos (kashmiri)

Taxonomy

Family: Moschidae

Conservation Status

IUCN: Vulnerable

CAMP: Critical

IWPA: Schedule I

CITES: Appendix-I

U.S. ESA: Endangered

All along the southern side of the Greater Himalaya between 2,500m to 'treeline' in Jammu & Kashmir, Himachal Pradesh, Uttaranchal, Sikkim & Arunachal Pradesh. Upper Temperate, Subalpine forests, alpine scrub and meadow habitats. Two sub species of Himalayan musk deer occur in India, M.c.chrysogaster distributed in western Himalaya and M.c.leucogaster distributed in eastern Himalaya. Two other species, the Black Musk deer M.fuscus and the Dwarf Musk deer M.berevoskii are also reported to occur in some parts of Arunachal Pradesh that are close to China and Myanmar borders, but needs confirmation.

Not a true deer, but a primitive deer-like ruminant. Differs from other deer by not having antlers and facial glands. Has gall bladder, caudal gland and musk gland which no other deer possess. Canines are greatly developed especially in males. Stockily built animal with small head having hare-like long ears, arched back and bounding gait. Hind legs are 5 cm longer than the forelegs. Well-developed dew claws or lateral hooves. The general body colour is grey-brown to light-brownish yellow or dark yellow or dark brown with two white throat stripes. The colour of the ear tips range from dark brown to ivory-yellow or white. Rump and thigh are darker and the belly pale brown. Genital regions are white and the tail is naked except for a tuft of hair at the tip. Fur coat is thick and wavy giving it a deceptively heavy built appearance.

Musk deer is a Small Solitary Forest Ruminant (SSFR) that inhabits the upper temperate, subalpine and alpine habitats between 2,500 m and 'treeline'. It is a sedentary animal and is either nocturnal or crepuscular spending most of the day under dense undergrowth and come out of cover for feeding in open alpine grasslands during night but seldom stray far away from escape cover. Wild predators of musk deer include snow and common leopards, Himalayan yellow-throated marten, and possibly Red fox.

It makes a non-vocal alarm call "Hiss" and stot on sensing danger. Man has persecuted this species for centuries for its musk. Being a SSFR, musk deer rely largely on communication by olfaction which is by means of scent marking behaviour and that includes defecating at defecation sites and by pasting with the secretions of the caudal gland by both sexes, and in case of males by the secretion of musk in urine. Musk deer has high-energy requirement per unit of body weight and it must select high quality food. It is called a "nibbler" rather than browser as it selectively feed on young leaves, buds, fruits, flowers of dicots, mosses and lichen.

KASHMIR STAG

Cervus elaphus hanglu Linnaeus 1758

Vernacular/other Names: hangul, honglu (Hindi/Kashmiri)

Taxonomy

Family: Cervidae

Subfamily: Cervinae

Conservation Status

IUCN:Endangered

CAMP:-

IWPA: Schedule I

CITES: Appendix-I

U.S. ESA: Endangered

At present occurs only in the Dachigam National Park and a few isolated pockets in Jammu & Kashmir State of India. In the past, it was distributed in mountains of Kashmir and in Chamba District of Himachal Pradesh. Subalpine forests, temperate broad leaved oak and conifer mixed forests, riverine forests, grasslands and scrub habitats

A subspecies of the Red deer of Europe that is distinctly different from the Red deer in body size, colour, and antler size and shape. Hangul is dark grey and dark brown rather than reddish and unlike Red deer, the antler bay tine is normally larger than brow and has much of cup. In Hangul, 10-point head is the normal one and any greater number of points is far more usual than in the case of Red deer. The coat colour ranges from light to dark brown, fading to dingy white on lips, chin, underparts and anal region. The white rump patch does not extend much above the tail and is divided by a broad median stripe extending down to the base of the tail and sometimes to its extremity. Coat colour fades during summer, but tones up with denser coat in winter, which in big males is very dark or rufous brown. Fawns are spotted. Old females may show white flecks. Antlers in adult males grow up to 1 m

Hangul is essential a forest animal found singly or in groups of about 10-15 individuals. It is diurnal and make distinct altitudinal migration from higher to lower elevations in winter. Predators are snow and common leopards. It is a selective feeder and feeds on a wide variety of plants that includes leaves/shoots of some trees and shrubs, grasses and herbs.

Another subspecies of the Red Deer that is reported in the Indian subcontinent is Shou or Sikkim stag (Cervus elaphus wallichi). It is reported to occur in Chumbi valley located close to the Indo-China border in Sikkim and there are unconfirmed reports of this subspecies being sighted occassionally in Pangolokha Wildlife Sanctuary

SPECIES OF THE TRANS-HIMALAYA AND OTHER ARID TRACTS

Rocky alpine steppe and the rugged tracts of the Central Asian mountains-from the Hindu Kush in Afganistan till the Sutluj gorge in Himachal Pradesh, India; and northwards along the Altai Shan and Tien Shan, into Mongolia and Russia. Within India in western Ladakh (Zanskar and Ladakh ranges) and Nubra in Jammu & Kashmir, and Lahul-Spiti in Himachal Pradesh. Covers ca. 25,000 km^2 within these two states.

Stocky built goat. Largest in the genus. The general colour of the pelage is a light tan, with the undersides lighter; the coat colouration however, varies widely across this ibex's range. In the Himalayan population during winter, mature males are much darker (dark chocolate brown; especially males older than 5 years), with patches of white on the neck and back. Dark dorsal stripe from lower neck till the tail pronounced in males.

The lighter ventral parts of females and young males are separated from the main body colour by a darker band which runs along the sides. Both sexes have a dark beard beneath the chin, although it is much less pronounced in females. Both sexes carry horns-in males they grow into massive arcs, which curl over the back and may even loop back on themselves, while in females they are small, almost parallel and slightly arched towards the rear. A male's horns have several large knobs on their frontal surface. Till the 7th-8th year two knobs are added each year; after which it is usually one every year.

The Siberian ibex live at high elevations, and often climb up to the vegetation line at 5,500m. In India, they usually occur between 2,500 and 5,500m. In many areas, they do not descend to lower elevations during winter. Uses primarily steep slopes, interspersed with 'escape terrain' in the form of rocky overhangs and cliffs, where they flee to escape predators such as snow leopard and the Tibetan wolf. In winter, partial to south facing slopes and areas where snow deposition is relatively lower such as windblown ridgelines, crests and avalanche paths. When snow cover is heavy, Siberian ibex find food by pawing at the snow with their forelegs in order to reach the vegetation concealed below.

Most hierarchy is established before the onset of the rut based on body and horn size, but when contests do take place they may extend for over three hours of clashes, body and shoulder pushing and horn entwining. During the clashes, a male would typically go upslope, rear on its hind limbs and clash down at the lowered horns of the opponent, often trying to dislodge it.

Occur in small groups-mean around 11 animals per group; occasional congregations of 70-100 animals may occur in spring. Principally a diurnal animal, the Siberian ibex has alternating periods of resting and activity throughout the day. Usually forage in early forenoon and late afternoon, but have a distinctly unimodal foraging peak during the noontime in peak winters. Adult males primarily separate into 'all-male groups' during the summer.

Is an intermediate forager, feeding primarily on grasses, forbs, leaves and shoots of shrubs and also trees.

FLARE HORNED OR KASHMIR MARKHOR

Capra falconeri, Wagner 1839

Vernacular Names: markhor (Punjab and Kashmir), raphoche (male) rawache (female)

Taxonomy

Family: Bovidae

Sub family: Caprinae

Tribe: Caprini

Conservation Status

IUCN: Endangered

CAMP:Critical

IWPA: Schedule I

CITES: Appendix I

US ESA: Endangered ...

Sparsely wooded mountainous regions in the western Himalayan Pir Panjal range at an elevation of 600-3,600 m. In India, they occur only in a few pockets of the Kashmir valley, notably the Kisthwar National Park, in the Greater Himalaya, with possibilities of their occurrence in the Pangi valley of Himachal Pradesh too. Bulk of the distribution is however in the Trans-Himalayan areas, now in the PoK. Other subspecies of markhor occur in the Salt, Safed Koh, Hindu Kush and Kirthar ranges in Pakistan, in eastern Afghanistan and southern Tajikistan.

The grizzled light brown to black coat is smooth and short in summer, growing longer and thicker in winter. Males have long hair on the chin, throat, chest, and shanks, while females have smaller fringes. The lower legs have a black and white pattern. Males have loosely curled, corkscrew-like horns, starting close together at the head, but spreading towards the tips. In males, they can grow up to 160 cm, and up to 25 cm in females. Female horns are also slightly twisted. A dark lateral stripe is present in males and is usually fainter in females.

Occurs in low to mid elevation, open and slightly wooded arid tracts in the Trans-Himalaya and parts of the Greater Himalaya. May migrate up to 4,000m in summer, but essentially remain in areas where rugged valleys and mountains are available at ca. 2,200m. Distinctly avoid areas with high snow cover.

Lack underwool and thus avoid excessively cold areas, but can tolerate high temperatures reaching up to 45°C. The markhor's alarm call resembles the nasal "a" not very different from the common domestic goat. The primary natural predators are leopard, Tibetan wolf, snow leopard, and lynx. Markhor, a wild goat species, are efficient negotiators of steep cliffs and use this to escape predators

The markhor is mainly active in the early morning and late afternoon. An intermediate forager, it consumes primarily grasses and forbs during spring and summer months, while in the winter it turns primarily to browse for nourishment. Markhor often stand on their hind legs in order to reach high vegetation; they are known to climb the gnarled trees for foraging. During the rut, males fight for breeding rights. These competitions involve lunging and locking the horns, followed by the combatants twisting and pushing in an attempt to make the other lose his balance.

Females and young live in herds of around 9 animals; adult males are usually solitary.

BHARAL, HIMALAYAN BLUE SHEEP

Pseudois nayaur, Hodgson 1833

Vernacular Names: Knabo (Ladakhi, Tibetan),nabo (Spiti), bharal (Hindi, Pahari)

Taxonomy

Family:Bovidae

Sub family: Caprinae

Tribe: Caprini

Conservation Status

IUCN: Low risk

CAMP: Low risk, least concern

IWPA: Schedule I

CITES: Not listed

US ESA: Not listed

Central Asian mountains-from Kunjereb in Pakistan in the west, to the Sichuan and Gansu provinces of China in the east, through bulk of the Tibetan plateau. Southern limit of distribution is along the Greater Himalayan chain in India, Nepal and Bhutan. Northern flank covers the Altai Shan, and parts of the Tien Shan. In India, found in Ladakh, Lahul-Spiti, and in some high alpine meadows of Kullu, Kinnaur, Uttaranchal, Sikkim, and the western Tawang region of Arunachal Pradesh covering ca. 30,000 km^2. Most of these, apart from Ladakh and Lahul-Spiti, are narrow regions on the southern slopes of the Greater Himalaya itself.

The adult male's coat is slate grey, sometimes with a bluish sheen. The underparts and back of the legs are white, while the chest and fronts of the legs are black. Separating the grey back and white belly is a black coloured stripe. The ears are small, and the bridge of the nose is dark.

The horns are found in both sexes, and have small ridges on the upper surface. In males, they grow upwards, then turn sideways and curve backwards, looking somewhat like a moustache. Females are light brown coloured with small horns, usually diverging at the top (important feature to distinguish with ibex females in areas where they are sympatric).

Bharal live at mid to high elevations, and may climb up to the vegetation line at 5,500 m. In India, they usually occur between 2,500 and 5,500 m, but usually below this upper limit. Uses primarily moderate to steep slopes, interspersed with 'escape terrain' in the form of rocky overhangs and cliffs, where they flee to escape predators such as snow leopard and the Tibetan wolf.

Habitat similar to ibex but can occur in more open slopes and in much moister areas on the southern slopes of the Himalaya. In winter, may descend if possible or remain partial to south facing slopes and areas where snow deposition is relatively lower such as windblown ridgelines, crests and avalanche paths.

Occurs in small groups of less than 20 animals. Sexual segregation is most common in summer, when males may use more open meadows at higher elevations. Bharal are active during the day, with a bimodal peak during morning and late afternoon.

Intermediate forager, diet consists primarily of grasses, hardy herbaceous plants, also some shrubs.

LADAKH URIAL

Ovis vignei vignei, Blyth 1841

Vernacular Names: Shapo (male), Shammo, Shanmar (female) (Ladakhi)

Taxonomy

Family: Bovidae

Sub family:Caprinae

Tribe:Caprini

Conservation Status

IUCN: Endangered

CAMP: Endangered

IWPA: Schedule I

CITES: Appendix I

US ESA: Endangered

A subspecies endemic to the Ladakh region. Occurs is relatively less steep and rolling slopes usually below 4,200m-mainly along the Indus River and the Shyok River and their tributaries. Within India, occurs along the Indus almost continuously from Upshi in the east till Dha-Hanu; a side population also occurs in the Wanla-Lamayuru-Nindum area towards the south and in the Markha Valley. The Shyok population is mostly concentrated around Tirit-Sumur and some occur further upstream along the Nubra River and along the Diskit-Khalsar area. Distribution in India covers ca. 2,000km2. Small populations also reported from the Shigar valley, Gilgit and Skardu regions of PoK. Other related subspecies are distributed in the Kirthar, Safed Koh and Hindu Kush ranges in Pakistan and in parts of eastern Afghanistan and Tajakistan.

Smallest wild sheep species. Adult urial are grey-brown in winter coat, but are rufous grey or brown during the rest of the year. Adult rams sport a black or grizzled ruff, which grows from the side of the chin and meets below and extends down the throat. The ruff is more pronounced during winter and in males older than about 5 years. In adult rams, a dirty white and indistinct saddle patch is present. They have a dark spot under the foreleg that may extend on to a lateral stripe in some males. Females are similar, but lack the saddle patch and invariable have just a dark spot under their forelegs. Underparts and rump patch in all age-sex classes are white. Male horns curve up, back, downwards and in large males turn a bit inwards. Females have short, parallel horns and are not divergent as in bharal and argali. Grey patches on face from the eye till the chin is present in both sexes.

Ladakh urial are primarily animals of the lower slopes, usually below 4,200 m; rarely occur up to 4,800 m as in the proposed Nindum Wildlife Sanctuary. Occur on gradual to moderate slopes, but have probably been pushed to use steeper and rockier gorges along the side valleys of Indus due to excessive anthropogenic pressures. Has long, lithe limbs that facilitate fast flight from potential danger. They are also known to retreat into cliffs or steep slopes to escape predators such as wolf and snow leopard. Usually occur in small groups of 5-12 animals, however, in certain areas and in seasons such as spring may occur in larger groups of ca. 80 animals. Sexual segregation is reported during much of the year barring the rutting period.

Is an intermediate forager, consuming grasses, forbs and shrubs in different seasons. During the rut, solitary males may travel vast distances in search of oesterous females. Contests between males are in the typical form of sheep, where two opposing rams clash into each other from some distance producing a loud clack. They may then involve in shoulder pushing and horn entwining.

TIBETAN ARGALI

Ovis ammon hodgsoni, Blyth 1840

Vernacular Names: Nayan, nyan (Ladakh, Tibetan, Spiti)

Taxonomy

Family: Bovidae

Sub family: Caprinae

Tribe: Caprini

Conservation Status

IUCN: Vulnerable

CAMP: Critically endangered

IWPA: Schedule I

CITES: Appendix I

US ESA:Endangered

Open, rolling high altitude slopes and plateaus in Central Asia. Different subspecies are spread from the Pamirs in the west to the eastern Tibetan plateau; and from the areas just north of the Greater Himalaya, to Mongolia, in the north. In India less than 300 might be surviving in its range in Ladakh with smaller portions of the range also covered in Sikkim, totaling to ca. 12,000 km^2.

Largest wild sheep in the world. Long limbs, with a pronounced shoulder and a large chest. The general colouration of argali is variable, ranging from a light buff to darker grey-brown in winter. The underparts are whitish, usually separated from the darker parts by a blackish stripe. In addition, males have a whitish neck ruff, and a dorsal crest, both of which are more prominent in the winter coat. Argali has a whitish, large rump patch. Adult males carry two enormous, ribbed, horns, which turn upwards, back, down, and then forward and outwards and can reach 145-190 cm when measured along the spiral. The basal circumference of the horns may measure up to 40cm. Females also bear horns, although these are much smaller, rarely exceeding 30 cm in length. These are however thicker and more divergent than other sympatric caprine female horns.

Usually occurs at the highest elevations in the Tibetan Plateau (4,500-5,500m), using the open mesic alpine meadows. While local migrations may occur in autumn and spring, argali may not descend much in winters, but may chose areas with less snow (they primarily occur is regions where winter precipitation is naturally not very high). With relatively long legs, argalis are fast runners and flee away from their primarily cursorial predators, the Tibetan wolf.

However, refuge is occasionally taken on steep mountain slopes. The primary vocalizations are an alarm whistle and a warning hiss made by blowing air through the nostrils. When competing, males rear up on their hind legs and, leaning forward, race towards their opponent, crashing horns in the process.

Occur usually in small groups 2-15 animals, but occasional aggregations of about 40 animals also reported. Herds are sexually segregated for most of the year, except the rutting season. Is an intermediate forager feeding on herbs, sedges, grasses and shrubs. Some recent studies suggest that they rely to a greater extent on forbs and shrubs.

TIBETAN ANTELOPE

Pantholops hodgsonii, Abel 1826

Vernacular Names: Tstosh (Ladakhi, Tibetan), chiru (parts of Tibet)

Taxonomy

Family: Bovidae

Sub family: Panthalopinae

Tribe: Saigini

Conservation Status

IUCN: Endangered

CAMP: Critical

IWPA: Schedule I

CITES: Appendix I

US ESA: Not listed

The Tibetan steppe at elevations of 4,000-5,500 metres in open, plains and rolling mountains. Occurs in the Chang Thang plains in northern Tibet, Xinjiang and Qinghai. Smaller populations occur in central Tibet. Small groups of female and young from the northern Chang Thang population from Tibet are known to migrate into Indian territories in the Aksai Chin (Daulat Beg Uldi-Lingti-Tsiang plains) and males in the Changchenmo valley during June till autumn. The combined distribution range within India will be less than 300km^2.

The dense coat is very soft and woolly, and is very good insulation against the cold Tibetan weather. The coat of adult males is reddish fawn with light grey and brown tones grading to creamy white undersides.

The fronts of the slender legs and the face (including the forehead, bridge of the nose, and upper cheeks) are dark brown. By October the males acquire the more striking winter pelage. The face and the front of the legs are now black, and the marking from the foreleg goes over the shoulder and from the hindlegs extends around the margins of the rump patch.

The rest of the body is light gray and tan. Females are smaller, and the coat is fawn-almost pinkish, often with rust brown in the nape that blends into the lighter underside. Males alone carry the slightly S-shaped horns which grow 50-70 cm in length. Black in colour and ridged on their lower half, they rise nearly vertically from the head. Another distinctive feature is the presence of walnut sized airsacs on each side of the nostril, that gives the muzzle a blunt and enlarged look. The fawn-coloured underwool or shahtoosh produced by this species is the finest wool known to man.

TIBETAN GAZELLE

Procapra picticaudata, Hodgson, 1846

Vernacular Names: Gowa (Ladakhi, Tibetan)

Taxonomy

Family: Bovidae

Sub family: Antilopinae

Tribe: Antilopini

Conservation Status

IUCN: Low risk

CAMP: Critical

IWPA: Schedule I

CITES: Not listed

US ESA: Not listed

Open, rolling plateaus, slopes and valleys, with mesic alpine meadow/steppe vegetation communities, usually above an elevation of 4,200 m. Global range extends in much of the Tibetan Plateau and the Xinjiang, Quinghai and Gansu provinces of China. In India, small populations occur in 3, possibly 4 places in eastern Ladakh (Hanle, Chushul, Chumur and Changchenmo) and northern parts of Sikkim (near Gyaum Chhona and Changri meadows). The overall occurrence may be in less than 500 km^2 in the country.

The gazelle is a small animal with slender legs weighing between 13 and 15kg. Its coat varies from sandy brown to grayish brown, and is greyer in summer.

The underparts and insides of the legs are white. A prominent feature is the large white heart shaped rump patch, which covers much of the rump. A rust-brown band surrounds the rump patch. Only males have horns. These slender horns go up, curve back and then up again. They are ridged till the distal quarter and are slightly divergent at the top and may again bend inwards.

Species of the open plateaus and mountains occurring between elevations of 4,200 and 5,500m. Primarily occur in the mesic alpine meadows and steppe vegetation. Rarely also occurs in desert steppes. Is a lithe animal that relies on quick detection and flight from predators like the Tibetan wolf and, and rarely wild dog and snow leopard.

Little altitudinal migration is reported, but generally occur in their lowest range in the spring. Winter is a hard time for this small ungulate, especially in years with heavy snowfall when heavy mortality may occur.

The gazelle usually occurs in small groups of 4-5 animals, and rarely larger concentrations may occur. In India the total population is likely to be less than 50 in three small populations and seeing large groups any where is extremely difficult. During rutting, males may hold small territories where they maintain small harems. These sites are often marked by 'laterine sites'.

The gazelle tends to be a 'concentrate forager' feeding on more nutritious forbs and lush sedges during all periods, except winter, when it switches to the only forage which is coarse for its survival.

YAK

Bos grunniens, Linnaeus 1766

Vernacular Names: Dong (Ladakhi, Tibetan)

Taxonomy

Family: Bovidae

Sub family:-

Tribe: Bovini

Conservation Status

IUCN: Vulnerable

CAMP: Critical

IWPA: Schedule I

CITES: Not listed

US ESA: Endangered

Montane regions of Tibet at an altitude of 4,000-5,400m on relatively moist grass and sedge dominated slopes and valleys. Distribution is somewhat restricted compared with other Tibetan ungulates to the northern parts of Tibetan Chang Thang, extending into the Xinjiang province in the north and the western extremity of the Quinghai province. Good populations are reported from the Aru Basin in the Changthang Nature Preserve. In India, the distribution is restricted to small portions in the Changchenmo valley in Ladakh, just north of the Pongong Tso where some 40 animals may exist.

The dark black-brown coat is dense, wooly, and extremely shaggy, although the colour is variable in domestic yaks. 'Golden' wild yaks are also known, but are rare. The shoulders are high and humped, with a broad, drooping head.

The short legs have broad hooves and large dewclaws as an adaptation to mountainous environments. Long mantles of hair drape down from the neck and flanks, often almost completely covering the legs. The tails are large and bushy. The horns are found in both sexes, though those of the females are considerably smaller and shorter. The curved horns grow out from the sides of the head and curve upwards. The wild yak horns are on an average larger than the domestic ones and have a distinctive white splashes on the muzzle.

Occur at high elevations (4,000 to the limit of vegetation at ca. 5,400m) on mesic to moist meadows and rarely on more arid areas. Prefers rolling slopes and flat plains or plateaus. Coarse/bulk forager requiring lot of forage every day, it survives on grasses, sedges, and occasionally lichens and tubers.

Due to the scarcity and unpredictability of vegetation in their habitat, wild yaks must travel great distances in order to obtain sufficient nourishment. In July, there is a general downward shift from the high plateaus to the lower plains, where swamp vegetation is at their peak growth.

As the temperature rises in August, the herds head back up to the plateaus, even retiring to snowy regions to beat the heat. Although sensitive to warm temperatures, wild yaks can easily tolerate temperatures of-40°C. Generally wary, if a herd is disturbed they will flee for a long distance, galloping with their tails held erect.

The only natural predator is the Tibetan wolf, but may have limited success of killing an adult yak. When cornered, or when young are present in the group, yaks may actively defend them against any potential danger.

In spite of their bulky, awkward appearance, yaks are excellent, sure-footed climbers. One of the few vocalizations is a loud grunt, made during the breeding season by wild yaks.

Domestic yaks, however, "grunt" throughout the year-hence the specific name 'grunniens'.

Solitary animals and herds of 10-50 are most common; occasionally 200 individuals are also seen. Aggregations of over 80 animals are commonly seen in some areas such as the Aru basin in Tibet.

TIBETAN WILD ASS OR KIANG

Equus kiang

Vernacular Names: Kiang (Ladakhi, Tibetan)

Taxonomy

Family: Equidae

Sub family:-

Tribe:-

Conservation Status

IUCN: Data deficient

CAMP: Vulnerable

IWPA: Schedule I

CITES: Appendix II

US ESA: Not listed

Occurs all along the rolling mountains and valleys of the Tibetan Plateau between 4,000 and 5,200 m. Distributed from Ladakh in the west to the Quinghai province of China in the east; and from the plateau regions on the northern fringe of the Greater Himalaya, till the Xinjiang province of China. In India, kiang are reported from the Chang Thang plateau of Ladakh and the northern cold desert areas of Sikkim.

The largest of the wild asses, the kiang is a robust animal. The head is large, the muzzle blunt and the nose convex. The mane is upright and relatively short. The coat is a rich chestnut colour or dark brown in winter, turning to reddish brown in summer. The legs, the ventral part of the body, including the neck, inside of the ears and the muzzle are white. A dark dorsal stripe extends from the neck till the base of the tail. The tips of the ears and a narrow band along the hooves are also black. Little sexual dimorphism exists in the species, but the males are slightly larger than females.

Occurs usually from 4,000 m till the limit of vegetation at ca. 5,200 m, but within this range it is largely confined to flat plains, plateaus and rolling smooth slopes. Kiang use alpine meadows and alpine steppes dominated by grasses and sedges, but also occur on drier desert steppes.

Kiang may show minor seasonal migrations, most of it being altitudinal-migrating to higher regions in summer and to lower ones in winter. Within the Indian region, kiang are often seen in the moister wide river valleys and lake basins of the Chang Thang during the winter; an area also used by the nomadic domestic sheep-goat herders of the region. Kiang is large and swift-footed animal and predation on adults by wild carnivores is rare.

The natural predator of the region is the Tibetan wolf; and man also takes a toll-hunting of kiang is still known to be prevalent in Tibet, but not in the Indian parts of its range. On approaching, kiang typically flee with its head up and wheel around after running 80-100 m to look back at the potential danger. Often, they appear inquisitive and begin approaching the intruder.

Kiang normally occurs in small groups of 8-10 animals. Solitary animals, mostly stallions are also common. Occasionally, they may form large aggregations of 200-300 animals. Such aggregations are most common during autumn and winter when animals congregate on meadows with better forage quantity. Males tend to maintain small temporary harems during the rutting period and may rarely also show site fidelity suggesting some territoriality in the species.

Kiang are 'bulk foragers' and require larger quantities of forage, but not necessarily of good quality. Thus, it survives on relatively poor quality diet of sedges and grasses during the entire year.

Female Characters

- Unlike males, Caprini females are often difficult to identify due to their similarities. Here are a few cues to distinguish between them.
- In general, Capra females have a more stocky built compared to Ovis & Pseudois.
- Ibex females have thin and parallel horns-usually larger than most Ovis (except argali) and Capra; have a distinct dark lateral stripe; often females also have a small beard
- Bharal are similar, but the horns are slightly divergent
- Urial horns are similar to ibex, but the horns are shorter and instead of a lateral stripe, they have just a black spot under the foreleg
- Argali females are bigger than all other similar Ovis and Capra. The horns are relatively large and divergent
- Markhor females have slightly divergent and twisted horns; lateral stripe is thin and sometimes indistinct.

9

Mountain Ungulates in the Himalayan and Trans-Himalayan Protected Areas of India

In all, 20 ungulate species belonging to four families viz., Cervidae, Moschidae, Bovidae and Equidae occur in the Himalaya. Of these, three species, viz., Sambar, Barking deer and Wild pig are widely distributed in the India and are not confined to the Himalayan region alone. The Himalayan ungulates are represented by 17 species and the members of the Sub Family Caprinae dominate (9 species). About 5,13,089 km^2 of India's geographical area is covered by the Himalayas and the hills of north-east India. There are about 75 Protected Areas (PAs) covering approximately 40,329.65 km^2 (7.86% of the region) in which the mountain ungulates occur. These include: 6 PAs in the Trans-Himalayan zone, 58 in the Himalayan zone, 3 in the Gangetic Plain, and 8 in North-East India. The Central Himalayan province (2C) has the highest percentage of PA coverage while the province of North-East Hills (9B) has the lowest PA coverage.

Protected Area Coverage

a. PA Coverage in different Biogeographic Regions: An analysis of area covered under the PA network in each biogeographic zone (i.e, area available for conservation of mountain ungulates and other species) reveals that the Eastern Himalaya (2D) has the highest (10,700.57 km^2) coverage while the North-East Hills has the lowest (1,249.69 km^2). The area covered under the PA network in other provinces are as follows: 1A-Ladakh Mountains (9,775 km2), 2B-West Himalaya (6,028.48 km^2), 1B-Tibetan Plateau (5,443 km^2), 2A-North-West Himalaya (3,419.09 km2), 2C-Central Himalaya (2,071.82 km^2) and in 7A-Upper Gangetic Plain (1,642 km^2).

b. PA Size Distribution (for some selected species): The mountain ungulate species found in various PAs and the potential areas available for each species are as follows: Himalayan ibex reported in 8 PAs (11,854.70 km^2), Ladakh urial in 2 PAs (9,100 km^2), Tibetan argali in 2 PAs (8,100 km^2), Bharal in 17 PAs (17,540.76 km^2), Tibetan wild ass in 1 PA (4,000 km^2), Himalayan musk deer in 37 PAs (17,831.48 km^2), Hangul in 5 PAs (1,178 km^2), Himalayan tahr in 17 PAs (5,953.61 km^2), Goral in 54 PAs (22,757.08 km^2), Serow in 43 PAs (18,434.61 km^2), Markhor in 1 PA (400 km^2), Takin in 6 PAs (5,561.50 km^2).

The mean PA size for PAs in Provinces 2A and 9B are low while it is higher for 1A and 1B. Over 36% of these PAs are <100 km^2 and about 40% PAs are in the category of 101-500 km^2. In other words, 76% of PAs that afford protection to mountain ungulates are smaller in size. There is a need for large PAs to maintain viable populations of mountain ungulates for long-term conservation.

Ungulate Species Richness in Protected Areas

Goral seems to be the most common mountain ungulate in the Himalaya as it is reported from 54 PAs, while the Tibetan wild ass and Markhor are found only in one PA each. Information on the distribution of species such as Tibetan gazelle, Chiru and Wild yak is lacking.

The highest mountain ungulate species richness is in the biotic province North-west Himalaya (8 species) and the minimum species richness is in the biotic province Upper Gangetic Plain (1 species). The state of Jammu & Kashmir has the most number of mountain ungulate species (10 species) while the states of Nagaland and Manipur have the least (1 species each).

MOUNTAIN UNGULATES OF LADAKH, JAMMU & KASHMIR

Ladakh-'the Land of Passes' (La-passes, dakh-land) is the largest in area when compared to the three main regions of the Jammu & Kashmir State viz., Jammu, Kashmir and Ladakh. This region falls under the districts of Ladakh and Kargil. The most striking feature of Ladakh region is the mountain ranges that stretch from the southeast to the northeast. Although most of Ladakh is mountainous, there are many valleys lying in the lap of the mountain ranges such as the Great Himalayan range, the Zanskar range, the Ladakh range and the Karakoram Range. As like all other high altitude mountainous region, Ladakh is sparsely populated (ca. 1,50,000) i.e., only two persons/ km2. Although life is difficult at high altitudes (2,900-5,900 metres), yet both man and wildlife survive here comfortably as revealed by the rich diversity of wildlife.

The Ladakh landscape is characterized by snow-clad mountains, treeless arctic deserts and a few narrow fertile valleys, some of them breathtakingly beautiful. With the advent of summer, a miraculous change occurs when life-sustaining vegetation lends color to an otherwise bleak landscape. Ladakh is a large barren but beautiful region of intense sunlight and clear unpolluted air.

The temperature in summer may rise up to 37oC, but may also drop to-40oC degrees in winter. Dras in Kargil district experiences the lowest winter temperatures. There is very low rainfall in the region is about 92 mm/annum because it is situated in the rain shadow region of the Greater Himalayas. Most of the water source is the frozen snow or ice.

Fauna of Ladakh

The Fauna of Ladakh is a mixture of Palearctic and Oriented regions and comprises mostly of mammals and birds. Ladakh has poor representation of reptiles and amphibians. The mammalian fauna comprises mainly of ungulates, rodents and carnivores. Ladakh is well recognized for its mountain ungulate diversity. Information on the status and distribution of these mountain ungulates in Ladakh are presented below.

Wild Yak

The most notable animal of the Ladakh, Tibet and adjacent parts of central Asia is the Wild Yak. It is a large animal weighting about a ton. It has long black hair, which is tinged with gray at the muzzle. The horns are curved and long which may grow up to 75 cm in length. The wild yak, which moves in herds, spends the summer at great heights and descends to lower altitudes in winter. Prior to 1962, the Wild Yak was distributed in plang darpo and kuenlum into Tibet westwards in Ladakh. As per the local people, the animals were found near Pangong Lake, Changchenmo Valley, Tsoogsalu, Daulat Beg Olde and Chushul areas. Since then, their distribution range has drastically shrunken and number has greatly declined due to massive hunting.

There were no official reports on the presence of Wild Yak in Ladakh for the last thirty years. A survey was conducted by a team of six members in the Karakoram Range of (a corridor between India & China) Changchenmo Valley, North-East of Ladakh during July-August 1996 in order to confirm the presence of Wild Yak. About 300 km were covered during surveys of which 170 km were by vehicle and the rest on foot. One male was sighted at Satlung Yogma and herd of 47 Yaks were sighted at Satlung Parma area in the Karakoram range, Changchenmo Valley. This survey confirmed the presence of Wild Yak in this area.

Tibetan Antelope

The Chiru or Tibetan antelope (Tsoros-Ladakhi)-is a valuable species that inhabits high altitudes of Ladakh. It is slender but stout looking due to the thick coat of interwoven pale-brown hair. The color varies from season to season and from individual to individual. They roam the eastern fringe of Ladakh and inhabit Aksaichin and Tibetan plateau above 5,000 metres. Their horns measure up to 70 cm and are black having knots indicating the animal's age. In case of male front legs has a strip of black or dark brownish in colour The Chiru is persecuted in large numbers for the sake of under fleece-shahtoosh-from which the famous shahtoosh shawls or 'ring shawls' are made. Hardly a pound of under fleece is obtained from one animal. These shawls are the highly priced, softest and warmest quality product.

It was reported that the Tibetan antelope was extinct as no reports of sightings were made during the period 1960-1990. In 1984, the Chiru were reported to occur in the Aksai chin and Tibetan plateau. The Chiru are migratory and come in to Indian Territory in the Changchenmo valley and DBO during summer. In 1991, the Indian Army reported the presence of Chiru in DBO (Daulat Beg Olde) falling in the Karakoram Wildlife Sanctuary located along the border with China. In 1994, Mr. N.A. Kitchloo, Wildlife Warden, Leh, deputed a survey team of 9 person headed by Mr. Amchuk, R.O. to DBO and reported the sighting of Chiru.

The Chiru population was estimated to be between 250 and 300. In India, the Chiru is found in the Changchenmo DBO (Daulat Beg Olde) valley of northern Ladakh between 3,700-5,500 metres from where it crosses from Tibet through Lanak Ia (pass) at the head of the valley. After this survey, it was certain that the animal is not killed in the Indian Territory i.e., DBO and Changchenmo-a fact supplemented by the security forces as well. In Ladakh, the illegal trade was reportedly carried out through the border of Changthang. No trade is reported from DBO and Changchenmo valley where the animals are found at present in Ladakh, the reason being that the area is not inhabited up to at least 180 km from Phobrang village to, Changchenmo and silk head to DBO (Daulat Beg Olde).

The population of Chiru has declined drastically by excessive poaching and disturbance of its natural habitats in Tibet as has been reported by various agencies. These animals come into this area during summer season (May to September) and they migrate to the lower elevations across the international border to Winter. They breed there in November-December and the young ones are born in May which is followed by their migration to higher elevations. The Chiru is a ruminant and feeds mostly during early mornings and late evenings especially along grassy edges and glacial streams. During day, it spends resting and before resting it first digs or scraps shallow pit in sand/ gravel and lies in side for concealment.

Tibetan Argali

Another pride of Ladakh is Nayan or Tibetan Argali found at a height of about 4,500m. A male may weigh up to a quintal. Lt. General Moti Dar has reported their number to be around 200 in eastern Ladakh.

Ladakh Urial

A close relative of Nayan is Shapo or Ladakh Urial. It is smaller than Nayan a large one weighing around 80 kg. It prefers heights between 3,000 to 4,000 m.

Blue Sheep

The bharal or Blue sheep is a strange looking creature, half-sheep and half-goat. It differs from the goat in that it doesn't have a beard. Likewise it differs from the sheep in the complete absence of glands on the face. The Bharal are found at an altitude of 6,000 metres. In summer, they graze in large herds on rich and abundant grass of the meadows.

Asiatic Ibex

The Asiatic Ibex is the most beautiful of all mountain goats. It supports two long scimitar-shaped horns marked with bold transverse knots on the front surface. They may be over a metre long. The mature males have a long beard and weigh over a quintal. They move in herds of 10 to 16 and prefer precipitous rocks and cliffs. In winter, they descend to the lower altitudes for food and shelter.

Tibetan Gazelle and Tibetan Wild Ass

The Tibetan Gazelle (Goa) is a small mountain ungulate that is distributed in eastern Ladakh. The Tibetan wild ass (Kiang) is a relative of the wild ass of the Rann of Kutch. It has a wide distribution. Besides Ladakh it is found in Tibet, Turkistan and Mongolia. Kiang is shy but an inquisitive animal. It inhabits plain and rocky grounds and can gallop at a good speed. Solitary, animals or groups of 10-12 animals can be seen.

The coloring of the upper portion of the body is chestnut or red and the under parts are white. There is a dark brown dorsal stripe extended from the stiff black mane to the tuft of the tail.

Other Herbivores

Among the other herbivores of Ladakh are the Himalayan mouse hare, Tibetan woolly hare, marmot and many other rodents. Marmots are common rodents found above the tree line. They live in burrows and produce shrill ringing calls. They hibernate during winter. Marmots and the hares form important prey base for snow leopard, lynx, fox and large birds of prey.

Conservation Issues

Despite the extremely harsh environment and sparse vegetation, wildlife in Ladakh thrived well prior to India's independence. This was mainly due to the Buddhist philosophy of non-violence. Construction of roads for defence purposes and development of the region ironically provided greater opportunities for killing the wildlife. The defence personnel also had a share in the killings because of their occasional indulgence in Shikar, a legacy of the Raj days. In short, the opening up of Ladakh to the rest of the world has exposed its Wildlife. Skins of the Snow Leopard and under fleece of Tibetan antelope and gazelle fetch fabulous prices, which has rendered wildlife vulnerable to poaching.

The mountainous state of Himachal Pradesh, with elevations ranging from 300 to over 6000 m, accounts 17% of the area of the north-western Himalayas. Bio-geographically the state can be divided into four distinct regions: the Trans-Himalaya (Biotic provinces 1A & 1B), which include the cold deserts of northern Lahul and Spiti districts; the Greater Himalayas ((Biotic provinces 2A & 2B), high and middle mountains covering most of the state; and the semi Arid zone (Biotic province 4A), consisting the hot dry foot hills in the south (Rodgers et al. 2000). The biotic provinces 1A (Ladkah mountains) and 1B (Tibetan Plateau) have mammals of international conservation significance such as the Snow leopard, Tibetan argali and Tibetan gazelle.

The biotic provinces 2A (North-west Himalaya) and 2B (Western Himalaya) also have species of international conservation significance such as the Hangul or Kashmir stag and pheasants such as the Wesern Tragopan and Cheer (Rodgers & Panwar 1988). Two National Parks and 32 Wildlife Sanctuaries have been set up so far in Himachal Pradesh covering 10.37% of the state area with proposals for new PAs that would add another 1.08% coverage (Rodgers et al. 2000).

Himachal Pradesh has a rich assemblage of over 74 species of mammals (excluding Chiropterans) belonging to eight Orders and 21 Families / Sub Families. Of these, 17 species are unconfirmed although they are most likely to occur in this state. Seven species of caprids are reported to occur in Himachal Pradesh. They are: Tibetan Argali (Ovis ammon), Bharal or Blue Sheep (Pseudois nayaur), Asiatic ibex (Capra ibex), Himalayan tahr (Hemitraghus jemlahicus), Serow (Nemorhaedus sumatraensis) and Goral (Nemorhaedus goral). Himalayan Musk deer (Moschus chrysogaster), and Tibetan Gazelle (Procapra piticaudata), are the other mountain ungulates that are present in this statea. The Hangul or Kashmir Stag (Cervus elaphus hanglu) was reported to occur in the northern parts of this state (Chamba district), particularly in the forested areas (2,500-3,200m) in and around the Gamgul-Siahbehi WS. There are no recent reports of this species in this state in the recent past. Based on the results of the Wildlife Surveys conducted in Sutlej and Beas catchments, the information on some caprid species in Himachal Pradesh is given below.

Goral (Nemorhaedus goral)

In Sutlej and Beas river catchments, Goral is very common. During a wildlife abundance estimation exercise in February 1990, I estimated a density of 1.2 goral/km^2 in Daranghati Wildlife Sanctuary. An estimate of 1.47 goral/km^2 was obtained for Rupi Bhaba Wildlife Sanctuary in Kinnaur district. Goral has been reported from Sangla Valley Wildlife Sanctuary and short of Lippa Asrang Wildlife Sanctuary, both in Kinnaur district of Himachal Pradesh.

A good population of goral exists in the proposed Rupi Bhaba Wildlife Sanctuary in Shimla and Kinnaur districts. In Kanawar Wildlife Sanctuary, 18 gorals were sighted in a 2 km^2 area during December 1989 wildlife survey. During March 2002, 48 gorals were counted in a day's walk in Rolla-Nara area (immediately after snow fall).

Serow (Nemorhaedus sumatraensis)

Serow is fairly common in Sutlej and Beas Catchments. Wildlife survey party could sight one animal in Rashi Thach of Daranghati Wildlife Sanctuary in February 1990. In Rupi Bhaba Wildlife Sanctuary (Kinnaur district), six animals were sighted in different nallahs and evidences for another three animals were recorded during the period, March 1989 to January 1990. Only one fourth of this sanctuary may be considered to be Serow habitat. The area around Srikhand peak is reported to hold good Serow populations. In Kullu district, Serow has been reported in Jiwa Nal and Sainj Nal catchments, and Nalchi forest of Parbati river catchment. Serow has been reported to occur in high abundance in Kalatop-Khajiar Wildlife Sanctuary in Chamba district.

Bharal (Pseudois Nayaur)

This species has wider distribution than any other member of Caprinae in the catchment of Sutlej and Beas rivers. The upper reaches of Kinnaur, Lahaul and Spiti and Kullu districts hold good Bharal populations. In a wildlife survey (last week of June, 1990), three groups of Bharal (of 7,5 and 4 individual respectively) were sighted about 4,000 metres on the extension of Hansbesin Massif which forms eastern boundary of Shimla and Kinnaur districts. During various wildlife surveys (1987-90), Bharal has been recorded from both the banks of Sutlej river in Kinnaur district. All the three Wildlife Sanctuaries of Kinnaur, namely Rupi Bhaba, Sangla Valley and Lippa Asrang have good Bharal populations.

In April, 1989, the wildlife survey party sighted 26 Bharal and 11 Ibex sharing same hillock in Lippa Asrang Sanctuary. The areas below Pandoswar Peak in Rupi Bhaba Wildlife Sanctuary and the adjoining areas of this sanctuary with Pin

Valley National Park and Great Himalayan National Park have good Bharal populations. The newly created Sangla Valley Sanctuary (which includes the earlier Rakcham Chitkhul Sanctuary) has forested as well as arid areas (Transition zone). The eastern part of this sanctuary (close to Indo-Tibet Border) has Bharal populations. In addition to these, Ropa Valley, Pooh, Rishi Dogri, Neshang, Nako and Sumdo are places in Kinnaur district where Bharal sightings have been made during 1988-90. It has also been sighted along the Shrikhand Dhar in the Rupi Bhaba Wildlife Sanctuary.

Bharal is principal species of left bank of Spiti river, though it has been sighted in good numbers on the right bank, too. During last week of November, 1989, the density of Bharal was estimated by the King's Method. A total of 28 Bharal were sighted on a stretch of 14 Kms road length, thus resulting in a density of 2 Bharal/km^2. This density increases dramatically, immediately after the snowfall when Bharal move down into the valley bottom. In Pin Valley National Park, bharal have been sighted in very low numbers. Only one Bharal was seen with a group of 25 male Ibex above Mud village during August, 1988. I could see a six feet high cairn made up of Bharal horns in November, 1989 near Tabo village in Spiti Valley. The local Buddhist people collect these horns to ward off the evil spirits.

There are positive reports of Bharal from the higher reaches of the Great Himalayan National Park in Kullu district. In October, 2001, a group of more than 45 bharals were sighted at Sartoo glacial lake in Jiwa-Nal valley of this Park (Pandey, pers. Observations). Regular sightings of bharal are reported from the Tirath area in the Tirthan valley. In Parbati river catchment. Bharal have been reported from above Tos Nal Forest on right bank and Tebla Thatch on left bank. In Lahaul, Bharal have been reported from near Bara Lach Pass.

Himalayan Tahr (Hemitrangus jamlahicus)

In Sutlej Valley, the Himalayan tahr has been sighted in Daranghati, Sangla Valley and Rupi Bhaba Wildlife Sanctuaries. A wildlife abundance estimation exercise conducted in Daranghati Part-II during January 1990 resulted in a density estimate of 2.26 tahr/ km2. The largest group size recorded was of 4 animals only. Its status in extended Rupi Bhaba sanctuary on the right bank of Sutlej river is quite good. However, its sightings, at present have become progressively less towards Rupi Bhaba and Sangla Valley Wildlife Sanctuaries beyond which arid zone areas of Kinnaur district start. The Kullu district in Beas catchment has good Himalayan Tahr population. During a wildlife survey in December 1989, in Kanawar Wildlife Sanctuary, a total of 130 Himalayan Tahr were seen in a 2 km^2 area. The largest group size of Himalayan Tahr was of 25 individuals.

This trend continues upto the Great Himalayan National Park though the habitat is quite fragmented in between the two PAs. During October 2000 surveys, 17 Himalayan Tahr were seen in one group along the dividing ridge between Sainj and Tirthan catchments.

Siberian Ibex (Capra ibex sibericus)

During 1987-90 wildlife surveys, Ibex was seen on the right bank of Sutlej river only. This fact confirms the statement of Prater (1971) that its eastern limits are set by the upper reaches of the Sutlej river, east of which it does not occur. However, a lager number of Ibex horns could be seen as offering to the temples in the Sangla valley which is in east of Sutlej river (i.e. on the left bank of the river) in Kinnaur district of Himachal Pradesh. No ibex was sighted on the left bank. It appears that the horns were collected and transported from the right bank of the river.

In Kinnaur district, Ibex were sighted in Lippa Asrang Wildlife Sanctuary in April 1989 (11 Ibex and 26 Bharal on the same aspect). The reported occurrence of Bharal in Rupi Bhaba and Dharangati Wildlife Sanctuaries is incorrect. The Pin Valley National Park is a stronghold of Ibex. In November 1989, a total of 174 animals were seen in about 76 km^2 which indicates an estimated density of 2.29 Ibex/km^2. Ibex is found on both the banks of Spiti river above Kaza. The areas of Ratang Valley near Losar and Kunzam Pass have good Ibex populations. Evidences of Ibex have been obtained from Chandra and

Penglang valleys. Recently, sightings of Ibex have been made in Manali Wildlife Sanctuary, Hamta Nala and Solang Nala in Kullu district. Its presence/absence is yet to be confirmed from the Great Himalayan National Park.

Nayan or Tibetan Argali (Ovis ammon)

The only confirmed place from where horns of Argali could be obtained is in Kibber Nala (Spiti Valley). The villagers told that at times Nayan cross over to Himachal area from the adjoining Jammu & Kashmir state. The usual route is along Parang La. Only a few individuals come (one or two or three) along with local sheep and goat. I have no other evidence of the presence of this species from Himachal Pradesh.

Astor or Straight-horned Markhor (Capra falconeri)

There is no confirmed evidence or sighting of Markhor from the Chenab river catchment in Himachal Pradesh.

10

Status, Distribution and Management of Mountain Ungulates in Uttaranchal

INTRODUCTION

Uttaranchal is very rich in Biodiversity and is represented by Biogeographic Zones 2B Western Himalaya and 7B Siwaliks in this region. The uniqueness of ecological diversity from high alpine areas to the Terai region interspersed with numerous rivers is unparalleled. Different forest types can be identified in the state that spreads over 34,661 Km^2. The Forest Department controls about 23,988 Km2 (64.81%). About 18.7% of the total area under the Forest Department has been clearly earmarked for Biodiversity conservation by the creation and management of 12 Protected Areas (PA) in the state. These PAs are:

National Parks (NP):

Sl NO	Name of the PA	Year of Establishment	Area (Km^2)	District(s)
1.	Corbett NP	1936	521	Garhwal
2.	Nanda Devi NP	1982	630	Chamoli
3.	Valley of Flowers NP	1982	87	Chamoli
4.	Rajaji NP	1983	820	Dehradun & Haridwar
5.	Gangotri NP	1989	2,390	Uttarkasi
6.	Govind NP	1990	472	Uttarkasi

The mammalian diversity in Uttaranchal is one of the richest in the country, exceeding 75 species; about 50% of these are threatened. A detailed analysis of the data shows that

37.8% of species fall under lower risk least concern category and 19.51% under lower risk not threatened status. The critically endangered species constitute 6.09%, while vulnerable species account for 12.91%.

Wildlife Sanctuaries (WLS):

Sl.NO	Name of the PA	Year of Establishment	Area (Km^2)	District
1.	Govind WLS	1955	521	Uttarkasi
2.	Kedarnath WLS	1972	957	Chamoli
3.	Askot WLS	1986	600	Pithoragarh
4.	Sonanadi WLS	1987	301	Garhwal
5.	Binsar WLS	1988	46	Almora
6.	Musoorie WLS	1993	11	Dehradun

The Mountain ungulates are quite varied in Uttaranchal. They are mostly distributed in Seven Protected Areas located in the Western Himalyas viz., Gangotri NP, Govind WLS and Govind NP, Kedarnath WLS, Nanda Devi NP, Valley of Flowers NP, Binsar WLS and Askot WLS.

The species include Himalayan Musk Deer (Moschus chrysogaster) Himalayan, Tahr (Hemitragus jemlahicus), Blue Sheep (Pseudois nayur), Serow. (Nemorhaedus sumatrensis) and Goral (Nemorhaedus goral). Sambar (Cervus unicolor) and Barking Deer (Muntiacus muntjac) also occur in the region, generally below 2,700m.

STATUS & DISTRIBUTION

The distribution and status of mountain ungulates in Uttaranchal in different PAs are as under (as per the record contained in the management plans of the PAs and information collected from the field).

Name of the Protected area	Name of the species	Status		
		Rare	Common	Abundant
Gangotri NP	1. Tahr		•	
	2. Serow			
	3. Goral		•	
	4. Musk deer		•	
	5. Barking deer			
	6. Blue sheep			

Kedarnath WLS	1. Tahr		•	
	2. Serow	•		
	3. Goral		•	
	4. Musk deer		•	
	5. Barking deer			•
	6. Blue sheep *			
Nanda Devi NP	1. Tahr			•
	2. Serow	•		
	3. Goral	•		
	4. Musk deer			•
	5. Blue sheep			•
Govind WLS and Govind NP	1. Tahr		•	
	2. Serow	•		
	3. Goral			•
	4. Musk deer		•	
	5. Blue sheep		•	
Valley of Flowers NP	1. Tahr		•	
	2. Serow	•		
	3. Goral	•		
	4. Musk deer	•		
	5. Blue sheep	•		
Binsar WLS	1. Tahr	•		
	2. Serow	•		
	3. Goral		•	
	4. Musk deer	•		
	5. Barking deer		•	
	6. Blue sheep	•		
Askot WLS	1. Tahr	•		
	2. Serow	•		
	3. Goral		•	
	4. Musk deer		•	
	5. Barking deer		•	
	6. Blue sheep	•		

Status Unknown

The following areas of Uttaranchal are mainly known to have Musk deer. However, these areas are only representative areas and further research and surveys are required to know the site specific locations and number of animals present in these areas:

In a survey conducted in 1968-72 the following estimates were made for some of the Musk Deer rich areas of Uttaranchal on the basis of field reports.

1. Almora Kapkot Between 20 and 30
2. Pithoragarh Dharchula Between 25 and 40
3. Tihri Garhwal Bhilangana Between 25 and 40
4. Uttarkasi-Purola & Naogaon Between 24 and 36
5. Chamoli-Raksi Between 15 and 30
6. Ukhimath Between 10 and 15
7. Tahrali Between 10 and 15

This survey was conducted many years ago. However on the basis of sightings and on the basis of frequency of sightings the number of three species have been steadily growing. These are Goral, Blue sheep and Tahr. The numbers of Barking deer is also on the rise. True status of Musk deer is still not very clear. However their number in the strictly protected areas like Nanda Devi NP has definitely taken an upward trend.

MANAGEMENT ISSUES

Main Issues

- Large scale killing of mountain ungulates in the past century specially musk deer, Tahr and Blue sheep.
- In winter the snow line drops. This is also the time of rutting. Some mountain ungulates migrate down to lower reaches and this provides an easy opportunity for the poachers to kill the animal.
- Degradation of habitat due to increase in biotic pressure.
- Lack of funds and infrastructure.

- Lack of intra state and inter state communication between the PAs and well chalked out conservation plan.
- Lack of special high altitude training and working facilities for the staff.
- Captive bred animals are not being utilized for optimum use.

On Going Measures

Creation of Protected Areas

Seven protected areas viz., Gangotri NP, Nanda Devi NP, Govind NP, Valley of Flowers NP, Kedarnath WLS, Askot WLS and Govind Pashu Vihar WLS have been created and special protection measures are being undertaken for the conservation of all the ungulates along with the associated flora and fauna in Uttaranchal.

Eco-development programmes are being taken up for better management of buffer zones so that local activities, such as livestock grazing, agriculture and the collection of forest produce, are contained within certain areas, while others, including representative patches of habitats of endangered ungulates such as the musk deer, are left undisturbed as "strict natural" or "wilderness" areas.

Preparation of Landscape Management Plans

Landscape management plans for all the seven PAs are being prepared taking into account all the areas near the PAs and the concerned stakeholders who have a bearing on conservation to facilitate better understanding and better awareness among all concerned parties.

Ex situ Conservation Management in Uttaranchal

In Uttaranchal, two Himalayan Musk deer Breeding Centres viz., Kanchula Kharakh (Chamoli) and Dharmaghar (Almora) have been created and managed. A few mountain ungulate species along with other high altitude fauna are housed and managed in the Naini Tal Zoo.

The status of these breeding centres are as follows:

Name of the Centre	Date of Establishment	Admn. Authority	Area	Elevation	Temp Rang	Number Animals
Musk Deer Research, Almora	1971	Central Council for Research in Ayurveda & Siddha	2 Acre	7,500 fl.	Max-31 C MIn- Below freezing	13.15.0 [mm.ff.yy]
Kanchula Kharakh Chamoli	1982	Forest Department	20 Ha.	9000 ft.	Max - 31 C Mm- Below freezing	9.6.0

The Challenges & the Conservation Strategy

Most PAs of Uttaranchal lack the financial and manpower resources to adequately protect the mountain ungulates and it's apex predator snow leopard and/or Common leopard. Additional constraints include extremely remote and rugged range, harsh climatic and environmental conditions that prevail in many areas, the long international borders that are accordingly difficult to patrol, and a severe lack of trained and motivated staff to conduct surveys, logistic and infrastructural support and management plans.

A large number of wild animals, including Musk deer, are found outside existing PAs. According to an estimate, 80% of wild animals may venture outside the PAs. Presence of animals such as the Blue Sheep, Serow, Black Bear, Musk deer, Goral occurring outside the PAs is quite common.

Presence of wild animals particularly in the periphery is not only due to lack of prey animals and foraging site inside the park but due to sharp edge effects created by the villagers. Effective monitoring of ungulate populations outside PAs and proper documentation of every case of animal lifting, human loss or poaching will also help reduce the conflict with park managers

Bulk of the people of the region depend on cattle rearing. The potential impacts of excessive grazing by livestock include depletion of the scarce forage for wildlife, habitat degradation and disease transfer.

Abundance or population estimation of high altitude ungulates is a specialized job and it cannot be done in a routine way. Not only specialized equipments like light and powerful field glasses and cameras are required, but also involvement of technical staff and researchers is a must. For proper maintenance of records and analysis of field data Computers and Statistical software are also required.

General perception of the local people about endangered species and their importance in the ecosystem is poor. Efforts are needed to highlight biological and morphological importance of the PA in the context of human existence. Education camps and special trainings for the local N.G.Os, youth club members, Mahila Mangal Dal (Womens' Group) members will have to be provided. In addition to these, capacity of the local staff will also have to be developed to arrange grass root training camps on their own.

The mountain ungulates of Uttaranchal not only hold a great ecological value but they are also part and parcel of cultural ethos and heritage of this Himalayan state. All concerted efforts are being made to save them for posterity and for the healthy sustainable ecological balance. Challenges are many but the Wildlife wing of the Forest Department of Uttaranchal is all set to successfully handle these challenges.

MOUNTAIN UNGULATES IN SIKKIM

One of the smallest states in India, Sikkim lies between 27°5' to 28°9' N and 87°59' to 88°56' E, covering an area of 7,096 km2, extending approximately 114 km north-south and 64 km east-west. Wedged in between the Himalayan kingdoms of Nepal in the west and Bhutan in the east, Sikkim is bounded by Darjeeling District of West Bengal in the south and a stretch of Tibetan Plateau in the north. In this land of vast altitude variation (ca. 300m-8,586m) within very short distances, elevation has played a major role in fashioning the various eco-regions.

This is evident from the presence of the sub-tropical Rangit Valley Sal forests with Wild boar and Indian muntjac in the south, to the temperate fir forests harbouring Himalayan tahr and Musk deer in the north, beyond which lie the Trans-Himalayas and cold desert of the Tibetan plateau supporting Kiang and Nayan. Sikkim is classified as part of the biogeographic province 2C (Central Himalayas), which in India includes the Darjeeling district of West Bengal with Temperate-Broadleaf biome, with the north of Sikkim as biogeographic province 1B (Trans-Himalayas-Tibetan plateau) with biota of Palaearctic affinity. The latter area is high-altitude cold desert in the rain-shadow of the main Himalayan range with typically Tibetan flora and fauna.

As per the 2002 Annual Administrative Report of the Department, about 2,177 km^2 or 30.68 % of the total geographical area of the state is under wildlife protection, which is perhaps the highest in the country. The largest Protected Area (PA) in the state, the Khangchendzonga Biosphere Reserve was notified in February 2000. It is spread over North and West districts encompassing 1,784 km^2 of Khangchendzonga National Park (KNP) and 835.9 km^2 over four buffer zones totaling an area of 2,619.9 km^2. These buffer zones are Lhonak Valley, West Chungthang-Lachen, Tholung Valley and Rangit and Tista Catchments. Pangolakha Wildlife Sanctuary was recently declared on the Bhutan-China (Tibet)-India (Sikkim and West Bengal) tri-junction. There is also another proposal for declaration of a cold desert protected area in north Sikkim.

Mountain Ungulate Surveys in Sikkim

Over the last three decades, the State Forest Department conducted sporadic management surveys of which no detailed records were kept. Some such patrols were anti-poaching or 'Operation Trap Demolition' expeditions in the Khangchendzonga National Park (KNP) to dismantle vast stretches of live rhododendron shrubs worked for kilometres into traps for Musk deer. In a 1993 Tiger Census in north and east Sikkim, other species of wildlife encountered including ungulates, were also recorded. The following areas were specifically covered in KNP (Lachungpa, C. pers. comm.):

i. Yuksom-Dzongri-Goecha La, Lampokhari trekking trail (W)

ii. Tholung Valley (N)
iii. Chungthang-Menshithang-Bikmatar, Phimphu (N)
iv. Lachen-Zema-Green Lake (N)
v. Thangu-Muguthang-Green Lake (N)

In the last decades, two surveys were conducted specifically for mountain ungulates in Sikkim. Between 1995-1997, Mr. C. Lachungpa, Divisional Forest Officer, with assistance from WWF-India surveyed the Pangolkha range for the Shou or Sikkim stag. The areas covered included Rachela, Phadamchen, Rigyap, Menmoitso and Menla. No shou was recorded (Lachungpa, C. pers. comm.) but there was one indistinct sighting of the Takin. It was based on this survey that the proposal for declaration of the area as Pangolakha National Park was moved and in 2002 the Pangolakha Wildlife Sanctuary was declared.

In 1996, Mr. C. Lachungpa as the first Kailash Sankhala Awardee, initiated another survey for the Himalayan Tahr locally called 'Shapi', in the KNP. He confirmed the existence of the species not only in the Phimphu area in north KNP but also in the western part of the park. (Lachungpa, C. pers. comm.). Much earlier around 1986-87, a group of foreign trekkers had reported sighting of the Tibetan argali in west KNP above Goecha La, (report not traceable) in a note to the Department but their observations could not be confirmed. In 1988, Mr. S. Z. Lucksom as Field Director (KNP) was the first to film the Shapi in Sikkim from the Phimphu area.

Opportunistic sightings of mountain ungulates were also recorded during the following departmental research surveys between 1988-2002. Information from these was used in relevant short publications, papers presented during seminars or as short unpublished departmental reports.

- Asian Waterfowl Counts in the Trans-Himalayan and alpine regions of north and east Sikkim, 1988-1994
- Short surveys for butterflies in all four districts, 1988-1994 (information used in Haribal, M. 1992)
- Cold desert wildlife surveys in north Sikkim 1988, 1991-1995

- Survey of birds of Fambong Lho Wildlife Sanctuary, east Sikkim, 1989
- Wildlife expedition to Lhonak Valley-Green Lake, north Sikkim, 1990
- Wildlife survey of Lhonak Valley, Lashar Valley and Tso Lhamo Plateau, north Sikkim, 1992
- Wildlife survey including bird ringing studies at Lashar-Sebu La-Yumesamdong-Tembawa and Dongkia La-Tso Lhamo Plateau, 1995
- Royal Botanic Garden Edinburgh expedition to Lashar-Sebu La-Yumesamdong-Tembawa and Lachung Valley, north Sikkim, Fambong Lho Wildlife Sanctuary (WLS), east Sikkim, July 1996
- Oriental Bird Club bird survey in Kitam and lowland forests, south Sikkim and Barsey Rhododendron Sanctuary, west Sikkim, Mar-Apr and Sep-Oct 1996
- Biodiversity survey of Maenam Wildlife Sanctuary, south Sikkim, in collaboration with the World Pheasant Association in April-May 1998
- Red Panda pilot survey for the WWF in and around PAs, Sep-Dec 1998
- Bird ringing studies in Fambong Lho WLS, Kyongnosla Alpine Sanctuary, Himalayan Zoological Park, east Sikkim, 1992-93, 1995-96, 2000
- Alpine Grassland Ecology Project of BNHS in sub-alpine, alpine and Trans-Himalayan areas of north Sikkim, 2000-2002, study sites being Tso Lhamo plateau, Thangu, Lhonak and Lashar valleys, Yumesamdong, Yumthang

As many as 15 species of wild mountain ungulates were recorded from this small portion of the Himalayas, ranging from the Tibetan Wild Ass Equus kiang and the (Globally Threatened) Nayan or Great Tibetan Sheep Ovis ammon hodgsoni on the Tibetan Plateau, to the Indian Muntjac Muntiacus muntjac and Wild Boar Sus scrofa in the sub-tropical south.

So far the State Forest Department has not recorded some species such as the Mouse-Deer, Pygmy Hog and Hog Deer reported in literature from 'Sikkim Terai', area which is no longer within the present limits of the state. Some Chital Axis axis from the Rustomjee Deer Park, Gangtok, were released into the lowland forests in the last decade and are still occasionally sighted.

Interestingly, single individuals of two other ungulates, Takin and Gaur were sighted as recently as 1999 and 2002 from Kyongnosla Alpine Sanctuary and the recently declared Pangolakha Wildlife Sanctuary both in east Sikkim (Departmental Report, in prep.). While the lone Takin was a novelty for most of the local people, the Gaur was found to be commonly called 'Mithun-Gai'. Both species are now known to occasionally stray over from the Bhutan border.

There are seven PAs in Sikkim, but none so far either in the lowland forests or Trans-Himalayan Sikkim, though Kitam Wildlife Sanctuary for peafowl in the south and a Cold Desert protected area for trans-border ungulates like nayan, kiang and Tibetan gazelle in the north have been proposed. The state also has feral ungulates in some of the PAs.

Table 1A: Legally Gazetted Wildlife Protected Areas in Sikkim

Name of the PA	District	Area in km^2	Date of Notification
National Park			
1. Khangchendzonga National Park	North and West	1,784	26.08.1977
Wildlife Sanctuaries			
1. Shingba Rhododendron Sanctuary	North	43	05.12.1992
2. Barsey Rhododendron Sanctuary	West	104	08.06.1996
3. Kyongnosia Alpine Sanctuary	East	31	05.12.1992
4. Fambong Lho Wildlife Sanctuary	East	51.76	02.04.1984
5. Maenam Wildlife Sanctuary	South	35.34	09.03.1987
6. Pangolakha Wildlife Sanctuary	East	128	07.11.2002

Table 1B: Proposed PAs

1. Tso Lhamo Cold Desert Conservation Area	North	2.00
2. Kitam Bird Sanctuary	South	6.00
3. Rabdentse Bird Sanctuary	West	2.00

Status and distribution of Mountain Ungulates of Sikkim.

Species	Wildlife Protected Areas							Outside	
	SRS (N)	KAS (E)	FBL (E)	PGL (E)	KNP (N&W)	BRS (W)	MNM (S)	Low land Forests (S)	Trans Himachal (N)
Equidae									
Equus kiang Tibetan wild ass	-	-	-	-	-	-	-	-	R
Suidae									
Sus scrofa Wild boar	-	-	C	C	C	C	C	A	-
Moschidae									
Moschus chrysogaster Himalayan musk deer	R	R	-	R	R	R	R	-	-
Cervidae									
Axis axis Chital, Axis deer	-	-	-	-	-	-	-	R	-
Cervus eiaphus Shou	-	-	-	?	-	-	-	-	-
Cervus unicoior Sambur	-q	-	-	R	?	-	?	?	-
Muntiacus muntjac 'Indian muntjac, Barking deer	-	R	C	C	C	C	C	A	-
Bovidae									
Bos *gaurus* Gaur, Indian bison	-	-	-	R	-	-	-	-	-
Bos *grunniens* Domestic yak .	C	C	-	R	C	C	-	-	C
Budorcas taxicolor Takin	R	R	-	R	-	-	-	-	-
Procapra picticaudata Tibetan gazelle	-	-	-	-	-	-	-	-	R
Naemorhedus goral Himalayan goral, Common goral	C	C	R	C	C	C	C	R	-
N. sumatraensis Southern serow. Mainland serow	R	R	R	R	C	R	C	R	-
Hemitragus jemlahicus Himalayan tahr	-	-	-	-	R	-	-	-	-
Ovis ammon Nayan Great Tibetan sheep, Argali	-	-	-	-	R	-	-	-	R
Pseudois nayaur Bharal, Blue sheep	C	R	-	R	C	7	-	-	R

11

Wildlife Management in Sikkim

In the biodiversity hotspot that is Sikkim, wildlife management practices are area and not species specific. The present management practices followed are:

1. Habitat oriented management:
   a. Habitat improvement: afforestation of wildlife amenable species using gap plantation in degraded areas and block plantation in forest blanks
   b. Water regime improvement: creation of waterholes, revitalization of existing lakes and ponds
   c. Reducing fire hazards: with help from the Eco Development Committees around PAs
2. Law enforcement: implementation of Wildlife (Protection) Act (1972, 2002), creation of information network with help from Ecodevelopment Committees (EDC), reduction of grazing, liasoning with the Indian Army, Border Roads Organisation
3. Research and Development: field surveys, mapping of PAs using remote sensing & GIS (newly initiated)
4. Survey and demarcation: installation of boundary pillars around PAs

The Department carries out regular patrolling for monitoring of habitat to control wildlife offences inside the PAs. However there is no effective monitoring of ungulate populations outside PAs.

One of the main threats being faced by wildlife (especially mountain ungulates) as perceived by the State Forest

Department is lack of awareness, especially in the remote areas. Barking deer, Goral, Serow occasionally fall prey to traps laid for crop protection and their hides were used to make small stools (mudas) for domestic use.

There have also been instances of discarded wire and metal being used to snare Blue Sheep in restricted areas where road construction and maintenance take priority and temporary settlements of non-native labourers are located. Along the international border where national defence takes priority, Nayan fall prey along with Kiang and Yak to land mines. Also, all wildlife especially ungulates are plagued by the problem of stray and feral dogs near army installations.

These and other issues are being addressed in a study presently underway for development of a conservation strategy for the alpine grasslands of Sikkim, in collaboration with the Bombay Natural History Society. The issue has also been addressed in the National Biodiversity Strategy and Action Plan (NBSAP) where a separate SAP has been written for the Indian Army in Sikkim.

With newer areas under the PA network, many more management initiatives are being proposed such as intensive scientific research, strengthening of EDC network, training of forest staff, creation of alternative livelihoods for people dependent on forest resources and preparation of detailed management plans for the PAs.

Mountain ungulates such as Goral and Bharal are also covered under an ex situ management programme in the Himalayan Zoological Park at Bulbuley, Gangtok.

There are however many limitations for wildlife conservation in Sikkim, the leading one being those imposed by international border restrictions (Nepal, Tibet and Bhutan), difficult terrain and harsh, high altitudes, followed by lack of awareness, of motivation, of infrastructure and logistics (barracks, range offices, vehicles, ammunition and communication), lack of skilled manpower, lack of research and lack of funds. This severely limits options for patrolling wildlife outside PAs especially in the Trans-Himalayan area of north Sikkim.

INTRODUCTION

The present Arunachal Pradesh was part of Assam till 1914, and was known as the North-East Frontier Tract till 1954 and as the North East Frontier Agency (NEFA) up to 1972 when it was given its present name. It is situated between 260 28' N & 290 30' N and 910 30' E & 970 30' E. It covers a geographical area of 83,743 km2. It is the largest state in the northeastern part of India. The state is predominantly hilly and mountainous. It is flanked by Tibet to the north separated by the McMohan line, Bhutan to the west, China and Myanmar to the east, and the Indian states of Assam and Nagaland to the south. It is predominantly a tribal state consisting of 82 major tribes and sub-tribes of Indo-Mongoloid and Mongoloid lineage. (Singh,1999). The tribal communities are fully dependent on natural resources for their sustenance and due to sparse population density, 13 persons/km2 (Anon. 2001) and large tracts of hilly forest, pressures on the forest and wildlife were minimal despite traditional hunting. In recent times, however, this has rapidly changed because of pressure from increasing human population within the state, the market forces from outside the state and large development projects taken up to give a boost to the region's economy to improve the quality of life of its people. Most of the land area of the state is under tribal ownership which is managed under their customary practices.

Physiographically, a major portion of state is divided into two sections, viz., the flood plains of the Brahmaputra and its tributaries, and the Arunachal Himalayas. The Arunachal Himalayas is further sub-divided into three sub-regions-the foothills, the Greater & the Lesser sub-Himalayan Ranges, Siwaliks and Purvanchal (Singh, 1999). The hills of the Naga-Patkai ranges are included in Purvanchal.

The flora and fauna of the state predominantly have Oriental affinities. As per Rodgers and Panwar's (1988) Bio-geographic Classification the state has is classified under the 'Eastern Himalaya-Province 2D (Rodgers et. al. 2002). Tirap and parts of Changlang district falling south of Chowkhan Pass and Noa-Dehing (Diyun) river is part of the Naga-Patkai mountain ranges. As such, bio-geographically, this belt of the state should have been included in the North East Hills (9B) Bio-geographic province of the North-East India zone in the classification of Rodgers et al. (2002). This state is also bio-geographically important because it falls in the transition zone between Indian subcontinent and Indo-Chinese bio-geographical regions (Dinnersten et al. 1997). It is the gateway to India's rich biodiversity and is among the world's 25 global biodiversity hotspots, and identified as being among 200 globally important eco-regions.

The state has a wide altitudinal variation ranging from 300 m in the foothills to about 7000 m along the Greater Himalayan Peaks in the north. The areas having altitudes more than 4,500 m are generally under perpetual snow cover. Arunachal Pradesh falls under the Upper Brahmaputra River System constituted by six river basins namely Kameng, Subansiri, Siang (the Tsangpo in Tibet), Dibang, Lohit-Tellu and Tirap river basins including sub-basins of Tawang, Sessiri and Tiso (Singh, 1999).

In addition to the variations in the climate at the local level due to relief conditions and drainage patterns, the climate of Arunachal Pradesh can be classified into three major types: the hot and humid sub-tropical climate of the South (foothills), cooler temperature zone of Lesser Himalaya, and alpine zone of the Greater Himalaya adjacent to Tibetan plateau.

It is located in one of the heaviest rainfall zones of the country. Due to complex relief features and drainage systems the rainfall pattern in the state is very complex. The annual rainfall is spread over 8-9 months and varies from 1,000 mm in higher reaches to 5,000 mm in the foothills. While it is 4,000 mm in the low land areas of Siang-Lohit valleys, it goes up to 5,000 mm in the lower parts of Siang and Dibang rivers. The Western and North-Western parts of the state receive moderate rainfall ranging from 2,500 mm to 1,000 mm annually. The pre-monsoon showers start from March. The monsoon is active from May to September. The retreating monsoon is active during October and November. The humidity during the rainy season goes up to 90%. (Singh, 1999).

The bulk of the region consists of shales, schist and conglomerates. The soil is acidic in the lower elevations of the valleys due to high rainfall. However, it is rich in humus contents.

The vegetation can be classified in six forest types-five broad types with a distinct sixth secondary forests type, which is largely man made (Anon.,1999). They are:

1. Tropical Forests
    (a) Tropical Evergreen Forests
    (b) Tropical Semi-evergreen Forests
2. Sub-Tropical Forests
3. Pine Forests
4. Temperate Forests
    (a) Temperate Broad Leaved Forests
    (b) Temperate Conifer Forests
5. Alpine Forests
6. Secondary Forests
    (a) Degraded Forests
    (b) Bamboo Forests
    (c) Grasslands

Its location adjacent to the Tibetan Plateau and the wide variation in climatic and altitudinal conditions offer congenial environments for a wide variety of fauna including mountain ungulates. However, information about their status and the individual species present in the state is poor, because of the remote mountainous habitat and also the lack of requisite infrastructure available with the Forest Department. The research and inventory works carried out by the Forest Department and other agencies active in the field of wildlife conservation is negligible and so, the information available today does not provide the correct picture about the status of mountain ungulates. Therefore, an attempt has been made to assess the status of the mountain ungulates in Arunachal Pradesh on the basis of the Management Plans / Working

Plans, Forest Department publications and records as well as field information and other relevant publications.

Arunachal Pradesh has two National Parks and 11 Wildlife Sanctuaries spread over 9,897 km2 (11.81% of geographical area of the state) for protection and conservation of its flora and fauna. The state has more PAs in its southern parts covering foothill tropical evergreen forests and mid-elevation subtropical forests. The mountain ungulates are residents of higher altitudes and its habitat is mostly along the Northern parts of the state bordering the Tibetan plateau. It has not been protected adequately under the PA network. There are more mountain ungulate habitats outside the protected areas than inside. Therefore, the status of mountain ungulates outside the protected area should also be looked into.

The ideal habitats of mountain ungulates are the high altitude areas in the northern portion of the state bordering the Tibetan Plateau. The Zoological Survey of India has recorded presence of Serow (Nemorhaedus sumatraensis), Red Goral (Nemorhaedus baileyi), Mishmi Takin (Budorcas taxicolor), Musk Deer (Moschus chrysogaster) and Bharal (Pseudois nayaur) in the state (Ghosh et.al, 1987). The wild Yak (Bos grunniens) is found in the higher reaches of the state particularly areas bordering Tibetan plateau (sighted and photographed by the Author). However, the ecological status in the wild is not clear. The Musk Deer is found through out the state in the alpine zone. The local people of the Dibang Valley district have informed the author about the occurrence of two varieties of musk deer. One of them is bigger and is found at lower elevations and has bigger musk pods whereas the other variety is a smaller one and is found at higher elevations but have smaller musk pods. This fact however needs to be substantiated.

For better protection of these high altitude fauna outside the present protected area network, the Wildlife Institute of India has recommended extension of some existing PAs and creation of few new one's (Rodgers and Panwar, 1988). Based on these recommendations the Forest Department has identified some high priority conservation areas, that includes: Zimithang, Jang, Thingbu-Mukto, Taksing, Mechuka, Jorging, Metang,

Maibung and Ditchu. These areas do not have much human presence and can be easily taken up for conservation purposes under protected area network.

THREATS

The main threats to the conservation of mountain ungulates in the state are:

1. Poaching: The tribal people of the state practice hunting of mountain ungulates for meat, hide and trophies. The traditional conservation ethics amongst local tribal communities, included taboos on hunting of wild animal with younger calves or pregnant females. However, nowadays these taboos are fast eroding. Moreover, due to use of firearms for hunting-instead of bows and arrows, traps and snares-which were used earlier, hunting intensity has increased. In the high altitudes, the alternatives available for food are limited. Therefore, mountain ungulates are one of the major source of protein for the tribal people. In the past, the low population density of the tribal people compared with large forest area did not pose any immediate threat to wild populations. However, over the years, due to various reasons, the population of the people has gone up thereby increasing the demand and the consequent pressure on the mountain ungulates among others. In the case of the musk deer, it is the high economic value of musk in international markets and lack of other income-generation opportunities for local people which have considerably increased its poaching for musk.
2. Absence of Forest Personnel: The northern portion of the state does not have the minimum basic network of Forest Beat and Range Offices for this vast area. Most of these areas do not have any presence of the forest personnel in whatever manner. In the existing few Range and Beat Offices the sanctioned posts of the field personnel are negligible compared to the vast territorial jurisdiction earmarked for that Beat/ Range for protection. The communication facilities are non-

existent-no communication sets, no vehicles, no roads. Out of few sanctioned posts, many posts continue to remain vacant for years. The staff posted do not join duty because of adverse and harsh conditions prevailing in those areas. There is nothing to cater their basic necessities like medical facilities, school, communication and other basic facilities. As a result of this, the pressure of poaching and hunting in the interiors of the state is very high and the entire area is practically unguarded and unprotected.

3. Shifting Cultivation: Shifting cultivation (Slash and Burn) in the state is practiced up to an altitude of 2,000m covering around 2,705 km2 area which accounts for 3.2% of its geographic area (Singh, 1999). The shifting cultivation is very common along the slopes in the valleys of Ranga, Subansiri, Siang, Dibang and Tirap in the Subansiri, Papumpare, Siang, Lohit, Tirap and Changlang districts. It covers areas from tropical wet evergreen forests to pine forests. Earlier, the cycle of shifting cultivation was 3 years in Tirap and Changlang districts, 6 years in Lohit and Siang districts and 10 years in the Subansiri district. However, it has now come down to 2 to 4 years almost everywhere. This is responsible for the reduction and also fragmentation of the habitat. In the past, when the interval cycle of shifting cultivation was long, it was somewhat beneficial for some of the mountain ungulates. However, in its present form it is causing immense damage to the habitat of mountain ungulates.
4. Developmental Activities: The planners and leaders of this remote and backward state are trying hard to develop the infrastructure sector in the state to accelerate the pace of economic development. Consequently, construction of roads, bridges, dams, hydel power projects and development of townships has been taken up on a large scale. Such developmental projects in these hilly areas have, however, been taken up without adequate environmental considerations. The result is

deforestation, soil erosion and damage to the ecological balance. Horticultural plantations and agriculture is being taken up along steep slopes. All these activities are a potent threat to the future of ungulates. The tribal people of the region are backward and their quality of life needs to be improved definitely to keep them in the national mainstream and also at par with the developments taking place in the other parts of the country. However, a judicious balance needs to be maintained between developmental and environmental considerations for the benefit of one and all.

5. Awareness Programmes: The tribal people living in the higher reaches of the state are not aware of the provisions of the Wildlife (Protection) Act, 1972 and other legal enactments in this regard. Most of the habitat of the mountain ungulates is categorized as Unclassed State Forests (USF). The individual tribal communities have been exercising traditional rights over these areas since long. The attempts of the Forest Department to control and manage the USF areas are being met with strong resistance from the local communities. Moreover, in dealing with such cases the tribal customary law is given preference over the statutory law. They still feel that the wildlife available in their areas is meant for their use, as has been the practice since generations. As such they feel it as their right to freely use wildlife found in their areas for their sustenance. Therefore, awareness programmes in these areas have to be taken up by the agencies other than the Forest Department also on a large scale. Moreover, other alternatives for these people have to be introduced to remove the demand and to save the mountain ungulates.

Arunachal Pradesh is economically not developed. This state does not have its own resources to generate enough revenue to meet the demands for its all round development. It depends upon the Central grants and assistance for its ongoing development projects. The financial resources available with the state are spent upon priority areas like infrastructure and social security. As such, the state is not left with any surplus resources at its command to spare for forestry and the wildlife sector. For a backward state like Arunachal Pradesh, the investment on forestry and wildlife is not on its priority. Therefore, the allocation for the forestry and wildlife sector in the annual plans of the state is negligible. The result is complete neglect of this sector. The Government of India and other conservation agencies should come forward to help the state government set up infrastructure needed for this sector. The state government on its own is not in a position to provide necessary financial requirements for the forestry and wildlife sector.

The research, survey and conservation education activities in the state have to be strengthened. For this purpose, different Government agencies and non-governmental organizations working in the field of biodiversity conservation should come forward to undertake/initiate research and conservation education/awareness programmes in the remote and inaccessible areas of the state. This is required to create at least baseline data which would help for the planning of the required protection measures on sound scientific principles.

12

Snow Leopard Conservation in the Indian Trans-Himalaya

INTRODUCTION

Wildlife in India, especially the large mammals are primarily concentrated in the Protected Areas (PAs), which to have become habitat islands, isolated by vast stretches of unsuitable habitat for wildlife. Human population has been constantly increasing in the country and has recently crossed the one billion mark. At present about 4.7% of the country's 3.3 million km2 geographic area is under National Parks (NPs) and Wildlife Sanctuaries (WLS), and there are plans to increase this to ca. 5.7% in order to make the PA network biogeographically more representative (Rodgers et al. 2000).

The human pressure on India's wild lands has been constantly increasing, with more and more cases of serious conflicts between people and parks being reported. Wildlife conservation in India has a long history of management through 'policing' the PAs.

It is only in the past two decades or so that conservationists and park managers have realized that exclusion of people completely from PAs is not a viable option-a realization that has thrown up numerous challenges. The fact that a majority of Indian PAs have not been legally gazetted due to non settlement of the rights and concessions of local communities residing inside the PAs also calls for a review of this situation. Fortunately, the amendment to the Indian Wildlife Protection Act (2002) by inclusion of two additional categories of PAs viz.

Conservation Reserve and Community Reserve would provide a pragmatic solution to this hitherto unresolved issue through rationalization of PA boundaries.

PAs in India and elsewhere are meant to preserve and protect a range of conservation values. Each PA has specific objectives of management. Many of the objectives and conservation issues are common to a vast variety of PAs. One such objective for most Trans-Himalayan PAs is the conservation and maintenance of a viable snow leopard (Uncia uncia) population as a 'flagship species' (Anon. 1988).

Further, when conservation objectives and issues are similar, solutions may be as well, although adaptations for local conditions may be necessary. Often, managing and monitoring all aspects of biodiversity in a PA is difficult and hence, managers tend to concentrate on focal species that guide conservation efforts for the area (Simberloff 1998).

As per a critique on the single species management approach by Simberloff (1998), these species may be 'flagship species'; one that is 'normally a charismatic large vertebrate, one that can be used to anchor a conservation campaign because it arouses public interest and sympathy'.

Or it may be an indicator species, one that is usually sensitive to disturbance in the ecosystem that they represent and their population abundance is indicative of a healthy ecosystem. A third species oriented approach is to have an 'umbrella species', which needs such large tracts for its conservation that saving this species automatically saves an entire range of species occurring within its habitat.

The snow leopard is a charismatic large carnivore, distributed over most of the Trans-Himalaya and the Greater Himalaya. The sympathy and appeal that the snow leopard has drawn internationally is self-evident. The International Snow Leopard Trust (ISLT), an organization completely dedicated to the cause of the snow leopard conservation has been in existence for over two decades now, with programmes in several of the 12 range countries including India.

Within India as well, an entire conservation and management program focused on the snow leopard was proposed several years ago, some what along the lines of Project Tiger (Anon. 1988). Apart from its appeal in garnering public support and funding, which renders it a valuable flagship species for conservation, its large home ranges and ubiquitous distribution in the Indian Trans-Himalaya make the snow leopard a suitable umbrella species as well.

Importantly, the serious conservation issues in the Trans-Himalayan region-livestock grazing and associated out-competition of wild prey as well as livestock depredation-both involve or affect the snow leopard directly or indirectly. It is therefore imperative that the snow leopard conservation in the Trans-Himalaya should have a regional perspective involving range states and line agencies, which influence its conservation status in one way or the other.

BOX: Snow Leopard-An Elusive Carnivore

Snow leopard is an elusive cat with a potential range of approximately 2.4 million km2 in the arid mountain tracts of Central Asia, the Trans-Himalaya and the Himalaya (Jackson and Hunter 1996). Even though it has a relatively large global range, it has gone extinct locally at many places and at present are distributed in fragmented populations spread over less than 1.6 million km2 (Jackson and Hunter 1996). A coarse, but best possible estimate of its global population is 3,500-7,500 animals. In India, it ranges over some 75,000 km2, yet number only 200 to 600 (Fox 1994). Because of this precarious status, the snow leopard is included in the Schedule I of the Indian Wildlife (Protection) Act 1972 (Anon. 1992) and as 'endangered' in the IUCN's Red List (Nowell and Jackson 1996).

Snow leopard prefers rugged mountain tracts with abundant prey and stalking cover (Schaller 1977, Jackson and Ahlborn 1984, Chundawat 1992, McCarthy 2000). However, in much of the Tibetan plateau and Mongolia, snow leopard occurs in open, rolling habitats where shrubs and outcrops offer cover for stalking of abundant prey (Mallon 1984, Schaller et al. 1988, McCarthy 2000). The primary prey species of snow leopard in its range are bharal (Pseudois nayaur) and ibex (Capra ibex sibirica), although others such as urial (Ovis vignei), argali (Ovis ammon), markhor (Capra falconeri), wild goat (Capra agegrus) and marmot (Marmota spp.) may also be important locally (Schaller 1977, Chundawat and Rawat 1994). Estimates suggest that each snow leopard needs approximately 20 to 30 adult bharal annually (Jackson and Ahlborn 1984). Other estimates suggest that snow leopards need ca. 730 kg of meat annually from their large prey species such as bharal, and other smaller ones such as domestic sheep, goats, marmots and birds (Chundawat and Rawat 1994). Snow leopard distribution and status in the wild may be adversely impacted by low prey density, leading to increased depredation on domestic stock, thus causing conflicts with resident herders (Oli et al. 1994, Mishra 1997, Jackson 2000).

While a limited number of studies have yielded modest information on snow leopard ecology (Chundawat 1992, Jackson 1996, McCarthy 2000), even less information on population status across the range is available. The population and range figures above are largely educated guesses, however, snow leopard most certainly occurs in small and isolated populations, thus increasing the threat of the extinction (Jackson and Ahlborn 1990). Information on population status and structure is however very important to determine viability of populations. The reason for the lack of information on populations of snow leopard is because of the elusive nature of the species and the harsh habitat that it occupies. Snow leopard tends to move, bed and mark along linear geographical features such as crests, major ridgelines, at the base of cliffs and in gullies. Monitoring for signs along these features is the best possible way at present of estimating snow leopard population trends in an area (Jackson and Hunter 1996). This practice is however not in wide use at present. Use of genetic tools and camera trapping are other viable alternatives for gathering information on snow leopard abundance but are expensive.

The fact that the snow leopard has a wide distribution in the Trans-Himalaya and that it is the apex predator in most of this region enables the species to be used as a 'flagship species' and an 'umbrella species' to guide conservation efforts in the region, as was recognized by the Government of India in the 1980's (Anon. 1988). In this paper, we reckon that all conservation activities directed at snow leopards would benefit the ecosystem, and any conservation activity in the region including livelihood support to the local communities will also benefit the snow leopard directly or indirectly.

In this paper, we use the above reasoning to say that the snow leopard qualifies both as a flagship and an umbrella species representing the Trans-Himalayan ecosystem and that its conservation would mean the conservation of the Trans-Himalayan region as a whole. We also try to detail how the resource-deficient Trans-Himalayan region is special, where most of the region still has wildlife values and where communities or individual families have traditional rights over all usable land.

Hence, conservation challenges of the region will not be addressed by merely increasing the area under PA network, but by ensuring effective conservation measures in the larger region and by increasing the stake of the local communities in snow leopard conservation by providing viable livelihood support options.

THE TRANS-HIMALAYAN LANDSCAPE

The Trans-Himalayan region is a cold, arid, mountainous landscape that covers the rain shadow regions immediately north of the Himalaya. The region is characterized by severe winters lasting over six months, with temperatures dropping to as low as-50°C in some places. Another characteristic of the region is the short plant growth season of merely two to three months, when productivity is usually low. These harsh conditions have given rise to hardy and highly adapted flora, fauna and people.

Within India, the Himalaya and Trans-Himalaya are included in six states. Of these, the Ladakh region of Jammu and Kashmir, Lahul-Spiti region of Himachal Pradesh, and northern Sikkim have Trans-Himalayan areas that cover approximately 1.85 lakh km^2 (Rodgers et al. 2000). Uttaranchal and Arunachal Pradesh, along with the other three states mentioned above, have alpine and high arid areas on their northern boundaries that also comprise snow leopard range in India.

The entire Himalayan block (2.1 lakh km^2) is classified as the Biogeographic Zone 02 (Province A to D), or 'Himalaya' (Rodgers and Panwar 1988), but the higher reaches, the Greater Himalaya, that constitutes the snow leopard range, is a narrow belt quite distinct in topography, climate and vegetation from the rest of the Himalaya-being much colder, arid and being devoid of forests.

The Trans-Himalayan region in India forms the catchment of three major rivers. In the northwest, the Indus, with its major tributaries-Zanskar and Shyok, drains the entire Ladakh region. South of this, the Chenab river, with its tributaries, the Chandra and Bhaga rivers, drains the Lahul valley. East of Lahul is the Spiti valley that drains into the Sutluj river, which passes through the Kinnaur region. Within India two provinces in the Trans-Himalaya are recognized (Rodgers and Panwar 1988).

The 'Ladakh Mountains' constitute approximately 60% of the Trans-Himalayan zone and is spread in the Kargil, Zanskar, Leh, Nubra, and Lahul-Spiti regions of Jammu and Kashmir and Himachal Pradesh. These areas are mostly rugged mountains and valleys and have a large altitudinal range from 2,200m in the Kargil and Nubra regions to over 7,000m in the Karakorum range. The second province is the 'Tibetan Plateau' that constitutes the remaining 40% of the Trans-Himalaya. This region includes Changthang in Ladakh, parts of Spiti and the northern plateaus of Sikkim and is characterized by vast plains, rolling mountains and some large high-altitude lakes. Most of this region lies above an elevation of 4,200m.

In spite of the overall low numbers of species of plants and animals in the Trans-Himalaya (Das 1966), the region is home to an array of highly specialized assemblage of flora and fauna.

There are over 600 flowering plants and numerous species of graminoids many with significant ethnobotanical value as medicinal plants, forage for livestock, or fuel (Kala 2001). The region is also home to over 225 bird species, including numerous breeding waterfowl (Pfister 1998, Singh and Jayapal 2001).

Large mammals of the Indian Trans-Himalaya along with their legal conservation status

Species	**Scientific Name**	**Indian Wildlife Protection Act 1972**	**IUCN Category (CAMP Workshop – Anon 1998b)**
Ungulates			
Siberian ibex	*Capra ibex sibirica*	I	*Vulnerable*
Tibetan argali	*Ovis ammon hodgsoni*	I	Critical
Ladakh urial	*Ovis orientalis vignii*	I	Endangered
Bharal	*Pseudois nayaur*	I	Low Risk
Tibetan antelope	*Pantholops hodgsoni*	I	Critical
Tibetan gazelle	*Procapra picticaudata*	I	Critical
Tibetan wild ass	*Equus kiang*	I	Vulnerable
Wild yak	*Bos grunniens*	I	Critical
Large carnivores			
Snow leopard	*Uncia uncia*	I	Endangered
Lynx	*Lynx isabellina*	I	?
Tibetan wolf	*Canis lupus chanko*	I	Vulnerable
Wild dog	*Cuon alpinus*	?	Critical
Red fox	*Vulpus vulpus*	?	Low Risk
Brown bear	*Ursus arctos*	I	Low Risk

Some of these species, such as the black necked crane (Grus nigricollis) and the bar headed geese (Anser indicus) are of considerable conservation significance. The region has gained further importance as it has over six species and sub-species of wild sheep and goats that are an important genetic resource from the region. There are numerous mammal species in the region that are classified in the Schedule I and II of the Indian Wildlife (Protection) Act 1972 and some of these are listed in Appendix 1 of CITES. Ecological information on all species from India is scarce, however, some details about bharal and snow leopard are known (Chundawat 1992). Ibex ecology was described by Bhatnagar (1997) and Manjrekar (1997). Information on the status and distribution of species have been reported by Fox et al. (1991), Mallon (1991), Shah (1994, 1996), Chundawat and Qureshi (1999) and Bhatnagar and Wangchuk (2001). Although data on land ownership are not easily available, bulk of the land is State owned with traditional rights of use held by communities or individuals. Most usable land is already utilized as pastures, agricultural land, and for the collection of fuel, fodder and housing material.

Existing Conservation Scenario in the Trans Himalaya-Wildlife Protected Areas in the Region

Keeping our focus on snow leopard conservation, we mention here PAs in the Himalaya and the Trans-Himalaya. However, realizing that a relatively small portion of the Himalaya would qualify as snow leopard habitat, the discussion in the subsequent sections primarily deals with the Trans-Himalayan region.

Reliable information regarding the presence of snow leopard is absent for most PAs in the Indian Himalaya. Based on information that we have gleaned from literature and our own studies, there are 25 PAs within India that have potential for snow leopard occurrence (Mallon 1987, Anon. 1988, Fox et al. 1988, Bhatnagar 1997).

There are two National Parks (NP) and three Wildlife Sanctuaries (WLS) in the Trans-Himalaya, together constituting ca. 15,000 km2 or 8.2 % of the Trans-Himalayan zone in India (Table 1). There are nine NPs and 11 WLS in the Greater Himalayan zone with coverage of a further ca. 15,000 km2 (7.6 % of the zone 02) that may have snow leopards. Most of the PAs in the Greater Himalaya have very small portions in snow leopard habitat and the extent of such areas is not yet documented. Further, in at least three NPs and five WLS of this region with an area of 6,600 km^2, the presence of snow leopard is very doubtful. There are a few other erstwhile Hunting Reserves in the Kargil District of Ladakh, however their present status after the adoption of the Jammu & Kashmir Wildlife (Protection) Act (2002) is not clear.

It is evident from Table that 17 of the 25 PAs (68%) with a potential for snow leopards are smaller than 1000 km^2, with five of them being smaller than 100 km^2. There are a further three PAs in the 1001 to 2000 km^2, two in the 2001 to 4000 km^2, and three in the > 4000 km^2 range. In areas where PAs are habitat 'islands' the smaller PAs, especially those smaller than 100km^2, have little potential for long-term maintenance of viable snow leopard populations (Jackson and Ahlborn 1990). Even within the larger PAs there are numerous limitations at present. It is apparent that the PA network in the Trans-Himalayan and the Greater Himalayan zones is comparatively large in extent. Also, it is evident that the region has some of the largest PAs in the country (Rodgers et al. 2000). However, the following facts need to be critically examined:

1. Some PAs such as the Karakorum WLS are large, but have unclear boundary demarcation. There are over 15 towns and villages and numerous military establishments within the area. The human population in the region is over 10,000 (Anon. 1998a). There is also a great amount of military activity and vehicular traffic in the area, and all these factors render the area barely qualified as a wildlife sanctuary. This, and other similar areas, however, inflate the proportion of area under PA network in the zone.
2. Most PAs have up to 50% of their area under permanent ice or glaciers, shear and large rock faces, most of which have little wildlife values, thus further inflating the size, but not contributing to the wildlife values directly.
3. There are no Reserve Forests in the Trans-Himalaya that usually buffer disturbances in most wildlife PAs elsewhere in the country. Hence it is only the PAs in the Trans-Himalayan areas that have any legal status for the conservation of the native biodiversity.

Table 1: Protected Areas in the Trans-Himalaya in India and the Greater Himalaya (adjacent to the Trans Himalaya and with potential for snow leopard occurrence). Figures in parenthesis are percentage of the PA category in the biogeographic zone. Total land area in the Trans-Himalaya is *ca.* 1,84,900 km2 and in the Zone 2, that includes the Greater Himalaya is *ca.* 2,10,600 km2.

	Trans-Himalaya			
1	Hemis NP	1A, Jammu & Kashmir (J&K)	4100	
2	Pin Valley NP	1A, Himachal Pradesh (HP)	675	
	Total (National Park)		**= Sum(ABOVE) 4,775,** (2.6%)	
3	Karakorum WLS	1A, J&K	5000	Boundaries not well demarcated
4	Changthang WLS	1B, J&K	4000	Small portion of PA is snow leopard habitat
5	Kibber WLS	1B, HP	1401	
	Total (Wildlife Sanctuary)		**= Sum(ABOVE) 10,401,** (5.6%)	
	Grand total for Trans-Himalaya		**15,176,** (8.2%)	
	Greater Himalaya			
6	Gangotri NP	2B, Uttaranchal (UT)	2390	Small portion of PA is snow leopard habitat
7	Kanchendzonga NP	1B, 2C, Sikkim	1784	
8	Great Himalayan NP	2A, HP	754	Small portion of PA is snow leopard habitat
9	Nanda Devi NP	2B, UT	630	
10	Govind NP	2B, UT	472	
11	Kisthwar NP	2A, J&K	400	
12	Dachigam NP	2A, J&K	141	?
13	Valley of Flowers NP	2B, UT	88	?
14	Namdapha NP	2D, Arunachal Pradesh (AP)	1985	?
	Total (National Park)		**= Sum(ABOVE) 8,644,** (4.1%)	

* Information based on Rodgers et al. (2000)

? Snow leopard presence doubtful

13

Conservation Issues in the Trans-Himalaya

A variety of physical, biotic and political characteristics of the Trans-Himalaya influence conservation issues that are peculiar to the region. Chief among the challenges is the limited resources available to the native population of the region. These populations which mostly occur at low to moderate densities of <2 persons per km2, are primarily agro-pastoral, or, as in the Tibetan Plateau zone, are largely nomadic pastoralists. Human populations are increasing in the region with the breakup of the traditional polyandrous system and with fewer people opting for becoming celibate monks and nuns (Anon. 1998a, Mishra 2000). An important factor that needs to be considered is that in the harsh Trans-Himalayan landscape there is hardly any area that is not already in use by people at some time or the other during the year. Arable land is mostly limited to alluvial fans, and some stable areas in the valley bottoms.

Almost all the available arable land is already under cultivation and all pastures are grazed by the domestic stocks at least seasonally. Addition of newer areas under some poverty alleviation schemes incorporate development of expensive and long flow irrigation systems. Our observations show that these most frequently end up as failures since most of such channels are damaged by avalanches or are washed away by floods or simply break up due to the unstable substrate. Thus in spite of numerous efforts any significant addition of arable land is remote. National parks and sanctuaries in India do not permit consumptive use and require resettlement of people outside such areas (Anon. 1992). The point that we are driving at is that the Trans-Himalayan region has very specific and limited area for cultivation or use as pastures and thus offers no or very few alternatives for resettlement of people outside PAs.

The region has other peculiarities such as very poor road access, power supply, and difficult communication, apart from a harsh climate during much of the year. These features of the region thus do not allow scope for conventional industrial development and employment in the region, as is possible in other regions of the country.

As far as the wildlife values are concerned a very important characteristic of the Trans-Himalayan area is that it provides almost continuous wildlife habitat (Fox et al. 1991, Chundawat and Qureshi 1999, Bhatnagar and Wangchuk 2001). Almost the entire landscape has large mammals, including the snow leopard and wolf, but the densities may vary greatly from very poor areas to small pockets that may be rich in some large mammals. This means that a large amount of wildlife may actually be occurring outside existing PAs. In Nepal, for example, over 60% of the snow leopards are thought to occur outside PAs. In India, our coarse estimate is that of the probable maximum of 600 snow leopards in India (Fox 1994), ca. 80% may be occurring outside PAs. Among other endangered wildlife species such as the Tibetan antelope, Tibetan gazelle, Tibetan argali, brown bear, and kiang, the entire or substantial populations occur outside existing PAs (Chundawat and Qureshi 1999, Bhatnagar and Wangchuk 2001, Sathyakumar & Qureshi 2002). Mishra, (2001). has found that in Spiti, the Tabo area that is not within any PA has bharal densities that are higher than the Kibber Wildlife Sanctuary.

Shah (1996) has found remnant populations of the highly endangered Tibetan gazelle and argali in unprotected areas in northern Sikkim. The paradox here is that in spite of a very large proportion of the Trans Himalaya being under the PA network, numerous endangered species continue to occur outside. With this, and the fact that the region in general is resource deficient, with few livelihood options for the local herders we need to reconsider the approach of having large national parks and wildlife sanctuaries as 'inviolate areas' in the region. This is a challenging situation and the lack of a vision for conservation, as usually defined by Management Plans for PAs is absent at present.

Conservation issues common to the area primarily relate to deficiencies of infrastructure and staff for PA management, grazing competition between wild and domestic herbivores, conflicts relating to damage to crops and livestock by wildlife, some levels of poaching of snow leopard and prey species, wildlife diseases and political issues.

These issues were also flagged as the most important ones in a meeting between scientists and managers at Leh (Mathur 2001) and of numerous snow leopard experts from all over the snow leopard range countries (McCarthy and Chapron 2003). We now examine these issues in some detail:

Infrastructure and Staff for PA Management

In the harsh environs of the region, there is a severe shortage of staff, effective infrastructure and funds for the management of the PAs. For example Ladakh has ca. 13,100 km^2 under its PA network with a total park staff of merely about 20. This translates to 655 km^2 to every park staff-a completely ineffective strength to manage the region under any circumstance, but especially so under the difficult climatic and topograhic conditions in the Trans-Himalaya.

The numerous existing tasks of the Wildlife Department range from protection, tourism management, verification of compensation claims to nature education activities in the PAs spread all over the ca. 45,000 km^2 Ladakh region. We also understand that most park staff lack the necessary clothing, equipment and housing necessary for effective work in the region. The situation in Lahul & Spiti is not very different. It is an urgent requirement for the Centre and State Governments to provision the necessary resources to these areas for effective conservation in the region.

Grazing Competition between Wild and Domestic Herbivores

The entire region has heavy dependence on livestock. While some of the people are agro-pastoralists, many are entirely pastoral. Estimates range from 10 to a few hundred livestock heads per household in the region (Mishra 1997, Richard 1999, Bhatnagar and Wangchuk 2001). Livestock population in the Indian Trans-Himalaya has been growing continuously in the past decades, as evidenced by data available from Ladakh, were the livestock population has almost doubled between 1972 and 1992 (Anon. 1998a, Bhatnagar and Wangchuk 2001). Even though conclusive information on habitat degradation, and direct competition between domestic and wild herbivores from the region has just started coming (Mishra 2001), it is evident from some preliminary studies that the present livestock grazing levels in areas such as eastern Ladakh and Spiti may already be unsustainable (Mishra 2001, Bhatnagar and Wangchuk 2001, Raghavan 2003, Namgail 2003). The potential impacts of excessive grazing by livestock include depletion of the scarce forage for wildlife, habitat degradation, disease transfer, and reduction in the breeding performance of both wildlife and domestic stock (Mishra 2001).

Conclusive studies to ascertain impacts of livestock grazing need to be taken up at many sites. There is also an urgent need to see how the pastoral and agro-pastoral communities of the region can be drawn into a trade-off that reduces their dependence on large livestock holdings, while at the same time helps in improving their standard of living. An example for such an effort was made by the Nature Conservation Foundation, Mysore, and details are given below.

Kibber Grazing Reserve

The Nature Conservation Foundation, a science and conservation organization based in Mysore, signed a written agreement with the village council of Kibber in Spiti in the year 2000, where both these institutions resolved to protect a 5 km2 area exclusively for wildlife by agreeing not to graze their livestock in that region.

The rangeland area has been traditionally used for livestock grazing and collection of fuel, and medicinal plants. Two years of protection is already showing signs of wildlife recovery, as indicated by the increased use of the area by bharal. The compensation costs for lost grazing are being met with by the Van Tienhoven Foundation in the Netherlands, and the project is being implemented voluntarily by scientists associated with the Nature Conservation Foundation and the Wageningen University. The International Snow Leopard Trust has recently joined hands with the initiative, and these institutions are working together towards off-setting the costs that the local people are bearing for living with wildlife (through programs in conservation education, supporting self managed insurance schemes, value addition to local handicrafts), and towards enabling the local people to benefit from the wildlife they share their resources with (wildlife tourism).

Conflicts Relating to Damage of Crops and Pastures by Wild Herbivores

The Jammu and Kashmir Department of Wildlife Protection staff in Leh has been receiving compensation claims for damage to crops by species such as bharal and urial.

The extent of such damage is not yet clear, but there is an increasing trend in such claims. There is a need to have a better record of conflict cases. 'Hotspots' of such conflict zones should be clearly identified and if any are found, participatory exercises should be taken up to minimize the losses.

In a surprising development some nomads and state Govt. officials claim that the kiang are now damaging the winter pastures of the valuable pashmina or Cashmire goats in Changthang (Fox et al. 1991, Richard 1999).

It has been argued that such claims are largely baseless and are probably a result of reduced tolerence levels among the people in recent times (Richard 1999, Bhatnagar and Wangchuk 2001).

Livestock Depredation by Wild Carnivores

Livestock depredation seems to be a serious conservation issue in the Trans-Himalayan region. As indicated earlier, livestock rearing at present forms an important part of the local economy and any loss to livestock results in a direct monetary loss to the local herders. Park staff in Ladakh report that often up to 60% of their annual outlay goes in meeting the livestock depredation compensation claims filed by people (Rauf Zargar, Wildlife Warden, Leh, Pers. Comm.). Damage to livestock takes place in the pastures as well as in the night time corrals. In India's Trans-Himalayan zone only four studies have as yet quantified the extent of livestock damage due to depredation by wild carnivores. These studies are by Mishra (1997) from Spiti, Bhatnagar et al. (1999) from the Hemis NP, Ladakh, and by Jayapal (2001) and Sathyakumar (2001) from Zanskar, Ladakh. The damage to livestock in many of these areas is quite high and in some villages up to 14 animals per household have been lost in an year. The monetary loss to households in the Hemis NP averaged ca. Rs. 12,000/-during 1996-97 (Bhatnagar et al. 1999). This study also showed that over 40% of the losses were taking place in the corrals, an aspect that can be dealt with more easily than the damage in pastures. Small and effective means of alleviating these conflicts have been developed by ISLT and SLC, along with local NGOs and the Wildlife Department in Hemis NP, which has potential for replication elsewhere (Jackson and Jain 1999).

Integration of Efforts by Different Government Departments and Non-Government Organizations

Owing to the remoteness of the Trans-Himalayan region, the state governments have resorted to a system of governance that is called 'Single Line Administration'. Under this system, the district head, the District Commissioner (DC) or the Additional District Commissioner (ADC) becomes the head of all Government Departments working in the region. In addition, the Ladakh region, that constitutes bulk of the Trans-Himalayan region in India, has a Ladakh Autonomous Hill Development Council (LAHDC), a form of local Government.

After consultation with the Wildlife Department in Ladakh, it was apparent that inter-agency cooperation and coordination in the region is lacking, leading to inefficient functioning by the Wildlife Department (Mathur 2001). Examples of major developmental activities being undertaken inside wildlife PAs were cited as cases when the Wildlife Department had to stop such activities when they were well underway. This earned the ire of the local people as well as the respective Government Departments undertaking the work. For these reasons, we feel that the 'Single Line Administration' would facilitate coordination between Departments more effectively, specially if there are relevant policies and practices in place that make it imperative on the respective DCs or ADCs to keep wildlife conservation interest in mind before approval of any development schemes.

The Ladakh region has an added advantage of the existence of numerous non-government organizations (NGOs), many of which have a good reputation of grassroots work in the fields of alternative sources of energy, organic agriculture, and education. This is a resource that should be effectively tapped for conservation related work.

Political Issues

The entire Trans-Himalayan region has international borders. Ladakh has a large and hostile border along the west and northwest with Pakistan held Kashmir called the Line of Control (LoC). On the north and east is the international border and the Line of Actual Control (LAC) with China. Himachal Pradesh and Sikkim also share borders with China. Numerous stretches along these borders are disputed territory. Species such as the Tibetan antelope, argali, kiang and Tibetan gazelle occur at numerous places along and across the border with China (Fox et al. 1991, Shah 1996, Chundawat and Qureshi 1999, Bhatnagar and Wangchuk 2001). Good snow leopard, ibex and urial habitat occurs along the LoC. Often due to the sensitive nature of the region the Wildlife Departments have little control over the region. There is heavy presence of defence forces on both sides and wildlife of the region might also be a casualty to the frequent skirmishes. The problem is compounded when these may be the only places within the country where a species occurs. Trans-border conservation of these species should thus be given high priority.

Jammu and Kashmir has a separate Wildlife Protection Act, which had placed endangered species such as the Tibetan antelope and brown bear under Schedule II, for which hunting licenses could be given. The amended Act is however at par with the National legislation (Anon. 2002). The entire Trans Himalayan region spreads across three states and inter-state collaboration in conservation efforts though difficult, is nevertheless necessary.

What we want to stress here is that the political dimension is important to consider while planning any large-scale conservation effort in the Trans-Himalayan region, a region replete with sensitive borders spreading over three states.

Poaching of Snow Leopard and Prey Species

Sport hunting was quite widespread during the British period in the Trans-Himalaya (Stockley 1928, Ranjitsinh 1981). Even after independence the trend continued till the early 1980's when the defense forces, Government officials and others were known to hunt in various parts of the Trans-Himalaya, especially in Ladakh. This had decimated the populations of numerous species in the region (Ranjitsinh 1981, Fox et al. 1991). Recently, however, there is evidence of a decline in hunting in many parts of the Trans-Himalaya, with the revival of some wildlife populations in the region such as the Ladakh urial (Chundawat and Qureshi 1999).

Buddhism is the dominant religion in most of the Trans-Himalayan region in India and hunting is generally not practiced, unless it is in retaliation for some damage to their property. However, in western Ladakh and in Lahul, hunting might still be an issue. Again, little information exists on the extent of poaching going on in the region. Some illegal trade in wildlife products, including snow leopard parts and shahtoosh, may be occurring in the region (Wright and Kumar 1997). We understand from the Wildlife Department in Leh that no hunting license has been issued since the mid-1980's. Until trends in poaching and wildlife trade in the region are better documented and understood suitable measures cannot be devised and undertaken to minimize the problem.

Wildlife Diseases

Wildlife disease can be damaging and may even lead to the extinction of small populations. This is particularly true for small, isolated populations as the Tibetan gazelle in Ladakh, and snow leopard in parts of the Trans-Himalaya. Information on wildlife disease from the region is, however, completely absent and there is an urgent need to generate such information. The reports of infectious diseases such as PPR and FMD in livestock of the region increase the threat of an epidemic in the wild herbivore populations. It is suspected that the frequent imports of livestock from the plains by the armed forces for meat could be a source of exotic diseases in the region. Effective quarantine and screening of all imported animals and vaccination programmes for livestock are needed for the entire region, but on priority for areas in and around the PAs or areas with endangered species.

The way Forward

Some measures that could be undertaken in the region to aid conservation have already been discussed above in the section dealing with conservation issues in the Trans-Himalaya. What we give below is an indicative way of planning wildlife conservation in the region as a whole. We understand that these ideas will have to be fine tuned through wider stakeholder consultations. What we have tried to argue so far is that:

- Even though there are some large PAs in the Trans-Himalaya, bulk of these are occupied by permanent ice and sheer rock faces-the effective areas important for wildlife within them are usually small. Some of them may not even qualify as a PA.
- For existing PAs an effective vision for management is mostly absent.
- Most of the large mammals in the Trans-Himalaya, need large areas given the sparse resources, and seasonal

movements. Further, wildlife in this region is mostly outside the existing PAs and simply adding more areas under the PA network may not be a viable solution.

- Areas in PAs usually form an important resource for native people, for whom few alternative livelihood options are available. Traditional concept of large inviolate PAs is not practical in the region.

Based on the conservation issues presented above, and the almost continuous wildlife distribution in the region, we feel that conservation in the Trans-Himalaya has to be planned with a regional perspective, in which the native people are taken as an integral part of the conservation efforts. Having large inviolate national parks and sanctuaries does not seem viable in the region. The shift of focus for conservation in private lands is a need recognized by conservationists worldwide (Knight 1999, Norton, 2000). Using this line of thinking, we feel that continuing with the existing scheme of PAs may not work in the Trans-Himalayas and we now need an alternate paradigm for wildlife conservation in the region. One of the ways of moving ahead is to carefully work on the zonation of existing PAs and of the larger Trans-Himalayan landscape in general.

AN ALTERNATE ZONATION CONCEPT

Zonation within Existing PAs

PAs in India have zones of varying landuse, such as a core zone, which is inviolate, and a buffer zone that may have multiple-use (Anon. 1992, Sawarkar 1995). The latter zone further may have areas earmarked for forestry operations, tourism and other consumptive uses. Our information suggests that none of the existing PAs in the Trans-Himalaya have cores and buffers delineated. The NPs are essentially 'core zones' in their entirety. With the enhancement in the legal status of the WLS following the 1991 amendment of the Wildlife (Protection) Act, 1972, all the PAs constituting ca. 15,000 km^2 have technically become 'core zones'. Continuing with this practice, as we have already seen, is not pragmatic. We thus suggest that for the existing five PAs in the Trans-Himalaya we change the management zonation approach by carefully delineating core zones in a mosaic, with a buffer area surrounding it. The difference from the existing scheme, primarily is that we do not take impractically large areas of a few thousand km^2 as inviolate core zones and we have multiple core zones within any PA based on its value.

The steps to be followed may be as follows:

- Carefully survey all PAs to determine areas that have high wildlife value, either in terms of presence of an endangered species such as snow leopard, Tibetan gazelle or argali, or in the presence of a large diversity of large mammals.
- Designate such area as a core zone using a participatory approach.
- Have at least one such core area for every 100 km^2 of the PA, although consideration of species movements may need to be included in their planning.
- The peoples rights may need to be settled using innovative schemes such as those outlined in Box 2 and in the section on conservation efforts below.
- The buffer zones would be all the remaining area in the PA where traditional use may continue. Attempts would however, be made to minimize the negative impacts of human use.
- Focused studies that help in determining suitable levels of use need to be encouraged.

In areas of the Trans-Himalaya outside existing PAs

The issue of conservation of wildlife outside PAs is more complex. As alluded to earlier, the need for this arises because:

- Endangered species like the snow leopard, Ladakh urial, Tibetan gazelle, argali and chiru occur mostly outside existing PAs
- Including all such areas under the PA network would mean that over 50% of the Trans Himalaya will need to come under the PA network
- Resources for managing such a large network, both material and human are not available

- It is likely to further increase people-park conflicts manifold

There is thus a need to recognize these areas for their importance and device strategies for their conservation. This is with the knowledge that local culture/values and the ow human population density have an important contribution in wildlife persisting in these areas. Zonation seems one clear means to develop this strategy. We realize that aspects of what we present below may be theoretical but will surely be useful in developing a framework. In the alternate approach, we suggest further four landuse zones, which have subtle differences in their management objectives. The first zone is the 'Conservation Zone' which is a small, carefully researched and selected area preferably measuring more than 10 km^2, and where ever possible, up to 100 km^2, where the local people agree to give up their rights in exchange of some development schemes. These are then surrounded by the 'Alternate Livelihood Zone', which would be the most widespread zone. Here the various Government departments' and NGOs work together to limit livestock numbers and dependence on natural resources so as to allow sustainable utilization of resources.

This zone can also have agro based and other non-polluting industries to create employment. The third zone can be 'Low Value Zone', which includes unusable areas under permanent ice and large rock faces. These areas will constitute a major portion of the area. The zone can also include narrow stretches of areas that have lost all value for maintenance of wildlife such as townships and excessively degraded areas.

These zones would go a long way in addressing the issue of conservation and development using a regional perspective.

Areas with Information Gaps and Indicative Actions

Additional Livelihood Options

At present, we have the options of cash crops such as green peas and potato that can be marketed as fresh vegetables in markets in the plains and locally. To minimize the loss through decay during transportation to markets, part of the produce could be processed locally into processed food products or health food. Another industry suggested is electronic industry that is usually less polluting to the environment. But issues regarding power and access need to be addressed first in order to make such ideas viable. The region needs better schools and colleges and has potential for establishment of national level educational institutions. For all these activities, enhancement of the present infrastructure is extremely important. Ladakh already attracts large number of international and domestic tourists. The benefits from tourism are however largely limited to a very small population within Ladakh. There is tremendous potential for development of ecotourism schemes in the region that would enable tourism to take place in a sustainable manner and with substantial benefits reaching local residents. The potential for the development of nature tourism and handicraft based industry should thus be explored as a means of alternative livelihoods. This however, should not be developed as the only means of sustenance of families.

Some highly innovative nature tourism schemes are being developed for Ladakh by organizations such as the Snow Leopard Conservancy, The Mountain Institute along with local organizations such as Ladakh Ecological Development Group (Jackson, Rodney and Jain Nandita, pers. comm.). More effort needs to be devoted to establish optimal stocking densities for livestock in different parts of the range. Grazing competition between livestock and wild herbivores seems to be a significant conservation issue. However, quantitative information on impacts of this is grossly lacking from the region. The studies should also try to determine stocking densities that enable wildlife to exist at levels that allow them to breed and sustain a healthy population. These studies will be crucial for recommendations for the permitted grazing in the multiple-use areas.

Levels of Perceived and Actual Conflict between Wildlife and People Need to be Established

Data on actual levels of conflicts, the wildlife species involved and conflict 'hotspots' is often lacking from the region. For designing any conflict resolution scheme, such data is of immense importance. With such information, mitigation measures such as corral improvement, in small, but effective ways should then be taken up to resolve the issues (Jackson and Jain 1999). Innovative livestock insurance schemes are also an important possibility. These can be taken up in conjunction with programmes that help in actual reduction of the damage. One such scheme has been designed in Baltistan where the community managed insurance funds are complemented by money generated through wildlife tourism (Hussain 2000). Another one is being formulated in Kibber wildlife sanctuary, Himachal Pradesh, India by the Nature Conservation Foundation-ISLT. Resolving conflicts effectively will have a two pronged benefit. One is that the monetary loss to the local herders will be reduced and second is that they will be more sensitive to conservation efforts.

CONSERVATION AWARENESS INITIATIVES

Conservation awareness initiatives that illustrate the peculiarities and fragility of the local environment need to be taken up for the local people, tourists and importantly, the district Government officials and politicians. For the latter these may be in the form of relevant directions from various Central Ministries for keeping wildlife conservation perspective in view when developing conservation schemes.

Proactive Policies and Guidelines from the Wildlife Department

The Wildlife Department, in collaboration with scientific organizations needs to develop Management Plans for the existing PAs with relevant zonations in place. All other potential areas that could serve as the revised 'Core Zones' need to be surveyed immediately. Issues relating to infrastructure need to be addressed to the Ministry of Environment and Forests. The revival and redrafting of the 'Snow Leopard Scheme' (Anon. 1988) could be an ideal opportunity to bring in the suggested changes in the conservation of the region.

The Wildlife Institute of India, Dehradun, along with its partners, the International Snow Leopard Trust and the US

Fish and Wildlife Service have already undertaken a step in the direction of generating information on the gap areas and also conservation efforts that enable better trained staff with sound management plans in place. The programme also intends to try and influence policy for conservation in the region (Anon. 2001).

CONCLUSIONS

The above mentioned is an indicative approach of reconciling conservation concerns with development planning that would lead to improved standards of living through increased employment, better education, increased agricultural returns, increased value for livestock products, and also increased ecotourism and wildlife viewing. Use of conflict alleviation measures would help build trust between conservation and local herders. These will constitute important steps towards providing suitable alternatives to people and enable them to give up the areas to be used as the small 'core zones'. The strategy would also reduce livestock grazing pressures in some areas; reduce human-wildlife conflicts, and, hopefully, lead to the revival of wildlife in most areas in a manner that is more acceptable to the local people, politicians and conservationists alike. Undoubtedly, a regional perspective for conservation and development cannot be developed overnight. What is however needed is a beginning of planning, integrating and implementing of a wide array of conservation measures, based on an understanding of the ecology, environment and developmental needs of the Indian Trans-Himalaya, which is a vast landscape with unique biodiversity.

It would also be essential to revive the 'Project Snow Leopard' to deal with the regional planning issue by evolving a framework for conservation and development in a participatory manner. The urgency of reviving the 'Project Snow Leopard' cannot be overemphasized given the conservation challenges facing the vast Trans-Himalayan landscape and the crisis for survival of snow leopard-the flagship species of the region.

14

Musk Deer: A Story of Himalayan Survival

Brought up in the East Africa, where I became enthralled by its 'big game', Mount Kenya was the first mountain that I ever set eyes on-often elusive but fleetingly glanced through the clouds.. Those early childhood inspirations led me to the Himalaya, first in Nepal and later India. Here I took up the challenge of trying to match my skills and endurance with some of its little-known ungulates in order to understand their lifestyles and explore my fascination for large animals in such a demanding and stunningly beautiful environment.

It was in Nepal that I first saw a musk deer while wading through knee-high rhododendron scrub in the upper Langtang Valley. I watched her for over ten minutes as she fed from crustose lichens-a spectacular and memorable sighting of her perched on a rock, silhouetted at dusk against the pink 6,391 m fluted peak of Gang Chenpo. That was my only sighting of musk deer during a fifteen-month survey of Langtang National Park.

Elusive and solitary, like many mountain peaks, the musk deer is the most valuable flagship species of animal or plant to be found in the Himalaya: its musk1, produced only by males2, is worth up to four times its weight in gold (US $ 45,000 kg-). Its value is reflected in the tremendous lengths that hunters will go to catch musk deer.

It was in 1976, while trekking through the little frequented Larke Khola in Langtang National Park, that I encountered several kilometres of trap-lines where the rhododendron and other scrub had been cut to make one-metre high barricades of brushwood that ran from the river up the valley sides to the alpine pastures, intersected by others traversing the slopes. Snares3 were set in openings through the barricades at 10-30 m intervals and, having removed 30 from along a 350 m stretch, I estimated there to be 100-600 snares /km2-more than enough, surely, to wipe out that musk deer population within a few years.

Most hunting is done by local hill people and, although they receive only a fraction of the international market price of musk, their revenue from one musk gland or pod can equate to their annual cash income. Just how the musk deer is able to able to survive such intense hunting pressures, while living in seemingly inhospitable environments and in competition with other mountain ungulates became more apparent during my subsequent three-year study (1979-81) of the Himalayan species (Moschus chrysogaster) in Kedarnath Wildlife Sanctuary4.

The musk deer proved to be a particularly elusive animal to study, being small (body weight about 10-13 kg) and solitary, and taking refuge in the dense undergrowth of montane forests and sub-alpine scrub during the daytime. This was reflected in my observations, limited to 151 sightings (totalling about 64 hours) or about one sighting for every 10 hours in the field. Most observations were made at night, with the aid of a nightscope, when musk deer often emerged from hiding to feed on the alpine pastures.

Telemetry would have helped immensely but I was singularly unsuccessful in capturing any animals to fit radio-collars, despite trying the traditional brushwood barricade but fitted with box traps, stalking with a dart-gun and driving animals into nets. However, tracking in snow during winter provided information about home ranges and regular monitoring of latrines, sites where musk deer repeatedly defaecate, told me much about their means of communication. I also collected hundreds of samples of pellets to find out what musk deer eat.

Coping with Hunters and Natural Predators

My observations confirmed that musk deer lead very solitary lives: only once did I ever encounter two when an older male, judging from its longer canines, was seen pursuing a younger one at night. They occupied adjacent territories and must have been engaged in a border dispute. The fact that I never saw females accompanied by their young, combined with the knowledge that the young become independent of their mothers by about six weeks, is further evidence of their solitary behaviour-a characteristic of small forest ruminants that rely on being inconspicuous to avoid predators. This becomes even more crucial in winter when snow blankets the ground layer of vegetation that otherwise typically affords good cover for musk deer. But in snow conditions they are adept at remaining concealed in rhododendron thickets during the day, not easily detected even by the trained eye. Once I followed the tracks of a female in deep soft snow to within 9 metres of where she lay under a bush in a gully without seeing her. The animal flushed only after I had unknowingly retreated from her sight, behind a rock.

Implicit with such solitary behaviour is the rapid onset of sexual maturity. Musk deer attain most of their adult body weight by six months and become sexually mature by 18 months of age. Females are capable of breeding in their first year and in the forest musk deer (M. berezovskii) and Siberian musk deer (M. moschiferus), but not the Himalayan species, the incidence of twins is higher than single births. Such reproductive strategies have undoubtedly enabled musk deer to combat the tremendous hunting pressures experienced over centuries.

Hunters use a variety of techniques to kill musk deer, which includes snaring and shooting, the latter sometimes aided by dogs. There is nothing within the musk deer's repertoire of anti-predator strategies to counter the use of brush barricades in conjunction with snares, unless the animal is able to learn to recognise the danger of snares, which seems particularly unlikely for a solitary species. But the musk deer's solitariness and ability to remain concealed, often in dense scrub on precipitous terrain, equip it with some chance of evading hunters with guns.

Musk deer usually take flight when approached to within 30 metres but often then stop in their tracks to look back and, presumably, take stock of their situation. While this trait may help prevent animals being attacked by natural predators, it does provide the hunter with an extra chance of a shot. In snow conditions, however, musk deer have a considerable advantage over both hunters and natural predators: it's dew claws are enlarged, helping to spread its body weight over a larger surface area and thereby minimising sinking in soft snow. Wading knee-deep through snow, I found that musk deer never sank more than 26 cm and usually only about half this depth.

Natural predators in the Tungnath study area include both common and snow leopard (Panthera pardus and P. uncia), fox (Vulpes vulpes) and Himalayan yellow-throated marten (Martes flavigula). The hair and hoof remains of musk deer were found in leopard and fox scats but none of 12 scats of martens. However, there were two instances of juvenile musk deer being attacked by martens, which more often than not were seen hunting in pairs and small family groups. Leopard and snow leopard were both seen in the study area but it was impossible to differentiate between their scats.

I shall never forget my sighting of a snow leopard in March 1979. My attention having been attracted by the barking from a group of six common langurs (Presbytis entellus) on some cliffs above the forest level at about 2,740 m, I then saw one member of the group of six being pursued by a leopard. Closer inspection, aided by a telescope, showed this to be a snow leopard with its characteristic pale to mid-grey coat and squat face. Remarkably, after the snow leopard had given up chasing its quarry and perched itself on a nearby rock, the langurs continued to bark from just 10 metres away and on occasion to charge to within 5 metres of the snow leopard. This continued for about half-an-hour after which the snow leopard moved off up a ravine, out of sight, with the langurs following it. Part of the strategy of the snow leopard would seem to be to wait patiently until a langur ventured too close. This is certainly born out by my analysis of leopard scats which showed langur to be the single most important prey item (21% by volume), followed by goral Nemorhaedus goral (18%), Himalayan tahr Hemitagus jemlahicus (16%) and serow Nemorhaedus sumatraensis (11%). Musk deer registered only 2% of the total volume of 28 leopard scats.

Keeping in Contact with each Other

Given their solitary nature, how do musk deer communicate with each other? Musk deer are essentially sedentary and, based on mapping their tracks in snow, range over areas of 15-32 ha. Males are territorial: their home ranges do not overlap with each other but they do overlap with those of females. Thus, animals may come into contact with each other from time to time by means of visual cues, but the likelihood is reduced by the dense nature of their forest or scrub habitat. Moreover, vocalisation, as a means of long-range communication, is presumed to be incompatible with an anti-predator strategy that relies on remaining inconspicuous.

Scent is the musk deer's key means of communication-droppings, urine and, in the case of males, secretions from the musk and caudal (tail) glands are used as scent marks. There is also the interdigital gland, found in the front feet of the male, but its role in communication remains unknown.

A striking characteristic of musk deer is the way in which it uses specific sites for defaecation. Over 58,400 pellets were counted from one latrine, sheltered from the rain by an overhanging rock, and I estimated that it must have been used at least 169 times over a period of at least seven years. I was amazed by the musk deer's ability to precisely relocate its latrines, reflecting its intimate knowledge of its home range. I once tracked an individual return to and use a latrine that had not been used for ten months. Not only did the latrine lie beneath 40 cm of snow but all the old pellets had long since disintegrated during the intervening monsoon.

By fortnightly monitoring the use of 120 latrines over a 27-month period, I found that their use is seasonal and peaks in

December at the height of the mating season (rut). Particularly intriguing is the musk deer's habit of often covering its pellets with leaf litter, soil and other adjacent debris during this season of peak use. This is the driest time of year and I concluded that musk deer deliberately try to keep their pellets moist and, therefore, smelly. There was no evidence from their distribution to suggest that latrines served as boundary markers. In fact measurements of pellet weights suggest that some latrines were used by exclusively by one individual while others were used by several. The extent to which latrines were shared corresponds to the degree of overlap between individuals' ranges. There was evidence of males sharing some latrines with females but not other males. Thus, latrines are communication centres providing information on the identification, whereabouts and perhaps even the reproductive condition of the occupant(s) of a particular home range or set of overlapping home ranges.

Surprisingly, given centuries of use of musk by societies and the farming of musk deer by the Chinese since 1958, very little is understood about the role of musk in scent-marking. The musk gland lies in the male's genital region, opening just a few millimetres anterior to the urethra. It seems that musk is used to scent the male's urine. While tracking males in winter, I noticed that the snow was often stained pink or red from their urine and had a sweet scent when warmed in the hands, whereas the urine of females stained the snow amber and did not smell sweet.

The caudal gland of the male occurs as a thickening at the base of the short (ca. 2.5 cm) tail. It exudes a viscous yellow secretion, with an offensive odour, from pores either side of the tail. Typically, male musk deer rub the base of their tail against the stems of bushes or dried herbs and grasses, which results in the tail being naked except at its end. I observed such pasting behaviour on a number of occasions. A more detailed study in Russia has shown that male musk deer mark in this way throughout their home ranges.

While poorly understood, it is clear that musk deer used a variety of scents to communicate over time and space. Over shorter distances, acoustic signals also play a role. For example,

I have heard a young musk deer bleating whilst in search of its mother, and when alarmed musk deer often emit a double hiss. Most extraordinary was the trill that I heard one night, reminiscent of peacock quivering its fanned feathers, after seeing a young male suddenly get up from resting and walk quickly out of sight towards the border of his home range. More amazing still was the whiff of musk, distinctive from its sweet scent, which reached me a few minutes later. I concluded that this male was seeing off another older male, known to occupy the adjacent home range.

Finding Enough Quality Food

Being small animals, musk deer have relatively high-energy requirements, and, therefore, are much more selective in their choice of food than other larger Himalayan ungulates. Due to the difficulty of observing animals in daylight, I resorted to identifying plant fragments from their droppings using a microscope. I also analysed the chemical composition of the droppings to ascertain the nutritional quality of the musk deer's diet. Essentially, musk deer are browsers and select easily digestible, nutritious foods that are high in protein and energy (sugars) and low in fibre. Forbs (i.e. herbs excluding grasses) and woody plants constitute the bulk of the diet in summer and winter, respectively. During winter, when food is in short supply, musk deer survive on poorer quality diets. Where available, musk deer may switch to feeding largely on arboreal lichens (Usnea spp.), which are low in protein but high in energy. Evergreen foliage, such as Rhododendron campanulatum, and arboreal lichens may be the only readily available food plants during winter when the snow may be a metre deep. This was certainly true in parts of the study area and, while tracking musk deer in snow, I often came across rhododendron bushes whose leaves had been eaten-up to 97 leaves per feeding bout.

The availability of food in winter is obviously crucial and, together with hunting, I believe explains why musk deer are no longer found in some parts of their former distribution. Overgrazing by domestic livestock is a widespread problem throughout the Himalaya. It can result in severe depletion of the forest understorey, leaving no shrubs for musk deer to browse during winter when snow covers the ground.

Competing with other Ungulates

Another interesting feature of the musk deer is its thick, coarse, wavy hair, which under the electron microscope is like a honeycomb of air-filled cells. The hair has a plastic-like appearance and seemingly is waterproof. No doubt, these modifications provide extremely good insulation from the cold, both in snow and rain conditions. Its ability to live in cold conditions and move easily through deep, soft snow provides it with a competitive advantage over other ungulates that share its habitat.

Goral, serow and sambar also reside in the Tungnath study area, but there is very little overlap in their use of habitat and in their diet. These ungulates, like musk deer, are essentially solitary, forest-dwellers that are active both during the day and at night. Sambar descend to lower altitudes in winter, leaving only three ungulate species to compete for resources during this critical season. While musk deer and goral are most similar in their use of the habitat in terms of vegetation cover, slope and to a lesser extent aspect (musk deer tend to use more northerly aspects than goral), their diets are the most different. Grasses make up the bulk of the goral's diet in spring and summer. During winter, when herbs are generally snow-covered other than on south-facing cliffs, the species switches to bamboo and to a lesser extent tree (oak) and shrub leaves. The only other ungulates found in the study area were wild boar (Sus scrofa) and Himalayan tahr5. Evidence of the former was rare, indicating that it was not a significant component of the ungulate community. Tahr inhabited the cliffs along the eastern edge of the study area and, sometimes, small herds emerged to graze the alpine pastures. My previous research in Langtang had shown their diet to comprise mainly grasses and other herbaceous plants.

Of Ungulates, Men and Mountains

India shares with a number of other countries the world's greatest mountain system, the Himalaya, and with them the responsibility to safeguard their natural resources and the cultural heritage and lifestyles of their inhabitants. The challenges are immense, the more so because mountains are particularly difficult environments to manage, being fragile in nature and demanding to work in for even the most intrepid.

Mountains bring out the best and worst in human nature, challenging and inspiring us to ever greater heights of physical feats and depths of personal development, while also providing the battle ground for ethnic and international conflicts. That 23 of today's 27 conflicts are taking place in mountain environments casts a dark shadow on this International Year of the Mountains, but says something about their enormous importance and value to societies around the world.

My own respect and love of mountains matured quickly through my work with tahr on an alp overlooked by the 6,581 m peak of Langtang II. Most of my limited skills in rock climbing were acquired out of necessity during my meagre attempts to keep track of these agile mountain goats. One afternoon I nearly came unstuck. Intent on following a herd of 21 tahr, I followed their route along a narrow ledge. Next I began to traverse a rock face but ran out of handholds. Looking down I realised the enormity of my situation-a sheer drop of perhaps a hundred metres. My arms and legs began to tremble, panic began to take hold me, and I knew that I only had a minute or two before losing all my strength. The way back was probably further than my strength would last-after a moment of prayer to regain my composure, I resolved to venture upwards, clinging somehow with all of my body onto the grain of the rock and aided by the odd grass tussock and wodge of moss. My resolve bore fruit and I vowed never again to be led astray by tahr!

That memory came flooding back ten years later when trying to reach Nanda Devi (7,832 m)6. I had admired this peak from afar for three years while studying musk deer. My chance to get a closer peep came in 1987 when I was asked by IUCN-The World Conservation Union to help evaluate the nomination of Nanda Devi National Park for World Heritage status. Not only was I thrilled by the prospect of seeing the magnificent glacial basin, ringed by such other famous peaks as Dunagiri

(7,066m), Changabang (6,864 m) and Trisul (7,120 m), but I also hoped to see another Himalayan ungulate for the first time-the so-called blue sheep or bharal (Pseudois nayaur). Access to this natural sanctuary is difficult and our route via Dharansi Col at 4,250 m involved a short section where the trail is narrow and hugs the side of the cliffs for 100 m or so. The frozen trail was covered in 20 cm of snow and, unprepared, we had no rope to fix to the pitons left by previous expeditions. Anyone slipping from the trail would have tumbled down the smooth rock face and then dropped a thousand metres towards the Rishi Gorge. My previous sobering experience with tahr got the better of my ambitions and so I slowly turned my back on Nanda Devi. It was a wretched decision but made easier because on this occasion the lives of others were also at stake-others who trusted me.

15

Nutrient Dynamics in Himalaya

The structure and function of Shisham (Dalbergia sissoo Roxb.) forests were investigated in relation to nutrient dynamics in 5-to 15-year-old stands growing in central Himalaya. Nutrient concentrations and storage in different layers of vegetation were in the order: tree > shrub > herb. Forest soil, litter and vegetation accounted for 80·1-91·9, 1·0-1·5 and 7·0-18·4 %, respectively, of the total nutrients in the system. There were considerable reductions (trees 32·8-43·1; shrubs 26·2-32·4; and herbs 18·8-22·2 %) in nutrient concentrations of leaves during senescence. Nutrient uptake by the vegetation as a whole and also by the different components, with and without adjustment for internal recycling, was investigated. Annual transfer of litter nutrients to the soil from vegetation was 74·8-108·4 kg ha-1 year-1 N, 5·6-8·4 kg ha-1 year-1 P and 38·7-46·9 kg ha-1 year-1 K. Turnover rate and time for different nutrients ranged between 56 and 66 % year-1 and 1·5 and 1·8 years, respectively.

The turnover rate of litter indicates that over 50 % of nutrients in litter on the forest floor are released, which ultimately enhances the productivity of the forest stand. The nutrient use efficiency in Shisham forests ranged from 136 to 143 kg ha-1 year-1 for N, 1441 to 1570 kg ha-1 year-1 for P and 305 to 311 kg ha-1 year-1 for K. Compared with natural oak forest (265 kg ha-1 year-1) and an exotic eucalypt plantation (18 kg ha-1 year-1), a higher proportion of nutrients was retranslocated in Shisham forests, largely because of higher leaf tissue nutrient concentrations. This indicates a lower nutrient use efficiency of Shisham compared with eucalypt and oak. Compartment models for nutrient dynamics have been developed to represent the distribution of nutrients pools and net annual fluxes within the system.

INTRODUCTION

Dry matter accumulation and productivity of forests are influenced by the presence of nutrients in soils and their recycling. Nutrient elements therefore limit forest productivity. Recycling of nutrients is one of the principal processes that supports organic matter production of forests. Thus, the functioning of a forest ecosystem in relation to dry matter production depends not only on the availability of nutrients but also on the pattern and rate of nutrient uptake by species occurring in the forest. According to Lodhiyal and Lodhiyal (1997), survival of tree species and the rate of nutrient uptake depend upon the availability of water. They pointed out that trees take up large quantities of nutrients from the soil system and, although much of the nutrient uptake is returned to the soil through litter fall, large amount of nutrients are also removed when trees are harvested. Thus, from the point of view of sustainability, studies on nutrient dynamics in Shisham forests which are harvested following short rotations are important for management of plantation forestry.

Nutrient accumulation and the pattern of distribution in different plants are affected by climate (Bazilevick and Rodin, 1966), and by the type and age of the species (Ovington, 1968). Lodhiyal et al. (1994) pointed out that the major macronutrients limiting the production of a forest crop are N, P and K. According to Chapin and Kedrowski (1983), nutrient availability is a major factor influencing the distribution of plant species. Most plants from low nutrient sites have a low nutrient requirement (Clarkson, 1967; Robinson, 1968; Grime, 1977; Chapin, 1980). Stachurski and Zimka (1975) and Tilton (1977) suggested that plants growing on nutritionally deficient sites minimize nutrient loss by retranslocating a greater fraction of N and P from senescing leaves. Uptake of nutrients was found to be much greater in deciduous plantations than in evergreen plantations (Lodhiyal and Lodhiyal, 1997).

On the basis of above-ground biomass production relative to N uptake, deciduous forests have a lower nutrient use efficiency (NUE) than evergreen forests (Waring and Schlesinger, 1985). However, NUE did not differ with forest type across local N mineralization gradients in mixed-species sequences (Nadelhoffer et al., 1985), and was poorly correlated with foliar life span across diverse ecosystems (Reich et al., 1992). According to Lodhiyal and Lodhiyal (1997), the high NUE is largely the result of: (a) higher soil nutrient availability, and (b) increased nutrient concentrations and amount of litter nutrient returned through litter fall to the soil. Unscientific thinning and harvesting of trees not only degrades forest soils but also removes nutrients from the ecosystem. Many studies have been carried out into nutrient storage and cycling in forests and plantations (Kan et al., 1965; Johri, 1977; Singh and Misra, 1978; Seth et al., 1983; Chaturvedi and Singh, 1987a, b; Rawat and Singh, 1988; Lodhiyal, 1990; Bargali et al., 1992; Jha, 1995; Lodhiyal et al., 1995b; Lodhiyal and Lodhiyal, 1997; Pacholi, 1997). The amounts of nutrients taken up depend on the demands of the plant species and on the availability of nutrients in the soil to supply that demand. Thus, dry matter production is generally based on the fertility of the soil and on extra inputs provided by management.

Increasingly, indigenous leguminous trees are being planted in India because of their high biomass per unit area, their survival on nutrient poor sites and for their nutrient conservation efficiency. The pressures of a growing population and adverse ecological changes in the natural Shisham forests necessitate investigations into their sustainability. Little is known about the nutrient cycling and nutrient use efficiency of Dalbergia sissoo which enable it to occupy Tarai (nutrient-rich sites) belts in central Himalaya. The present investigation aims to provide detailed information on the structure and functioning of Shisham forests growing in moist plains of central Himalayan mountains in India, with regards to nutrient cycling and the pattern of nutrient use.

The major objectives of this study were to describe: (a) the various aspects of nutrient cycling, such as nutrient uptake and nutrient retranslocation in different vegetation layers; (b) nutrient return to soils through litter (i.e. by trees, shrubs and herbs); (c) nutrient use efficiency in relation to dry matter production and net nutrient uptake; and (d) to compare estimates of nutrients in Shisham forests with those in exotic plantations and natural forests.

MATERIALS AND METHODS

Nutrient dynamics were investigated in 5-, 10-and 15-year-old Shisham forest stands in Tarai belts of central Himalaya; dry matter dynamics of these forests have been reported previously (Lodhiyal et al., 2002). Sal forest (mixed broad leaved species) was the original vegetation in the Tarai area (Champion and Seth, 1968). According to Lodhiyal et al. (1995a), most of this region was converted into arable land during the 1960s, and since the 1970s has been used for exotic tree plantations.

Details of the study site (i.e. topography, geology, soils, meteorological data and vegetation types) and methods of sampling tree, shrub and herb components are described by Lodhiyal et al. (2002).

Samples of different tree components, i.e. bole wood, bole bark, branch, twig, leaf, reproductive parts, coarse roots (stump root + lateral roots) and fine roots were collected from 12 harvested trees [three trees from each sub-plot, one from each dbh (diameter at breast height) class; see Lodhiyal et al. (2002)] for nutrient analysis (nutrient concentration and nutrient content) in each Shisham forest stand.

Tree and shrub components were sampled during September 1996, and herbs (above-and below-ground parts) were collected in each season, i.e. summer, winter and the rainy season.

Composite samples (samples of each component taken from the lower, middle and upper plant parts and mixed) for each of the tree, shrub and herb components were taken separately to the laboratory and oven-dried at 60°C to constant weight. Oven-dried samples were mill-ground for nutrient analysis.

Litter samples were collected using litter traps at monthly intervals in all forest stands. The composite litter samples (litter samples collected from each dbh class of tree and mixed to form a composite, separately for each component) for each litter component, i.e. leaf, wood, reproductive litter and other litter, were ground separately and analysed for nitrogen, phosphorus and potassium.

Five replicates of dry plant material (0·5 g each) were analysed for total nitrogen after digestion by 10 ml concentrated sulfuric acid using 5 g of a catalyst mixture (potassium sulfate and cupric sulfate in a 9: 1 ratio) in a quick digestion unit.

Total nitrogen was determined by the micro-Kjeldahl technique (Peach and Tracy, 1956; Misra, 1968; Lodhiyal et al., 1995b). Phosphorus and potassium were extracted by wet ashing 0·5 g plant material in an acid mixture consisting of 10 ml H_2SO_4 + 3 ml HNO_3 + 1 ml $HClO_4$, following the method of Jackson (1958). Phosphorus was determined by absorption spectrophotometry and potassium by flame photometry (Jackson, 1958).

The standing state of nutrients in trees, shrubs and herbs was computed separately by multiplying the dry weight of each component by the respective nutrient concentration. Nutrient values in trees, shrubs and herbs were summed to obtain the total standing state of nutrients in the vegetation.

The amount of nutrients (N, P and K) in the soil was determined by the micro-Kjeldahl technique for N (Peach and Tracy, 1956), absorption spectrophotometry for P and flame photometry for K (Jackson, 1958). The amount of nutrients in the top 30 cm of soil was calculated by summing values for 0-10, 10-20 and 20-30 cm soil depths in each forest stand. Soil volume multiplied by the respective average bulk density gave the weight of the soil, which was in turn multiplied by the corresponding nutrient concentration to obtain the amount of soil nutrients (N, P and K).

The mean nutrient concentration was multiplied by the weight of annual litter fall, i.e. leaf, wood, reproductive parts of trees, and leaves of shrubs and herbs to give the amount of nutrients transferred to the forest floor in vegetation in stands of different ages. The turnover rate (K) for each nutrient on the forest floor was estimated following Chaturvedi and Singh (1987b) and Lodhiyal and Lodhiyal (1997) as:

$$K = A/(A + F)$$

where A is the amount of nutrients added to the forest floor by litter fall and F is the nutrient content of the lowest value of standing crop of litter in the annual cycle. Turnover time (t) for nutrients was calculated as for standing litter biomass. Turnover time is the reciprocal of turnover rate (K).

Nutrient uptake by components of vegetation in stands of different age was calculated by multiplying the net primary productivity (NPP) of different components by their nutrient concentration. The values of nutrient uptake by trees, shrubs and herbs were summed to estimate the total annual uptake by the forest vegetation.

Some retranslocation of nutrients (N, P and K) occurred during senescence of foliage. This was assessed following Ralhan and Singh (1987), Rawat and Singh (1988), Lodhiyal et al. (1995b) and Lodhiyal and Lodhiyal (1997), i.e.

$$R = (X-Y)/X \times 100$$

where R is nutrient retranslocation (%), X is the nutrient mass in mature green leaves, and Y is the nutrient mass in senesced leaves. X and Y were calculated on the basis of nutrient per unit weight of mature green and senesced leaf, respectively, multiplied by total amount of leaf litter fall.

To estimate nutrient retranslocation, 120 mature green and freshly fallen senesced leaves were collected in September (peak month of leaf maturity) and December (leaf senescing period) 1997, respectively. Since rainfall is negligible in the region when leaves senesce (December), leaching is likely to have only a minimal effect on nutrient loss from the leaves (Ralhan and Singh, 1987). The nutrient use efficiency (E) per unit area of Shisham forests was calculated by:

$$E = P/U$$

where P is NPP and U is the net nutrient uptake in kg ha-1 year-1 by the trees.

RESULTS AND DISCUSSION

Nutrient Concentration

Table below summarizes N, P and K concentrations in the different components of vegetation (i.e. trees, shrubs and herbs) of Shisham forests growing in Tarai belts of the central Himalayan mountains in India. The concentration of nutrients in tree components was in the order: reproductive parts > leaf > twig > bole bark > branch > bole wood in above-ground parts, and fine roots > lateral roots > stump root in below-ground parts.

The nutrient concentrations in different components of Shisham trees were higher in 5-year-old stands than in 15-year-old stands. Thus, as trees age the percentage of nutrients (N, P and K) in the different components decreases. Similar trends in different components of fast-growing poplar and eucalypt trees were reported by Lodhiyal et al. (1995b), Lodhiyal and Lodhiyal (1997), and Bargali et al. (1992) in adjacent areas of central Himalaya.

Table. Concentration of nutrients (% ± s.e.) in different components of trees, shrubs and herbs, and in soils of Tarai Shisham forests in central Himalaya

		Age of Shisham forests (years)		
Components	Nutrient	5	10	15
Tree layer				
Bole wood	N	0·365 ± 0·012	0·340 ± 0·020	0·328 ± 0·014
	P	0·042 ± 0·015	0·039 ± 0·027	0·038 ± 0·018
	K	0·202 ± 0·017	0·198 ± 0·024	0·195 ± 0·010
Bole bark	N	1·410 ± 0·020	1·390 ± 0·025	1·380 ± 0·025
	P	0·089 ± 0·024	0·088 ± 0·020	0·085 ± 0·020
	K	0·588 ± 0·026	0·582 ± 0·020	0·562 ± 0·024
Branch*	N	0·980 ± 0·034	0·962 ± 0·041	0·940 ± 0·052
	P	0·095 ± 0·028	0·088 ± 0·038	0·071 ± 0·012
	K	0·200 ± 0·025	0·198 ± 0·039	0·195 ± 0·014
Twig	N	1·658 ± 0·031	1·625 ± 0·042	1·580 ± 0·025
	P	0·099 ± 0·038	0·096 ± 0·044	0·094 ± 0·020
	K	0·588 ± 0·034	0·582 ± 0·038	0·570 ± 0·025

Leaf	N	2·750 ± 0·055	2·680 ± 0·035	2·640 ± 0·40
	P	0·188 ± 0·059	0·175 ± 0·039	0·170 ± 0·034
	K	0·780 ± 0·062	0·762 ± 0·041	0·740 ± 0·030
Reproductive parts				
	N	3·254 ± 0·048	3·225 ± 0·050	3·118 ± 0·020
	P	0·340 ± 0·043	0·320 ± 0·058	0·312 ± 0·019
	K	0·925 ± 0·040	0·915 ± 0·052	0·908 ± 0·012
Stump root	N	0·570 ± 0·040	0·592 ± 0·030	0·550 ± 0·014
	P	0·042 ± 0·039	0·038 ± 0·024	0·035 ± 0·015
	K	0·378 ± 0·034	0·375 ± 0·025	0·370 ± 0·012
Lateral roots	N	0·610 ± 0·034	0·698 ± 0·034	0·595 ± 0·024
	P	0·068 ± 0·040	0·062 ± 0·032	0·058 ± 0·021
	K	0·550 ± 0·041	0·520 ± 0·028	0·480 ± 0·022
Fine roots	N	1·012 ± 0·055	0·998 ± 0·042	0·995 ± 0·030
	P	0·198 ± 0·059	0·598 ± 0·050	0·188 ± 0·026
	K	0·610 ± 0·059	0·598 ± 0·050	0·589 ± 0·020
Shrub layer				
Lantana camara				
Stem	N	0·705 ± 0·052	0·702 ± 0·184	0·701 ± 0·095
	P	0·079 ± 0·034	0·078 ± 0·098	0·076 ± 0·047
	K	0·510 ± 0·025	0·508 ± 0·075	0·504 ± 0·059
Foliage	N	2·348 ± 0·040	2·345 ± 0·094	2·340 ± 0·052
	P	0·155 ± 0·015	0·152 ± 0·084	0·150 ± 0·038
	K	0·738 ± 0·021	0·735 ± 0·070	0·730 ± 0·044
Roots	N	0·780 ± 0·058	0·778 ± 0·062	0·770 ± 0·074
	P	0·077 ± 0·028	0·075 ± 0·048	0·072 ± 0·046
	K	0·546 ± 0·036	0·540 ± 0·042	0·540 ± 0·070
Murraya koenighii				
Stem	N	0·675 ± 0·069	0·674 ± 0·084	0·670 ± 0·053
	P	0·047 ± 0·022	0·045 ± 0·046	0·044 ± 0·058
	K	0·350 ± 0·062	0·348 ± 0·078	0·340 ± 0·063
Foliage	N	1·252 ± 0·042	1·250 ± 0·043	1·246 ± 0·047
	P	0·118 ± 0·048	0·118 ± 0·034	0·118 ± 0·064
	K	0·750 ± 0·018	0·750 ± 0·048	0·746 ± 0·072
Roots	N	0·758 ± 0·018	0·755 ± 0·024	0·752 ± 0·034
	P	0·049 ± 0·027	0·046 ± 0·057	0·045 ± 0·094
	K	0·412 ± 0·044	0·410 ± 0·054	0·408 ± 0·050
Clerodendron viscosum				
Stem	N	0·642 ± 0·075	0·640 ± 0·046	0·638 ± 0·029
	P	0.051 ± 0·081	0·050 ± 0·054	0·050 ± 0·039
	K	0·335 ± 0·048	0·332 ± 0·070	0·350 ± 0·066

Foliage	N	1·158 ± 0·054	1·150 ± 0·028	1·152 ± 0·045
	P	0·130 ± 0·029	0·128 ± 0·038	0·127 ± 0·050
	K	0·678 ± 0·052	0·675 ± 0·056	0·673 ± 0·043
Roots	N	0·670 ± 0·035	0·667 ± 0·037	0·664 ± 0·032
	P	0·055 ± 0·024	0·052 ± 0·042	0·051 ± 0·047
	K	0·358 ± 0·054	0·352 ± 0·042	0·350 ± 0·052
Pogostemone benghalense				
Stem	N	0·681 ± 0·082	0·680 ± 0·094	0.675 ± 0.074
	P	0·054 ± 0·050	0·050 ± 0·045	0.046 ± 0.058
	K	0·342 ± 0·042	0·340 ± 0·072	0.334 ± 0.073
Foliage	N	1·180 ± 0·053	1·178 ± 0·057	1·175 ± 0·046
	P	0·139 ± 0·042	0·136 ± 0·028	0·135 ± 0·034
	K	0·684 ± 0·038	0·682 ± 0·065	0·677 ± 0·054
Roots	N	0·750 ± 0·042	0·740 ± 0·069	0·730 ± 0·063
	P	0·055 ± 0·034	0·054 ± 0·047	0·052 ± 0·050
	K	0·480 ± 0·026	0·479 ± 0·046	0·475 ± 0·042
Herb layer				
Above-ground				
	N	1·572 ± 0·068	1·540 ± 0·076	1·475 ± 0·082
	P	0·084 ± 0·049	0·082 ± 0·056	0·078 ± 0·044
	K	1·342 ± 0·063	1·314 ± 0·074	1·304 ± 0·064
Below-ground				
	N	1·221 ± 0·063	1·202 ± 0·058	1·165 ± 0·078
	P	0·065 ± 0·025	0·062 ± 0·042	0·060 ± 0·036
	K	1·142 ± 0·052	1·135 ± 0·063	1·124 ± 0·050
Soil (0-30 cm depth)				
	N	0·159 ± 0·30	0·156 ± 0·32	0·151 ± 0·39
	P	0·013 ± 0·26	0·013 ± 0·26	0·012 ± 0·39
	K	0·065 ± 0·38	0·061 ± 0·30	0·056 ± 0·40

* Large woody shoots with leaves.

Current shoots bearing leaves.

Main root with tap roots and parts of stem (stump bearing roots).

Lateral branches of main roots with diameter > 5 mm.

Roots of diameter < 5 mm and associated mycorrhizae.

Leaf to wood concentration ratios for N (7·5-8·0), P (4·5) and K (3·8-3·9) were similar to those found in natural forests of central Himalaya and fall within the range for N (11-12) and P (6-7) reported for poplar trees (Lodhiyal et al., 1995b) but are much lower than values reported for temperate forests

(Whittaker, 1975). Leaf nutrient concentrations are higher than in Populus deltoides plantations (Lodhiyal et al., 1995b) and Eucalyptus hybrid plantation (Bargali et al., 1992).

Soil nutrient concentration decreased with increasing forest age, possibly as a consequence of uptake and leaching of nutrients by the Shisham forests. Similar findings were also reported for Tarai poplar plantations in nearby areas (Lodhiyal et al., 1995b). However, loss of nutrients can be considerable during initial site preparation, which involves burning ground vegetation and litter and, as a result of soil disturbance which accompanies planting, especially when vegetation cover is sparse (Bormann and Likens, 1979).

STANDING STATE OF NUTRIENTS

The standing state of nutrients increased with forest age due to increased dry matter storage. Bole (wood + bark) had the greatest concentration of nutrients in the trees. The relative contribution to the standing state of nutrients in different above-ground parts was generally in the order: bole > leaf > branch > reproductive parts, and that in below-ground parts was: stump root > lateral roots > fine roots. Similar trends have been reported for eucalypt (Feller, 1980; Bargali et al., 1992) and poplar plantations (Lodhiyal et al., 1995b; Lodhiyal and Lodhiyal, 1997). The different nutrients in the total vegetation (trees + shrub + herbs) was in the order: N (488-1002 kg ha-1 year-1) > K (235-471 kg ha-1 year-1) > P (50-82 kg ha-1 year-1).

Table. Nutrient content (kg ha-1) in different vegetation layers of Shisham forests

	Age of Shisham forests (years)		
Components	5	10	15
Nitrogen			
Tree layer	402·1 (82·3)	692·2 (85·5)	877·3 (87·5)
% Allocation in			
bole*	43·4	45·3	45·0
branch	17·0	18·7	20·3

leaf	22·1	18·1	15·5
reproductive parts	4·3	4·4	5·5
coarse roots	11·3	11·3	11·2
fine roots	1·9	2·2	2·5
Shrub layer	44·4(9·1)	79·8 (9·8)	91·3 (9·1)
Herb layer	41·9 (8·6)	38·1 (4·7)	33·6 (3·4)
Total vegetation	488·4 (100)	810·1(100)	1002·2 (100)
Soil (0-30 cm depth)	4834·6	4945·4	5026·0
Phosphorus			
Tree layer	43·7 (87·8)	64·5 (88·3)	72·5 (88·7)
% Allocation in			
bole*	37·1	44·8	48·6
branch	12·6	15·5	16·8
leaf	13·9	12·7	12·0
reproductive parts	24·3	4·7	6·6
coarse roots	8·7	9·6	10·2
fine roots	3·4	12·7	5·8
Shrub layer	3·9 (7·8)	6·6(9·0)	7·4 (9·1)
Herb layer	2·2 (4·4)	2·0 (2·7)	1·8 (2·2)
Total vegetation	49·8 (100)	73·1 (100)	81·7 (100)
Soil (0-30 cm depth)	405·7	412·6	388·9
Potassium			
Tree layer	172·6 (73·6)	289·6 (79·0)	390·9 (83·1)
% Allocation in			
bole*	50·0	55·4	51·9
branch	10·7	6·4	12·6
leaf	14·6	12·3	9·7
reproductive parts	2·8	3·0	3·6
coarse roots	19·2	19·8	18·8
fine roots	2·7	3·1	3·4
Shrub layer	25·6(10·9)	43·7 (11·9)	49·5 (10·5)
Herb layer	36·4 (15·5)	33·2 (9·1)	30·3 (6·4)
Total vegetation	234·6 (100)	366·5 (100)	470·7 (100)
Soil (0-30 cm depth)	1968·4	1934·6	1872·1

Values in parentheses represent percentage contribution.

* Bole wood + bole bark, which accounted for 11·0-19·8 % of the values (N, P and K).

Branch + twig (new shoots bearing leaves), which accounted for 1·7-9·3 % of the values (N, P and K). Stump root (main root) + lateral roots (lateral branches of main roots, which accounted for 3·2-7·9 % of the values (N, P and K).}

Nutrient storage by shrubs accounted for 8-12 % of storage by the vegetation as a whole and increased with forest age, while nutrient storage by herbs (2-15 %) decreased with stand age.

Similar trends were also reported for fast-growing poplar plantations (Lodhiyal et al., 1995b). This is because the tree canopy affects the growth of herbs and also reduces the amount of light available and thus photosynthetic efficiency.

Nutrient Retranslocation

The retranslocation of nutrients from senesced leaves was in the order: K (40-43 %) > N (33-35 %) > P (28-30 %). These estimates of nutrient retranslocation are markedly higher than those reported for fast-growing exotic eucalypt plantations (18-25 %; Bargali et al., 1992).

However, the present estimates are lower than values reported for Tarai poplar plantations (42-64 %; Lodhiyal et al., 1995b), for Larix laricina, Alnus crispa and Betula papyrifera (44-81 %; Chapin and Kedrowski, 1983), for Populus tremuloides (42-65 %; Verry and Timmons, 1976) and Populus deltoides (74-89 %; Baker and Blackman, 1977).

However, our estimates are close to the 23-39 % reported for Quercus rubra (Grizzard et al., 1976) and 38-49 % for Betula alleghaniensis (Hoyle, 1965). The estimate of N retranslocation was 33 % in mixed northern hardwood species (Bormann et al., 1977), which is similar to the present N estimate.

Thus, on the basis of correlation between proportional nutrient retranslocation from senesced leaves and tree leaf nutrient concentrations, our findings are consistent with those of Chapin and Kedrowski (1983).

According to Lodhiyal and Lodhiyal (1997), the nutrient requirement of vegetation not only depends on stand age and soil nutrient level, but also on the nutrient concentration of foliage.

They noted that the greater the leaf tissue nutrient level, the higher the nutrient retranslocation capacity of forest trees would be.

Table. Magnitude of retranslocation of nutrient (%) in leaves of different vegetations layers of Shisham forests

		Age of Shisham forests (years)		
Vegetation	Nutrient	5	10	15
Tree layer	N	35·2	33·6	32·8
	P	30·3	28·8	28·1
	K	43·1	41·5	40·3
Shrub layer	N	32·4	30·3	28·8
	P	30·7	25·0	25·0
	K	30·2	28·7	26·2
Herb layer	N	22·2	21·6	20·8
	P	17·2	16·8	16·9
	K	19·8	19·4	18·8

Nutrient Uptake

The present estimates of gross nutrient uptake (kg ha-1 year-1) by vegetation ranged from 114 (5-year-old stand) to 167 (15-year-old stand) for N, 10 (5-year-old stand) to 14 (15-year-old stand) for P, and 70 (5-year-old stand) to 92 (15-year-old stand) for K. Of this, the tree layer accounted for 59-74 % N, 64-81 % P and 44-61 % K; the shrub layer for 5-6 % N, 6-14 % P and 4-6 % K; and the herb layer for 20-37 % N, 13-22 % P and 33-52 % K.

Table. Nutrient uptake (kg ha-1 year-1) by different vegetation layers of Shisham forests

	Age of Shisham forests (years)		
Components	5	10	15
Nitrogen			
Tree layer	67·1(63·7)	96·9 (91·5)	122·9(117·1)
% Allocation in			
bole*	45·1	41·3	40·4
branch	17·7	17·1	18·3
leaf	14·4	16·5	14·4

reproductive parts	3·0	7·7	6·6
coarse roots	11·7	9·2	12·2
fine roots	8·1	8·2	8·1
Shrub layer	5·4 (4·9)	9·3 (8·6)	10·2 (9·4)
Herb layer	41·9 (34·3)	38·1 (31·4)	33·6 (28·0)
Total vegetation	114·4 (102·9)	144·3 (131·5)	166·7 154·5)
Phosphorus			
Tree layer	6·4 (6·2)	8·9 (8·7)	10·9 (10·6)
% Allocation in			
bole*	44·1	41·2	40·3
branch	14·9	14·2	14·0
leaf	10·4	11·6	10·4
reproductive parts	3·3	8·2	7·4
coarse roots	10·5	7·4	10·9
fine roots	16·8	17·4	17·0
Shrub layer	1·4 (1·3)	0·75 (0·7)	0·8 (0·7)
Herb layer	2·2 (1·9)	2·0 (1·7)	1·8 (1·5)
Total vegetation	10·0 (9·4)	11·7 (11·1)	13·5 (12·8)
Potassium			
Tree layer	30·5 (29·3)	42·8 (40·9)	56.1 (54·0)
% Allocation in			
bole*	49·0	47·9	45·6
branch	10·5	10·6	11·1
leaf	9·0	10·6	8·8
reproductive parts	2·0	4·9	4·2
coarse roots	18·7	14·8	19·8
fine roots	10·8	11·2	10·5
Shrub layer	3·1 (2·9)	5·1(4·7)	5·5 (5·2)
Herb layer	36·4 (30·5)	33·1 (28·0)	30·3 (25·8)
Total vegetation	70·0 (62·7)	81·0 (73·6)	91·9 (85·1)

Values in parentheses represent nutrient uptake (kg ha-1 year-1) after adjustment for retranslocation.

* Bole wood + bole bark, which accounted for 11·9-19·6 % of the nutrient values (N, P and K).

Branch + twig (new shoots bearing leaves, which accounted for 4·9-8·3 % of the nutrient values (N, P and K).

Stump root (main root) + lateral roots (lateral branches of main root, which accounted for 2·2-10·3 % of the nutrient values (N, P and K).

Nutrient Return through Litter Fall

Of the net annual uptake of nutrients by trees, 56-69 % N, 63-72 % P and 31-46 % K is returned to the ground through litter fall. The total inputs of nutrients to the forest floor via tree litter fall and litter fall from the total vegetation were similar to those of a eucalypt plantation (56 % N, 51 % P and 47 % K; Bargali and Singh, 1991) and lower than those reported for Populus deltoides plantations (Lodhiyal et al., 1995b) in an adjacent area in the central Himalayan mountains.

Table. Mean nutrient concentration (% ± s.e.) in different litter components of vegetation of Shisham forests in Tarai of central Himalaya

	Age of Shisham forests (years)		
Components	5	10	15
Nitrogen			
Trees			
Leaf	1·783 ± 0·088	1·779 ± 0·084	1·774 ± 0·085
Wood	1·011 ± 0·050	0·982 ± 0·052	0·954 ± 0·051
Reproductive parts	1·952 ± 0·068	1·935 ± 0·078	1·870 ± 0·080
Shrubs*	1·003 ± 0·092	1·032 ± 0·090	1·055 ± 0·088
Herbs	1·572 ± 0·068	1·540 ± 0·076	1·475 ± 0·082
Phosphorus			
Tree			
Leaf	0·131 ± 0·042	0·124 ± 0·040	0·122 ± 0·045
Wood	0·070 ± 0·048	0·067 ± 0·046	0·066 ± 0·044
Reproductive parts	0·221 ± 0·068	0·208 ± 0·062	0·203 ± 0·064
Shrubs*	0·093 ± 0·068	0·099 ± 0·066	0·099 ± 0·067
Herbs	0·084 ± 0·049	0·082 ± 0·060	0·078 ± 0·044
Potassium			
Trees			
Leaf	0·443 ± 0·062	0·445 ± 0·056	0·440 ± 0·054
Wood	0·395 ± 0·070	0·390 ± 0·062	0·382 ± 0·066
Reproductive parts	0·509 ± 0·070	0·503 ± 0·068	0·499 ± 0·066
Shrubs*	0·497 ± 0·058	0·506 ± 0·054	0·521 ± 0·056
Herbs	1·342 ± 0·063	1·314 ± 0·074	1·304 ± 0·064

* This includes the composite mean nutrient concentrations (%) of leaves, twigs and reproductive parts of shrubs.

This includes the (%) nutrient concentration of leaves of herbs.

Table. Amount of nutrients (kg ha-1 year-1) returned through different litter components of vegetation

	Age of Shisham forests (years)		
Components	5	10	15
Nitrogen			
Trees	41·9 (56·0)	64·1 (65·6)	74·9 (69·0)
% Allocation in tree component			
Leaf	48·6	55·4	56·2
Wood	1·2	2·1	3·2
Reproductive parts	0·7	1·9	3·2
Roots	5·6	6·2	6·3
Shrubs	5·8 (7·8)	9·1 (9·3)	12·3 (11·3)
Herbs	27·0 (36·2)	24·5 (25·1)	21·3 (19·6)
Total vegetation	74·8 (100)	97·6 (100)	108·4 (100)
Phosphorus			
Trees	3·6 (63·3)	5·3 (70·1)	6·1 (72·4)
% Allocation in tree component			
Leaf	46·9	50·1	49·8
Wood	1·1	1·8	2·9
Reproductive parts	1·1	2·5	4·4
Roots	14·2	15·7	15·3
Shrubs	0·5 (9·5)	0·9 (11·6)	1·1 (13·6)
Herbs	1·5 (27·2)	1·4 (18·3)	1·2 (14·0)
Total vegetation	5·6 (100)	7·5 (100)	8·4 (100)
Potassium			
Trees	12·0 (31·0)	18·5 (41·5)	21·5 (45·9)
% Allocation in tree component			
Leaf	23·3	30·4	32·4
Wood	0·9	1·9	3·0
Reproductive parts	0·4	1·0	1·9
Roots	6·4	8·2	8·6
Shrubs	2·9 (7·5)	4·4 (10·0)	6·0 (13·0)
Herbs	23·8 (61·5)	21·5 (48·5)	19·3 (41·1)
Total vegetation	8·7 (100)	44·5 (100)	46·9 (100)

Values in parentheses are the percent contribution of the total vegetation.

Turnover of Nutrients on the Forest Floor

The turnover time of nutrients on the forest floor was longer (Table 8) than that of tropical dry deciduous forests (0·3-0·5 year; Pandey, 1980), eucalypt plantations (1·1-1·3 year; Bargali et al., 1992) and Populus deltoides plant ations (1·1-1·4 year; Lodhiyal et al., 1995b). This indicates that a small part of the forest floor litter biomass remained in steady state but this amount was less than in other deciduous forests. According to Lodhiyal and Lodhiyal (1997), a long turnover time shows that the forest floor litter biomass is in steady state because the annual decomposition rate of litter is low compared with the rate of litter input.

Table. Turnover rate (K, year-1) and turnover time (t, years) of nutrients on the forests floor

Nutrient	Age of Shisham forests (years)	5	10	15
N	K	0·65	0·66	0·63
	t	1·54	1·51	1·59
P	K	0·62	0·65	0·56
	t	1·61	1·54	1·79
K	K	0·64	0·66	0·61
	t	1·56	1·52	1·64

NUTRIENT USE EFFICIENCY

The nutrient use efficiency (NUE = NPP /net nutrient uptake) of Shisham trees ranged from 137-143 kg ha-1 year-1 for N, 1441-1570 kg ha-1 year-1 for P and 305-311 kg ha-1 year-1 for K (Table 9). According to Lodhiyal et al. (1995b), as stems and branches become larger the nutrient concentration of woody tissues declines, resulting in higher nutrient use efficiency. The availability of soil nutrients in the Shisham forests studied was found to be similar to that in nearby high and low density Populus deltoides plantations (Lodhiyal et al., 1994). This may be due to higher nutrient concentrations in tissues and increased amounts of nutrients returned through litter in Shisham forests.

Table : Nutrient use efficiency (kg ha-1 year-1) of Tarai Shisham forests in central Himalaya

	Age of Shisham forests (years)		
Nutrient	5	10	15
N	143 (113)	137 (111)	143 (112)
P	1484 (1177)	1441 (1170)	1570 (1228)
K	311 (247)	305 (240)	309 (242)

NUE = NPP/net nutrient uptake.

Values in parentheses are above-ground NUE.

Nitrogen NUE for N was lower in Shisham forests than in a nearby poplar plantation (Lodhiyal et al., 1994) while NUE for P and K was similar in both sites.

However, the NUE for N was higher than the value reported for an 8-year-old eucalypt stand (215 kg ha-1 year-1; Bargali and Singh, 1991) and 189-209 kg ha-1 year-1 for central Himalayan natural Sal (Shorea robusta), oak (Quercus leucotrichophora) and chir (Pinus roxburghii) forests (Singh and Singh, 1987).

This indicates that Shisham trees are preferable from the standpoint of NUE and their fast growth rate. Despite a proportional increase in nutrient retranslocation, Shisham forests have a similar NUE to eucalypt stands, largely because of higher tissue nutrient concentrations.

The soil nutrient extraction efficiency (nutrient uptake per unit nutrient present in soil) of the Shisham forests studied was 1·3-2·2 for N, 1·5-2·7 for P and 1·5-2·9 for K, and falls within the range reported for Populus deltoides plantations (1·8-3·4; Lodhiyal et al., 1994).

On the basis of the nutrient parameters above, Dalbergia sisoo is the most important species because it not only produces a higher amount of dry matter but also because it requires only small amounts of nutrients compared with exotic tree plantations and indigenous forest species in adjacent areas.

Thus, it is more suitable than other species not only for Tarai regions but also for plantations in areas of low nutrient status.

Thus, it is concluded that growing Shisham forests in the Tarai belt is advisable because of their relatively higher productivity, even in poor sites, than any other natural forest growing in adjacent areas. In addition, the species removes only small amounts of nutrients compared with the exotic fast-growing trees (poplar and eucalypt). Therefore, trees can be harvested in a shorter rotation period with higher wood biomass in this moist plain of central Himalaya.

NUTRIENT DYNAMICS

Compartment models of nutrient dynamics (pools and fluxes) for 5-and 15-year-old Shisham forests are presented in Fig. 1. Nutrients present in the soil to a depth of 30 cm are considered a source, while those associated with decomposition are released into the soil for re-use.

The direction of nutrient flux from soil to foliage indicates a one-way movement, although it is realised that the nutrients are utilized by the leaf in organic matter synthesis and that they are redistributed among different components at varying rates giving rise to internal recycling.

The amount of nutrients (N, P and K) stored in the vegetation was greater in 15-year-old than in 5-year-old forest stands. Of the total nutrients, the tree layer accounted for 74-88 % in the 5-year-old stand and 83-89 % in the 15-year-old stand. The total amount of P and K in the soil decreased, while the amount of N increased with increasing age of the forest.

The amount of nutrients (N, P and K) taken up by the different vegetational layers as a proportion of the total uptake was as follows: 5-year-old forest, trees (47-65 %) > herbs (20-49 %) > shrubs (5-14 %); 15-year-old forest, trees (64-82 %) > herbs (12-30 %) > shrubs (5-6 %).

The total amount of nutrients retranslocated from above-ground senescing plant parts of the tree layer increased with the age of forest from 3·4 (5-year-old stand) to 5·8 kg ha-1 year-

1 (15-year-old stand) for N, 0·2 (5-year-old stand) to 0·3 kg ha-1 year-1 (15-year-old stand) for P, and 1·2 (5-year-old stand) to 2·0 kg ha-1 year-1 (15-year-old stand) for K. In the shrub layer, the amount of N, P and K retranslocated was 0·37-0·84, 0·04-0·06 and 0·13-0·34 kg ha-1 year-1, respectively, and increased with the age of the stand.

However, in the herb layer, the amount of nutrients ranged from 5·6 to 7·7 for N, 0·2 to 0·3 for P and 4·5 to 5·9 kg ha-1 year-1 for K, and decreased with the age of the stand. Thus, a proportion of annual dry matter production of litter supports the whole pattern of nutrient transfer in Shisham forests and consequently reduces the nutrient demand on the soil system.

16

Valuation of Ecosystem Services of Himalaya Mountains Forests

Apart from timber and non-timber products, the forests also perform a number of ecosystem services, which are not only local and regional but also global in nature. These services include carbon-sequestration, recreational services, improvement of soil fertility, purification of soil and air, control over climate and others, and consist of flows of materials, energy and information from natural capital stocks that include various forms such as trees, soil, the atmosphere and others. With a growing realization of the importance of the life supporting ecosystem services in conservation and local livelihoods, market-based approaches to environmental services have become a focus of interest in recent years. Technically, such markets are an opportunity for people living in and around forests to enhance their livelihoods through not only economic benefits (rewards) but also through increased social and human capital (recognition). Globally, implementation of payments for environmental services (PES) initiatives has been increasing in popularity.

In this context, International Development Research Centre (IDRC), South Asia Regional Office (SARO) and ANSAB (Asia Network for Sustainable Agriculture and Bioresources) having worked together for a number of years realized the need to initiate a pilot project in the area of ecosystem services. The pilot project was designed and implemented from January 26, 2005 to November 26, 2006 with the purpose of facilitating conservation of the forest ecosystems and biodiversity by valuing their ecosystem services through creating awareness, capacity building, and policy interventions in Nepal and Uttaranchal, India.

This was an exploratory study, preparing a ground for bigger interventions in future. The project

(i) identified important ecosystem services, their providers and receivers;

(ii) assessed value of recreational services and forest carbon;

(iii) reviewed current practices and development on PES; and

(iv) raised broad level awareness on PES among policy makers and key stakeholders in Nepal and Uttaranchal India.

Community level interactions, national and regional workshops and meetings of concerned stakeholders representing government, non-government and research institutions, civil society and community federations in the pilot process has clearly indicated that there is a need to understand the opportunities and requirements of clean development mechanism (CDM) procedures and payment mechanisms, build the capacity of local communities to increase environmental services and participate in PES, and establish and/or strengthen national system and procedures required to implement the mechanism.

RESEARCH PROBLEM

Forests are home to about 80% of the global biodiversity and have similar proportions of biomass and carbon-stock. Forests are not only for timber and non-timber products, but also for a number of ecosystem services. The ecosystem services are defined here as services generated as a result of interactions between abiotic and biotic components of various ecosystems (Singh 2002). These services include carbon-sequestration, improvement of soil fertility, purification of soil and air, control over climate and others, and consist of flows of materials, energy and information from natural capital stocks that include various forms such as trees, soil and the atmosphere. Some of these services would be required to cope with the climatic change, and its causal connection to the rise in greenhouse emissions is now well established (King 2004).

Costanza et al (1997), while doing an exercise at global level, have shown that the total value of ecosystem services is about twice as much as global GNP. The forests of Himalaya mountains of Nepal and Uttaranchal India supply ecosystem services to most of the Gangetic Plains (GP) which is undoubtedly one of the most productive/fertile and populated regions of the world. It is but obvious that any impairment of the forest ecosystem services of the Himalaya Mountains is going to affect the life of over 500 million people living in the adjacent river basin. Somehow, it is taken for granted the flow of ecosystem services from these mountains to GP and seldom appreciated the intimate relationship between the health of forests of these mountains and the population supporting capacity of GP. This observation stresses that there is a need to recognize the scope of these services at various levels by considering various forest types differing in properties and developing a management plan based on them.

In spite of the importance of the forest ecosystem to provide all these services, deforestation (loss in forest area) and forest degradation (reduction in biomass of forest stands) in Tropics remains an environmental challenge with global ramifications. Mountains, which have some of the last of forest areas in tropics, are under great anthropogenic pressure, as forests of much of the nearby plains have already been converted into crop fields. The threats to these mountain forests continue to be high largely because of poverty of the people and lack of any alternative strategies for development. Forest stands in general, have a lower biomass and productivity than their potentials (Singh & Singh 1992), many species are failing to regenerate (e.g., Quercus semecarpifolia) and several forest stands consist of denuded tree stems and large branches because of the excessive lopping for firewood and fodder.

Overgrazing by domestic animals without concern for regeneration of forest growth, inappropriate harvesting practice for extraction of biomass to meet the day-to-day needs of firewood and fodder, frequent fires, poaching of wild animals and the spread of invasive/exotic plant species are some of the observations indicating that the forests are not healthy and liable to deteriorate further. Since more than 80% of the people depend on the forest biomass for day-to-day living in the Himalaya Mountains (Singh and Singh 1992), the biomass removal from forests is substantial and widespread, and the scope for further biomass extraction for local livelihoods is limited. Obviously, the people do not have enough capacity and incentives to conserve forests on their own.

Although the governments of Nepal and India have tried several measures to protect forest from deforestation and degradation, such as ban on green tree felling, restriction on use and trade of forest products and delineation of protected areas, they failed to generate the intended benefits in conservation. This has also resulted in worsening of the living conditions of rural communities, who depend on forest. Therefore, it is necessary to explore other possibilities of creating economic incentives to rural communities through payment or compensation and rewards for their stewardship and efforts in maintaining and conserving mountain forest ecosystems.

Getting payment from a standing forest represents a major advancement in conservation. All these years, forest managers have confined to working out the sustainable harvest rate of forests, whereas getting payments for forest ecosystem services represents making money without cutting or degrading forests. This approach of conservation is different from the one based on "polluter pays principle", which says that those who pollute environment should bear the costs. For example, owners of factories which dump their effluents in rivers should bear the costs of treating water and restoring rivers. The costs, however, are passed on to consumers of goods in the form of their increased prices. The ecosystem service-oriented approach holds that, those who provide an environmental benefits should be rewarded for doing so, and this can be referred to as "provider gets principle" (Pagiola et al 2002). Failure of its application is one of the principal causes of ecosystem degradation and loss of ecosystem services.

With this realization, International Development Research Centre (IDRC), South Asia Regional Office (SARO) and ANSAB (Asia Network for Sustainable Agriculture and Bioresources) having worked together for a number of years initiated a pilot project in the area of ecosystem services. A pilot collaborative project "Valuation of Ecosystem Services of Himalaya Mountains Forests for Conservation through Capacity Building and Policy Interventions-A Pilot Study of Nepal and Uttaranchal India" was designed and implemented from January 26, 2005 to November 26, 2006.

RESEARCH FINDINGS AND FULFILLMENT OF OBJECTIVES

The general objective of the pilot research project was to contribute towards conservation of the forest ecosystems and biodiversity by valuing their ecosystem services and raising awareness among key stakeholders on the possibilities of payment or compensation and rewards of ecosystem services. This was an exploratory study, preparing a ground for larger interventions in the future. The specific objectives were: i) to identify and assess ecosystem services of the mountain forests; ii) to educate, sensitize and interact with the decision makers and key stakeholders; and iii) to explore options for getting payment of ecosystem services of the mountain forests.

The pilot initiative consolidated and generated new knowledge in the field of ecosystem services from scientific and policy perspectives. With this research initiative, we have identified important ecosystem services of mountain forests in Nepal and Uttaranchal India, their providers and receivers; assessed value of recreational services and forest carbon; made a survey of studies, efforts, mechanisms and practices on payment of ecosystem services around the world; and facilitated to raise awareness among key stakeholders in Nepal and India. As reflected by concerned stakeholders at various forums and interactions, this exploratory study serves as a milestone for bigger interventions in future. The findings and scientific outputs of the research are grouped in the following four major headings.

Ecosystem Services in Himalaya: Identification, Survey of Payments and Policy Implications

Through exploratory exercises with multiple stakeholders, reviews of relevant literatures, and a series of interactions and discussions among research team members, a list of major ecosystem services that flow from the Himalayan forests was prepared, and these services were further exercised in detail to identify their providers and receivers. Among the key services, carbon sequestration, recreational services, biodiversity conservation, watershed protection, soil formation, colonisation and pollination services were found to be pertinent to consider for payment to mountain forest conservation communities in Nepal and India Himalaya.

Moreover, to explore suitable options for PES to our context, a continuous survey of similar experiences, learning, and initiatives was made during the pilot period. We found that the market-based mechanisms that involve ecosystem services are still in its initial stage of development. However, in a few thousand sites on the world the political institutions and market mechanisms for ecosystem service conservation are being developed at the moment. An example is the Habitat Conservation Plans in which land owners are required to make efforts to mitigate for the 'taking' of species protected by the U.S. Endangered Species Act. Using a valuable ecosystem on one place should require restoring the same habitat on another place. Other examples are the wetland banking in the United States and the now popular selling of carbon sequestration services of forest ecosystem in the international market.

Beneficiaries of the conservation can pay to the people who are conserving the ecosystem services. The payment needs to be enough to make it financially possible/attractive to people to conserve the ecosystem and have desired land use sustainability. An example is the Costa Rica watershed conservation. This example is very important with respect to the huge number of watersheds in Nepal and India. The people who conserve the ecosystem can also be given a new source of income. Products can be marketed with a premium on the prices for biodiversity conserving. The Shade-grown coffee of Mexico for example is sold for a higher price than the coffee that is not grown under soil protecting trees. Ecotourism is another possibility. Entry fees to protected areas and national parks can be charged to visitors.

Experiences of different parts of the world indicate that market-based payments are difficult to achieve, particularly in developing countries where poverty is still a major issue, and awareness is low. Ecosystem services in these countries suffer both from oversight by governments and lack of market mechanism. Governments would not need to assess the economic values of each of ecosystem services in precise terms, but accord some sort of their relative values in general.

Assessment of Forest Carbon Value of Nepal and Uttaranchal India

The project team assessed forest carbon and quantified contribution of forests to carbon-sequestration in Nepal and Uttaranchal based on the existing data and growing stock estimation. This was the best alternative to the more precise estimation in the given time limitation to make periodic assessments of tree growth over the years, financial resources, and scope and nature of the pilot study. The detail of the assessment and findings is given in Research Report section 2, and the highlight of the findings is given below.

The formation of community forest user groups (CFUGs) in Nepal has played a significant role in restoring degraded forests. In Uttaranchal the government has taken an initiative to put community forest in place. In terms of carbon sequestration of community forests, Tewari and Phartiyal (2006) taking two cases in Nepal and three cases in Uttaranchal recorded that an average of 2.1 t C/ha/yr (Nepal) and 3.7 t C/ha/yr (Uttaranchal) is sequestered. At this rate, a community forest area of 100 ha can yield about US $3,953 (IRs 166,000) in Uttaranchal, and US $2,730 (NRs 196,560) in Nepal (estimated at the rate of US $13 per t carbon). Though not a huge amount, this is can be a substantial cash income for poor local people.

In whole of Uttaranchal, in relatively undisturbed forests carbon sequestration rates in total biomass (above ground plus below ground) generally range between 4 and 5.6 t C /ha/yr, which are similar to those reported for tropical forests. However, the average value of sequestration for the region is about half as much as above.

This gives a total amount of sequestration in entire forest area of Uttaranchal, about 6.6 million t C per year. Its value at the rate of US $13 per ton carbon comes to US $85.5 million or about 3.1 billion Indian rupees or NRs 5 billion (1 US $= IRs. 46; 1 US $ = NRs. 72). In Kumaun region of Uttaranchal, Chirpine (Pinus roxburghii) forest is the largest contributor to carbon sequester, but at the state level temperate broad leaved forests, in which various Oaks dominate, account for the largest fraction of carbon accumulation.

Similarly, in Nepal, as for estimation of productivity we used appropriate quotients derived from studies in Uttaranchal and in certain sites of Nepal. Our estimation shows approximately 126 million t C is stored in the tree stems of Nepal forests. Since the forest soil pool is likely to be of a similar size, the total forest C pool can be assumed to be about 250 million t in Nepal.

The yearly C sequestration from all forest comes to about 10 million t, contributions being large from sal forests, oak forests, pine forests and fir forests. Since our estimates do not include branches, which may account for 20-40% of biomass in forest types like oak and other broadleaved species, we suggest that actual yearly carbon sequestration could easily be about 15 million t. Furthermore, this estimate does not include the additional revival of community forests, which have clearly shown signs of recovery during the last decade or so. National parks, sanctuaries and other protected areas have some of the least disturbed forests of Nepal. We estimate that at present forests in Nepal sequester about 20-25 million t C each year, which gives a value US $260-325 million.

Our study shows that forests managed by communities both in Uttaranchal and Nepal can sequester carbon in addition to meeting their needs of subsistence living, provided the area of forests under their control is sizeable. Payment for carbon sequestration may be used as an economic incentive for further improvement of the forest management.

Assessment of Recreational Service value of Nepal and Uttaranchal Mountain Forests

An important aspect of Himalayas and Himalayan forests is the recreational services provided by them. The Himalayan forests attract a number of local, regional and international tourists. In order to estimate the value of recreational services, an extensive study was carried out in Nepal and Uttaranchal.

The sites selected for the primary data collection were: Chitawan National Park, Nagarkot, Pokhara and Langtang National Park in Nepal and Nainital, Bhimtal, Sattal, Naukuchiatal, Mussoorie and Jim Corbett Park in Uttaranchal. A total of 369 tourists-242 domestic and 127 were selected at random from the sites in Nepal in the month of February and March 2006. In Uttaranchal, 279 local and 156 foreign tourists were selected at random in the months of April to June, 2006.

The analysis and results based on f the 4 sites in Nepal show that the value derived from domestic tourists in the Himalayan forests is to the tune of US $3.8 to 4.5 (NRs 273 to 323) per hectare. Accordingly, the total value of Himalayan forests for domestic tourists comes out to be US $60,000 to US $70,000 (NRs 4.06 million to 5.06 million). Similarly, the value of Himalayan forests for foreign tourists comes out to be US $1.04 to 1.85 million. The total tourism value from Himalayan forests falls between US $272-526 (NRs. 18,490 to 35,797) per hectare.

Similarly, the value of Himalayan forests for foreign tourists to six sites in Uttaranchal comes out to US $3.7 to 7.6 million. The total tourism value from foreign tourists comes out to US $48 to 102 (IRs 1,985 to 4,290) per hectare.

The findings are expected to be useful to the governments and other stakeholders of both the countries in terms of designing and planning participatory conservation initiatives;

strategizing buffer zone management approaches; determining conservation or entrance fee for tourists; and identifying roles and developing revenue sharing mechanisms among local communities, governments, and other stakeholders.

Sensitization, Interaction, and Capacity Building of the Decision Makers and Key Stakeholders

As payment or compensation and rewards of ecosystem services is a new area and recently budding concept in conservation, there has been a huge gap in understanding and realizing the ecosystem service oriented approach in view of conservation and poverty reduction. From the beginning of the pilot project, we made a continuous attempt to involve relevant stakeholders from government and non-government sectors, and organized and facilitated several forums including a regional level stakeholders' meeting in Delhi. These interactions and workshops were helpful to educate, sensitize, and share experiences and learning among relevant stakeholders of Nepal and Uttaranchal India.

We organized a country level meeting through Nepal NTFP Network (NNN) in Nepal on July 25, 2006 with the objectives of educating policy makers and other stakeholders on ecosystem services, and looking options for future collaboration in advancing the conservation movement.

The meeting was participated by a wide range of key stakeholders consisting of senior officials from government, Member of Parliament, representatives from non-government, community federations, and civil society. Prof. S.P. Singh, a research team member (renowned ecologist) along with other team members provided a training and facilitated sharing and discussion on PES.

Furthermore, to facilitate learning across the region, we organized a regional workshop in Delhi in August 22-23, 2006 involving key stakeholders of Nepal and Uttaranchal India, and the proceedings of the workshop was widely circulated among relevant individuals, institutions, and donors (for detail see the Workshop Proceedings included as a separate document along with this report). To give basic insights and make the stakeholders familiar with the recent trends, practices, and developments on the valuation and payments of ecosystem services around the world, a brief synopsis note was prepared and disseminated to outreach policy makers and pertinent stakeholders.

The synopsis note is also included in the proceedings. As reflected by most of the workshop participants, the workshop was very useful, insightful, and the presence of a wide range of stakeholders from Nepal and India made it possible to make common understanding, regional perspectives, and share ideas and strategies on possible actions and key issues in relation to PES. Most of the participants offered their commitment to move the PES initiatives ahead, and agreed to work together. They also opined that ANSAB should continue coordinating PES initiatives and program development involving all relevant stakeholders at regional level.

From these interactions, forums, and awareness activities, we found that there has been a mounting interest in payment for environmental services as a means to secure improved natural resource management in the cases of Nepal and Uttaranchal, where local forest management communities are not able to capture the resulting benefits. Among the reasons for this interest were its potential for improving upon past mechanisms that have had uneven success, and the possibility that it could offer impoverished rural forest management communities a market through which they can raise their incomes while also conserving the natural resource base.

In the process, we noticed that many researchers, community federations, and particularly advocates for the poor have become enthusiastic about the prospects for PES to play the role of conserving the natural resource base, raising land productivity, and alleviating poverty, but there were legitimate fears that PES risks becoming just another development fad because of enthusiasm about its potential outpacing analysis of what it could actually achieve. As expressed, perhaps the most critical element in making PES work and provide benefits to poor local forest management communities was to identify and mobilize users of environmental services who would be willing and able to pay the communities to provide services, with assurance that the service has been actually provided. The role of donor organizations, government officials, and policy makers to further promote and support on this agenda was felt crucial.

Apart from contributing towards making PES as a conservation agenda among stakeholders, all these interactions and consultations in the pilot initiative also identified a number of possibilities, opportunities and areas for further actions and collaborations. The pilot phase has clearly indicated that there is a need to understand the opportunities and requirements of CDM procedures and payment mechanisms, build the capacity of local communities to participate in PES, and establish and/or strengthen national system and procedures required to implement the mechanism.

PROJECT DESIGN AND IMPLEMENTATION

The project adopted a participatory process in all its research and capacity building activities. Based on the project proposal, a detail action plan was designed at the beginning with the inputs from key stakeholders and research team members from India and Nepal, which became a guide for the implementation of research activities. Regular interactions among research team members, workshops and meetings with stakeholders, and continuous support and advice from IDRC were useful to carry out the research activities.

Table: An outline of key activities and implementation

Key activities	Methods	Remarks
Identification of ecosystem services, their providers and receivers	Consultations, interaction and dialogues, literature reviews, review of on-going initiatives	Qualitative information; list of services, their providers, and receivers
Assessment of recreational services	Travel Cost Method	Primary survey in Nepal and Uttaranchal India
Assessment of forest carbon of Uttaranchal and Nepal	Periodical biomass estimate of the Himalayan Forests	Secondary Data: growing stock, density and basal area of tree species, composition etc.
Facilitation of dialogues and interactions on PES	Meeting, workshop, NNN forum	Dissemination of workshop proceedings, synopsis notes, ANSAB website
Review of similar initiatives and look for suitable models	Literature review, interaction with similar organizations, attending forums and meetings	Exploration of prospects of payment options to mountain communities, particularly carbon

Project Management

The research project activities took place as planned, and stakeholders from government and non-government both from Nepal and India were found enthusiastic in the research process. From project initiation to implementation and management, IDRC continuously encouraged us to take all planned actions, without which the research project would not have achieved its objectives. Not only as a donor, IDRC also provided a lot of technical advice, research inputs and managerial support, and allowed the project team to become innovative, adaptive and flexible to carry out the research work.

PROJECT OUTPUTS, IMPACTS, AND DISSEMINATION

The major outcomes of the project include:

(i) raised broad level awareness on PES among policy makers and key stakeholders in Nepal and Uttaranchal India,

(ii) identified important ecosystem services, their providers and receivers,

(iii) reviewed current practices and development on PES, and

(iv) assessed value of recreational services and forest carbon.

The last three outputs are found in a separate research report attached to it. As the exploratory study itself was among the pioneer initiatives in the field of ecosystem services, it has created an enabling ambience for the further research and action, and prepared foundation for upcoming relevant efforts made in this area to promote conservation and livelihood opportunities. Through this initiative, we found that there has been a growing interest in payment for environmental services as a means to secure improved natural resource management, as well as the possibility that it will offer impoverished rural forest management communities a market through which they can raise their incomes while also preserving the natural resource base. In this pilot process, we observed that many researchers, donor organizations, policy makers, community federations, and advocates for the poor have become enthusiastic about the prospects for PES to play the role of conserving the natural resource base, raising land productivity, and alleviating poverty.

Through organizing forums such as NNN and regional stakeholders meeting, production of proceedings and reports, as well as through sharing project activities and its findings at various forums, the outcomes of the project initiatives are being disseminated. Moreover, producing and disseminating the synopsis on PES to the target clients being undertaken continuously is helping to increase the level of awareness among the relevant stakeholders and policy makers.

OVERALL ASSESSMENT

Besides the contribution of the project in identifying major ecosystem services, their providers and receivers, assessing carbon stock and recreational services, and contributing to raise awareness among local and regional stakeholders, it was a learning opportunity for most of the stakeholders who participated in the process.

The activities took place as planned, and it received a strategic support from IDRC for the research process. From the time of its implementation, all the relevant stakeholders have realized that the PES initiative is crucial. Despite the fact that the research has been done in a small scale, short-term, and could not cover many services in terms of assessment, the approach and lessons learned made from the research stands for and can be applicable to other numerous cases and services. The research findings are expected to be useful to the governments and other relevant organizations to build on their works and it will be an important asset for the whole movement of conservation in the region. This has clearly created a foundation for the bigger interventions in the future.

RECOMMENDATIONS

Through multistakeholders processes and learning from the research activities, the pilot initiative identified a number of possibilities, opportunities and areas for further actions and interventions.

- With this initiative, there is a clear indication that there is a need of bigger intervention in the area of PES that incorporates strengthening the capacity of local communities to participate in PES, establishing and/or strengthening national system and institutional procedures required to implement the payment mechanism, and facilitating in understanding of the opportunities and requirements of CDM procedures.
- Moreover, to operationalize PES actually on the ground, it requires developing appropriate methods for assessing the value of ecosystem services appropriate to mountain terrain; preparing guidelines for local community forest management groups to enable them for claiming carbon sequestration and other social and environmental benefits in line with CDM; and providing technical assistance to the communities for taking measures to improve the flow of services and minimize carbon leakages. The local communities need further technical assistance in resources assessment, documentation, and making claims for PES.
- As some services are of local as well as regional in nature, there is a need to build alliance among key stakeholders, policy makers, and experts at national and regional levels.

17

Sino-Himalayan Mountain Forests

HIS region is made up of the mid-and high-elevation forests, scrub and grasslands that cloak the southern slopes of the Himalayas and the mountains of south-west China and northern Indochina. A total of 28 threatened species are confined (as breeding birds) to the Sino-Himalayan mountain forests, including six which are relatively widespread in distribution, and 22 which inhabit one of the region's six Endemic Bird Areas: Western Himalayas, Eastern Himalayas, Shanxi mountains, Central Sichuan mountains, West Sichuan mountains and Yunnan mountains. All 28 taxa are considered Vulnerable, apart from the Endangered White-browed Nuthatch, which has a tiny range, and the Critically Endangered Himalayan Quail, which has not been seen for over a century and may be extinct.

Key habitats Montane temperate, subtropical and subalpine forest, and associated grassland and scrub.

Altitude 350-4,500 m.

Countries and territories China (Tibet, Qinghai, Gansu, Sichuan, Yunnan, Guizhou, Shaanxi, Shanxi, Hebei, Beijing, Guangxi); Pakistan; India (Jammu and Kashmir, Himachal Pradesh, Uttaranchal, West Bengal, Sikkim, Arunachal Pradesh, Assam, Meghalaya, Nagaland, Manipur, Mizoram); Nepal; Bhutan; Myanmar; Thailand; Laos; Vietnam.

Eighteen IBAs have been selected, which together support populations of all threatened forest birds of this region apart from Himalayan Quail and possibly Rusty-throated Wren-babbler, and include some of the largest and richest forests remaining in the Sino-Himalayan mountains. Many other forest sites in this region with significant populations of threatened forest birds will be documented during BirdLife's ongoing IBA Project.

CURRENT STATUS OF HABITATS AND THREATENED SPECIES

The extent of forest loss varies widely within this region. In China, large-scale logging operations have clear-felled huge areas of forest, including subalpine forests up to the treeline. In Sichuan, forest cover declined from 19% to 12.6% between the early 1950s and 1988 and in Yunnan it declined from c.55% to c.30% between the early 1950s and 1975; subsequent loss of habitat in China has, if anything, been even more rapid (see F03: South-east Chinese forests). However, some extensive tracts of forest are protected in reserves (often established for charismatic mammals such as giant panda Ailuropoda melanoleuca and Yunnan snubnosed monkey Rhinopithecus bieti) or survive in unlogged areas, and in 1998 a national logging ban restricted logging to local subsistence needs. In the Himalayas, although natural habitat remains relatively secure at high altitudes, forests at mid-elevations tend to be under greater pressure, and are now highly fragmented in many areas.

Three quarters of original forest cover has been lost in the western Himalayas, and this figure is even higher for Nepal, where almost all lower-altitude subtropical forests have been lost or degraded. In north-east India and northern Myanmar the situation is less extreme, as large, almost continuous areas of mid-and high-altitude forests remain. However, forests were being rapidly logged in north-east India until a recent ban, and shifting cultivation has cleared or degraded large areas. In Bhutan an admirable national policy proposes to maintain forests over 60% of the country, although some localised habitat loss has been reported. Some montane forests in Myanmar, Thailand, Laos and Vietnam have been badly affected by clearance for permanent and (especially) shifting agriculture, as well as commercial timber extraction; the situation is particularly acute in Chin State, Myanmar, northern Laos and northwest Vietnam, but some large areas of relatively undisturbed forest remain, for example in northern Myanmar and the Annamite mountains in Laos and Vietnam.

CONSERVATION ISSUES AND STRATEGIC SOLUTIONS

Shifting Cultivation

Some parts of the region are populated by ethnic groups whose lifestyle is based on shifting or semi-shifting cultivation. Practised on a small scale using long clearing cycles, this has little lasting impact and the forest eventually recovers. However, in many areas increased population pressure and a reduction in the area of forest available have resulted in a rapid shortening of the cycle, and an increase in pioneer shifting cultivation, which is causing widespread forest loss and degradation, principally in the mountains of north-east India, Myanmar and northern Indochina. Often associated with shifting cultivation, fires have been one of biggest causes of montane forest loss in northern Vietnam and Laos.

There is an urgent need to promote sustainable forms of upland agriculture that do not result in net loss of natural forest, including improved agricultural and agroforestry practices that enable farmers to remain longer on established clearings, and thereby reduce their demand for new land. Efforts are needed to rehabilitate abandoned land, including the development of community forestry plantations. At selected key sites, projects should integrate conservation and land-use development, and work in collaboration with local people. Such projects could prevent shifting cultivation within core areas of reserves, and control it in buffer zones. Simple socio-economic incentives to replace destructive practices by shifting cultivators should be promoted through environmental awareness and training programmes.

Conversion to Agriculture and Plantations

Clearance for permanent agriculture and plantations has contributed to the reduction and fragmentation of natural forests in many areas. Deforestation for agriculture is now illegal in China, but small-scale encroachment still happens. Conversion for tea and other plantations is still taking place in north-east India. These activities need to be effectively banned within core areas of reserves, and controlled in buffer zones. In China (and probably elsewhere), disputes over administrative boundaries need to be resolved and land ownership and land-use rights clarified, to help strengthen forest management and prevent illegal conversion for agriculture.

Forestry and Illegal Logging

Until recently, commercial logging was a major reason for the diminution of natural forests in this region, particularly subtropical forests at mid-altitudes. The clearance and degradation of forests has caused major environmental problems, including erosion, which causes siltation of rivers, and damage to watersheds, which affects water supplies (causing periodic flooding and drought). A national logging ban was enacted in China in 1998, which limits logging to local subsistence needs. Following disastrous floods in 1992, logging was banned in North West Frontier Province, Pakistan; although the ban was lifted in 2001, strict new regulations have so far prevented the resumption of widescale logging. Logging and timber export was recently banned in Arunachal Pradesh and other north-east Indian states. These bans have greatly reduced the rate of forest loss, but some illegal logging continues, and in Arunachal Pradesh it is still legal to cut timber to supply plywood and veneer factories. In Laos and Vietnam, logging of the commercially very valuable conifer Fokienia hodginsii, mainly for export to Japan, affects montane areas. The commercial logging bans in China and India should be continued, and, where appropriate, similar restrictions promoted in other parts of the region. The ban in China allows the forestry authorities to work together with local communities, NGOs and conservationists to develop sustainable forestry under the National Forest Protection Program.

Measures are needed to minimise illegal logging, particularly in protected areas and other sites of high biodiversity value. Since the ban, forestry workers in Sichuan have been redeployed in replanting some of the steeper denuded slopes, mainly using seeds from local broadleaf trees; similar reforestation with appropriate mixtures of native tree species is needed elsewhere in the region. In Pakistan, the government is currently revising its Forest Working Plan, which provides an opportunity to prescribe extraction rates and logging practices which benefit local people and conserve biodiversity.

Exploitation of Forest Products

The collection of wood and other forest vegetation for fuel, construction material and fodder is causing forest degradation in many parts of the region. The collection of fuelwood from collective forests by local people is permitted in China, but poses a threat to forest ecosystems, particularly as logging waste is no longer available for fuel. In some areas of Nepal (and presumably also India), the cutting of fuelwood to provide heating and hot water for tourists is degrading forests near trekking routes. These activities need to be minimised throughout, and controlled within core zones of protected areas. Community or collective forests need to be established more widely, and their management improved and made more sustainable through training in forestry techniques for local people. Sustainable alternatives to fuelwood should be promoted, including the use of biogas (produced from livestock manure) and solar power.

Development (Urban, Industrial, Etc.)

New roads, dams, mines, buildings and other developments strongly contribute to habitat loss in this region, both by directly damaging forests, and indirectly by displacing people into forest areas. Construction of roads in highland areas may cause landslips, and provide improved access to remote montane habitats for shifting cultivators, illegal loggers, hunters and harvesters of forest products. Environmental impact assessments should be conducted for development projects (and associated new and upgraded access routes) that have the potential to damage forested areas, with appropriate mitigation plans. New developments should be avoided near protected areas and other sites of high biodiversity value.

Disturbance and Livestock Grazing

In addition to the permanent residents, there are seasonal influxes of large numbers of people, their livestock and dogs into montane habitats. In summer, flocks of sheep, goats or yaks are taken to the high-altitude forests and alpine grasslands, damaging vegetation structure, particularly the understorey; moreover, production of cheese from yak milk requires considerable fuelwood. The summer peak in both grazing and the (locally large-scale) collection of edible fungi and medicinal plants coincides with the bird breeding season, probably posing a threat to some threatened species (e.g. partridges and pheasants) through disturbance and hunting. New management measures are needed in areas where human disturbance and overgrazing are a problem; for example, in the Daliang Shan in Sichuan control of livestock movements through forests to grazing areas is required, along with restrictions on bamboo-shoot collecting.

PROTECTED AREAS COVERAGE AND MANAGEMENT

Gaps in Protected Areas System

There are many protected areas in this region, which together support populations of most threatened birds. However, it is unclear whether some of the more poorly known species, such as Himalayan Quail, Dark-rumped Swift, White-speckled Laughingthrush and Rusty-throated Wren-babbler, are adequately covered by existing reserves. The most important populations of Western Tragopan in northern Pakistan are currently unprotected, notably in the Palas valley; conservation measures are needed to protect these forests from high-impact commercial logging. Where surveys locate important populations of poorly known species, or reveal that current levels of protection are inadequate (as in the case of Hume's Pheasant in India), new reserves need to be established for the species in question.

Many protected areas are too small to support viable populations of the larger threatened species; to improve coverage of these low-density birds, selected reserves should be enlarged, and their buffer zones expanded. Villagers are often not opposed to the idea of protected areas, and indeed themselves confer some level of protection to montane forests in order to maintain their water supply and populations of prey species; such local protection could be reinforced and supported, by encouraging communities to establish village sanctuaries. The protected areas system in Myanmar is currently being reviewed and revised, and surveys are required in ornithologically undocumented areas to locate suitable sites for new reserves, for example in Shan State to safeguard Hume's Pheasant and Giant Nuthatch.

Weaknesses in Reserve Management

There are major problems with the management of protected areas, linked to a lack of resources and the practical difficulties associated with remote mountainous terrain, with forestry departments in most countries understaffed, underfunded and badly equipped. As a consequence, illegal activities are widespread in many reserves, including logging, mining, forest grazing, agricultural encroachment, hunting, etc. Increased resources and improved management planning and training of reserve staff are needed, with a particular focus on the most outstanding sites for threatened biodiversity. Appropriate funding and training of the governmental departments responsible for conservation are also required. In China, the National Endangered Plant and Wildlife Protection and Nature Reserve Construction Program is a new government initiative that has the potential to make these types of improvement.

EXPLOITATION OF WILDLIFE

Hunting and Trapping

Shooting and snaring of wildlife is common throughout much of this region, which is populated by ethnic groups whose lifestyle is based on shifting or semi shifting cultivation and hunting, although pressure is less intense in Bhutan and Tibet for cultural reasons. The larger forest species are probably most seriously affected, notably the hornbills, and partridges and pheasants, which have been much reduced in many areas. Improved law enforcement is required to prevent illegal hunting both inside and outside protected areas. Control of gun ownership is meeting with some success in Laos and Vietnam, and could be expanded to other countries in the region, particularly near important protected areas. Education programmes concerned with forest conservation, threatened species and the hunting laws could help reduce hunting pressure, possibly using the most charismatic threatened forest birds such as Blyth's Tragopan or Rufous-necked Hornbill as flagships. Community-based initiatives, including signing of stakeholder agreements with local households and establishment of patrolling groups, have helped control hunting at key sites in Vietnam, and should be tried in other areas of high biodiversity value.

GAPS IN KNOWLEDGE

Inadequate Data on Threatened Birds

Knowledge of the distribution and ecology of the threatened birds is very incomplete, including their tolerance of logging and other modifications of their habitats. Two Himalayan species-Himalayan Quail in the west and Rusty-throated Wren-babbler in the east-have gone unreported for years, and need to be searched for. Most other Eastern Himalayan species are poorly known, notably Chestnut-breasted Partridge, Dark-rumped Swift, Snowy-throated Babbler and Rusty-bellied Shortwing, and surveys are required throughout the remaining forests in the highlands of north-east India, Bhutan and northern Myanmar. In China, surveys are required for Whitespeckled Laughingthrush, to determine whether it has populations in any protected areas and, if not, which of its sites should be established as reserves. The threatened species of the West and Central Sichuan mountains EBAs are poorly known, most notably Rufous-headed Robin, Black-throated Blue Robin and Rusty-throated Parrotbill, and studies are required to investigate whether these birds are sufficiently protected by the network of reserves established for giant panda and other mammals.

FLORA AND VEGETATION OF AFGHANISTAN

Siegmar-W. Breckle

Afghanistan is a very mountainous country. It offers a big variety of ecological conditions, this means a big variety of vegetation types is covering land surface. These vegetation types are consisting of a high biodiversity, since the floristic influence from various neighbour regions is a considerable factor in floristic and vegetation pattern. On the other hand, Afghanistan is a very dry country with scarce rainfalls (Flohn 1969), but again very varying between north and south, west and east, lowlands and mountains.

Flora of Afghanistan

By far the most comprehensive source for the Afghanistan flora is Rechinger's "Flora Iranica", which started in 1963 (Breckle & Frey 1976c) and is now almost completed with about 180 deliveries of the various plant families. Additionally many other short research papers on the flora and vegetation of various parts have been published. Afghanistan is certainly a country which flora and vegetation has been studied quite in detail (Breckle et al. 1969, 1975, Breckle 1981, 1999), however, mainly before the critical times of the Sovjet imperialism and subsequent civil wars.

Though Afghanistan is a rather dry country with a high percentage of deserts and semideserts, the number of vascular plant species is distinctly higher than in the climatically more humid Germany. GROOMBRIDGE (1992) gives an estimate of 3500 species and 30-35% of endemics, as well as about 5-10% of species, which might be added by future new discoveries. Our estimate is about 5000 species and about 25-30% of endemics.

The chorological types include species with circumboreal, with holarctic, with central Asian, with himalayan, with irano-turanian, with sahara-sindian, with sudanian, with deccanic floristic relations, but then also those, which are more restricted to specific regions, as e.g. Pamir, Wakhan, Central Afghan mountains, Western, central and/or Eastern Hindu Kush. Endemism is a character to be restricted to a distinct geographical unit, not to a state. This makes it difficult to judge, since many floras are written to describe the occurence of species within political borders, which normally makes not much sense.

Precipitation and altitude are conditioning factors resulting in the diversity of the country's flora. A limited area in the east and southeast receives the impact of the Indian monsoons and belongs to the sub-tropical zone. Altitude, throughout all zones, may allow for the development of different strata of vegetation. Thus, diverse ecological conditions, ranging from barren deserts to lush sub-tropical regions to high alpine nival regions, have favored the establishment of a complex and varied flora. Common physiognomic features of the plants of the region are gray or white hairs, gray bark that is particularly thick at the base, reduction of leaf area and cushion growth that protects the plants against the strong insolation, dry wind and sand-drift that threaten to dry them out. Plants are often characterized by spiny stems and leaves or glands containing etheric (essential) oils or poisonous secondary compounds or other elements that render them unpalatable to the animals that for centuries have exerted heavy impact on the flora.

In order of numerical importance the following major families are found in Afghanistan. More than 500 species are known from the Asteraceae (Compositae) plant family, including about 100 species of Artemisia. The second biggest genus in the area is Cousinia after Astragalus. Within the Flora Iranica Rechinger (1972) mentions 355 species of Cousinia, describing not less than 61 as new species. From Afghanistan there are reported 144 species of Cousinia, 93 of them endemic to Afghanistan. 138 species from Iran, 40 from Turcomania, 31 from adjacent Pakistan, 21 from Iraq. The family Fabaceae (Leguminosae) is attested with some 400-500 species of which the genus Astragalus is by far most numerous. In the Brassicaceae (Cruciferae) family about 250 species are found, especially Brassica, which includes cabbage, mustard and radish. There are more than 150 species of the Poaceae (Gramineae) family including such important cultivated plants as wheat, rice, barley, maize and sugar cane. Other grasses include the genera Agropyron (wheatgrass), Poa (bluegrass), Arundo (grainreed), Cymbopogon (lemon grass) and Andropogon (bluestem). In the steppes many Festuca, Bromus, Stipa spp. occur as well. More than 180 species are recorded from the

Lamiaceae (Labiatae) family, including Phlomis (Jerusalem sage), Thymus (thyme), Mentha (mint), Nepeta (cat mint), Origanum and Eremostachys. The family Apiaceae (Umbelliferae) is represented by more than 100 species; most notable of which is Ferula assafoetida, an item of export and other giant hapaxanthic umbellifers from Ferula or Dorema. There are many other drugs derived from naturally occuring species in the area (Breckle 1979, 1982, Breckle & Unger 1977).

Chenopodiaceae halophytes are common, especially Salsola, Suaeda, Arthrophytum, Halostachys and Halocharis. On the other side the orchids (Orchidaceae), which are common in the Mediterranean and in the Himalaya spread only with few species to the area. From Afghanistan by Renz (1978) only 13 species are recorded (Iran: 48, Talysch: 28, Iraq 21, Flora Iranica total: 63). In Iridaceae, there are recorded 35 species in Afghanistan and the same number from Iran, 18 from Iraq, 10 from Turcomania, a total of 65 from the whole Flora Iranica region. A very typical genus of the drier mountain areas is Eremurus (steppe-lilies), where 23 species are known from the Flora Iranica area, 19 of those from Afghanistan and only 7 from Iran. The wild Tulipa (tulips) comprise 34 species in the Flora Iranica area, 17 in Afghanistan, 18 in Iran.

Vegetation of Afghanistan

Vegetation all over Afghanistan has been severely influenced by man and only a few high mountain and very dry desert areas retain a quasi natural vegetation cover. In most parts the vegetation depends on the winter rain, in the south winter rains are often irregular. Rainfall increases to the north and east resulting in better vegetation conditions in these parts. The eastern parts receive additionally some monsoon rains in summer. Vegetation types have been studied in detail by Freitag (1971a,b). His survey is still the most complete of the area, especially also for the eastern, monsoonal influenced more humid parts with Himalayan forest types.

The main vegetation types which are shown on the map (Vegetation of Afghanistan), are:

Calligonum-Aristida-Sanddesert (1a)

Haloxylon salicornicum-Desert (1b)

Other Deserts (rich in Chenopod.) (1c)

Ephemeral Desert (1d)

Dwarf Amygdalus-Semidesert (2)

Subtropical dry Scrub and Savannah (3)

Pistacia vera-Woodlands (4a)

Pistacia atlantica-Woodlands (4b)

Juniperus-Woodlands (5a)

Amygdalus-Woodlands (5b)

Sclerophyllous Oak Forests (6)

Conifer Forests (7)

Rhododendron-Krummholz (8)

Thorny Cushions, subalpine and alpine semideserts and meadows (9)

Nival belt, glaciers (10)

Azonal riverine vegetation (11a)

Swamps, Salt swamps, lakes (11b)

These vegetation types indicated on the map are the "natural potential vegetation", which would be the vegetation cover without human activities. It gives an idea on the natural potential and resources of the various regions. Today, by longlasting exploitation, grazing, agriculture and irrigation, deforestation, many of these original vegetation types are only left on few spots, remote places, and are replaced by substituted associations poorer in shape, diversity and productivity, as well as also the soils are often degraded, eroded or totally destroyed.

Desert Vegetation

The deserts of the north, west and south, in Registan and Dashte Margo contain active sand dune areas and dunes fixed by a rather open vegetation (1a). The flora here is scarcely modified by man. The main plants are Haloxylon persicum, Calligonum spp. and perennial Aristida spp. In lower lying saline areas, Chenopodiaceae are dominant (1c) and in the salt plains of Seistan the vegetation (1b) is characterized by Haloxylon salicornicum, Salsola spp., Ephedra scoparia and Tamarix spp. In some parts the ephemeral vegetation (1d) is very characteristic, in summer these areas look totally dry and dead. In saline flats in the north the black saxaul Haloxylon aphyllum can form open woodlands, but has been heavily used, see also paragraph azonal vegetation below. An overview on the Irano-Afghan deserts is given by Breckle (1983).

Steppe and Semidesert Vegetation

The steppes in Afghanistan are scarce in typical steppe grasses, they should be named semi-deserts. Anyhow, they are the most important grazing areas where large number of nomads graze their livestock on a seasonal basis. The low lying steppes and semideserts in the west and south are dominated by an open vegetation of Artemisia herba-alba and other species of this genus, Zygophyllum spp., other dwarf shrubs are spiny Amygdalus (2), partly Acantholimon spp., Acanthophyllum spp., Atriplex spp., Alhagi camelorum, and Cousinia spp., the graminoids are often reduced by heavy grazing, Poa, Agropyrum, Stipa, Festuca, Carex and others are more common only on remote or inaccesible areas. An Amygdalis brahuica community is found between 1000 and 2000 m altitude also in the dry valleys of the east.

Along dry river beds there are thorny belts of Stocksia brahuica, Amygdalus communis and Convolvulus spinosus. The floral composition is very variable and depends on humidity, length of winter, sand composition, wind force and grazing pressure. More humid azonal places have denser vegetation with a richer species composition (11a). In areas west of Herat with cold winters and in some parts in the north, Artemisia spp. and Ferula spp. dominate along with geophytes like Iris songarica, Tulipa, Iris and Allium spp.

The northern loess zone supports a grass steppe dominated by Poa bulbosa or Carex pachystylis with Bromus spp., Agropyron spp., Festuca spp., etc. Poppy and herbaceous bulbs such as Anemone, Gagea, Tulipa. Iris, Merendera and Muscari are the first flowering plants in spring. Shrubs are completely absent 1d). In the spring the ground cover is 30-90%, but most of the plants die back from lack of water in the summer.

In the higher mountains there are other areas of semi desert. Around Bamiyan they are dominated by Salsola spp. High level steppes benefit from a higher precipitation as well as lower evaporation. Overgrazing generally favors the less palatable Artemisia shrubs and annuals at the cost of the palatable perennials. In dry years when the annuals do not germinate, heavy mortality of domestic animals takes place.

Arid Sub-tropical Woodlands and Savannah

Perennial grasses and thorny evergreen shrubs and small trees predominate in the lower Kabul valley which experiences hot summers with few occasional monsoon rains and moderate winters. Heavy grazing and fuel wood collection have reduced the shrubs and led to an increase of annuals. A Zizyphus nummularia community occupies the lower regions up to 750 m. This is replaced at higher levels with a Salvia-Pistacia community. In the dry valley Acacia modesta penetrates the vegetation, it resembles already a subtropical savannah with a few C4-grasses (Aristida, Panicum). In Pakhtia also the dwarf palm Nanorhops ritchieana occurs, which leaves are heavily used for furniture and wattlework. Between 700 and 1300 m there is sometimes a Reptonia buxifolia and Olea ferruginea woodland which is heavily utilized for fodder and as pasture land.

Pistacia Woodlands

To the north of the Hindu Kush on the extensive loess plains between 600 and 1600 m woodlands of Pistacia vera (4a) with some Amygdalis bucharica and in the northeast remnants of Cercis griffithii are characteristic. On the lower slopes of the Hindu Kush open Pistacia woodlands replace the Amygdalus community in higher parts in the south, resp. the Juniperus woodlands in the north. The southern slopes of the Hindu Kush are characterized by 4-6 m high Pistacia atlantica (cabulica, khinjuk) (4b) and are rich in herbs like Gagea, Anemone and Allium spp.. On valley slopes Pistacia khinjuk and Cercis griffithii are sometimes found, especially in the Kabul and Logar Valleys. In the last century Cercis woodlands were much more common all around Kabul, also around Herat. The Pistacia vera and Juniperus excelsa woodlands are heavily exploited for charcoal production.

Amygdalus and Juniperus Scrublands

The upper part of the forest belt on the northern slopes of the Hindu Kush is formed by an open mixed woodland dominated by Juniperus excelsa, intermixed with other Juniperus species (5a).

On the same elevation between 2000 and 3000 m and in areas with more than 400 mm of precipitation in the south a 2.5-6 m high Amygdalus community (5b)is dominant; many scrub species and geophytes such as Eremurus, Corydalis, Rheum, Gagea, Tulipa, Iris, Allium spp. also occur in both types.

Amygdalus scrublands are often intermixed with the Pistacia woodlands, and can be intermediate between the semideserts of the south and west and the woodlands of the Hindu Kush. These areas are important for winter pasture. These woodlands are heavily used and badly degraded.

Himalayan type Evergreen Forests in East Afghanistan

Between 1200 and 2200 m the oak Quercus baloot (6) dominates a forest which is up to 15 m high; it has a rich undergrowth and several tree species including almonds Amygdalus kuramica and Pistacia khinjuk. It is heavily utilized for fodder, fruits and fuelwood and large parts have been destroyed to provide fuel for the main cities.

The remnants of Qu.baloot forest in the Panjshir valley, northeast of Kabul, forms the westernmost extension of the Himalayan forest belt. A few trees were even occuring near Top Dara in the Koh-e-Daman Plain near Charikar. Formerly also at the Latahband pass (some 25km east of Kabul) there were Qu.baloot remnants. In very humid places with high summer rainfall in the higher mountain belts Qu. baloot is replaced by Qu. dilatata and between 2400 and 2900 m by Qu.

semecarpifolia. Azonal associates in river valleys are Juglans regia, Acer turkestanicum and Pyrus pashia.

Temperate Coniferous Forests of East Afghanistan

The forest belt between 2200 and 2500 m in moderately humid parts is a 5-12 m high Pinus gerardiana woodland with local stands of Betula. A thorny Cotoneaster-Sophora-Rosa scrubland colonizes the areas after the pine has been felled.

Between 2500 and 3100 m Cedrus deodara forest is found. Depending on soil and humidity the cedars may be up to 30 m high and form a very dense forest. Large parts of the Cedrus forest have been exploited and replaced by a stable Artemisia community.

Logging has now reached even the western parts of Nuristan. In the humid areas the upper belt of the forest, up to an altitude of 3300 m, is formed by a 20-25 m high Picea smithiana-Abies webbiana forest, varying from valley to valley. In the dry areas a 10 m high Juniperus seravschanica-J. semiglobosa woodland is found. However, most areas have been cut for fuelwood and mature stands are rare. The herbaceous ground cover, especially along the streams is heavily grazed.

It is very interesting to note, that fossile conifer needles (similar to Pinus roxbourgii) and many other fossile leaves from a rather humid vegetation have been found in marl sediments at the Latahband Pass (Breckle 1967), probably being from about early Quaternary. This is indicating that monsoonal climate has reached much far to the west.

Krummholz

In areas of the east with monsoonal summer rains a dense 0.5-1 m high vegetation of Juniperus squamata, Rosa spp., Ribes spp. and Rhododendron spp. develops between 3000 and 3500 m, but only few sites are left. On deep soils, Salix spp. may dominate this community. On lower sites, at the tree line, the very rare Rhododendron afghanicum occured, but is extinct now (Breckle 1972). In parts of the Hindu Kush, a Juniperus nana community with many thorny dwarf shrubs occurs. Between 3600 and 4000 m in the dryer central and northern

Hindu Kush, there is a cushion scrubland with many different species of Acantholimon, Artemisia, Astragalus, Cousinia, Ephedra and Onobrychis. A similar thorny cushion shrubland, with very varying species composition changing from mountain ridge to mountain ridge is found in many of the Central Afghan high mountain areas (Paghman, Western Hindu Kush, Koh-e-Baba). Many endemics occur in this area.

Subalpine Thorny Cushions, Semideserts and Deserts, and Meadow Vegetation

On mountain ridges, above the tree line at about 3300 m subalpine and alpine shrublands, alpine heaths and meadows occur which offer good range forage for domestic animals. The subalpine and alpine vegetation of the Hindu Kush on dry sites is open and poor in species, but each slope may have another species pattern.

This belt is therefore typical for a high and endemic biodiversity. On wet sites (melting snow water etc.) a closed meadow canopy rich in species may occur. That of the Pamirs and Eastern Hindu Kush often is somehow denser with a great variety of herbs.

Usually, the alpine meadows, dominated by grasses and a variety of herbs, are heavily utilized during two months as summer pastures by nomads and the pastoral people. Studies on flora and ecology of vegetation have been performed by Breckle 1971b,e, 1973, 1974, 1975, 1988, 2002, 2004, Breckle & Frey 1974, 1976a,b. Additional data on the Wakhan and Pamir area are given in Agakhanjanz & Breckle 1995, 2002, 2004, Ahmadov et al. 2005, Breckle 2003, Breckle & Wucherer 2005, Breckle et al. 1969.

Nival Vegetation

In the Pamirs and in Central and Eastern Hindu Kush, the boundary with the nival zone is 4900 m on the northern exposed slopes and 5300-5400 on the southern exposed slopes. The higher peaks and ridges are not dominated by alpine heaths (Ericaceae), as it is sometimes wrongly recorded, but by a low and very open, very frost resistant herbaceous and semifruticose vegetation. The highest record of a vascular plant in Afghanistan is the beautiful Primula macrophylla in the central Hindu Kush at 5600 m. Sibbaldia cuneata is also known from about 5500m. There are 37 species recorded from above 5000m (Breckle 1974). Mosses and lichens occur even higher, up to the highest peaks on rocky surface.

Azonal vegetation: Rivers, Lakes

These systems have been drastically altered by human activity. The original forests of major river valleys have been replaced by irrigated crops. Dense vegetation is found in regularly flooded areas. This is dominated by Tamarix spp., Salix spp. and reeds (Phragmites australis, Typha) and, depending on the frequency of inundation, species such as Populus spp. Myricaria spp., Berberis spp., Crataegus spp., and Hippophaë.

Along the river beds (11b) on well drained areas with deep soils, many of the wild ancestors of cultivated fruit trees occur. These include the apple (Malus spp.), pear (Pyrus spp.) and almond (Amygdalus spp.) as well as grapes (Vitis spp.). Trees of Fraxinus spp., Acer spp., and Platanus spp. are also found here. But undisturbed natural riverine vegetation can not be found today. Little information is available on the vegetation of the lakes (11b) but Hamun-e-Puzak and Kol-e-Hashmat Khan are covered with reeds. One of the few higher plants in the Ab-e-Istada lake is the pondweed Ruppia maritima with colonies of Taraxacum monochlamydeum forming conspicious vegetation on mudflats around the lake. Some Characeae occur in Dasht-e-Nawar, as well as in Band-e-Amir.

Azonal Vegetation (saline flats)

Deserts are arid areas, where salinity close to the erosion basins is a common natural phenomenon. By irrigation without drainage in agricultural areas also salinity is enhanced, and after a few decades those fields are unproductive and have to be abandoned. They are taken over by a halophytic vegetation. The irano-turanian floristic region is very rich in halophytic species (Breckle 1986, 2000, 2002, Mirazai & Breckle 1978). It is an evolutionary center for Chenopodiaceae. Some of the above mentioned endorrheic lakes (Hamun-e-Puzak and Kol-e-Hashmat Khan, Ab-e-Istada, Dasht-e-Nawar etc.) are in part huge salt swamps, where a rich halophytic vegetation occurs with Salsola spp., Suaeda spp., Halocnemum strobilaceum, Halostachys caspica, spp., Halocharis spp., Halimocnemis spp., Gamanthus ssp., Seidlitzia rosmarinus and many other genera from Chenopodiaceae, but also Limonium spp., Zygophyllum, Nitraria, Frankenia spp., Tamarix spp., Reaumuria spp., Cressa cretica etc. are common.

Cited Literature (Additional citations, see Publication List Breckle on Afghanistan)

Flohn, H. 1969: Zum Klima und Wasserhaushalt des Hindukusch und der benachbarten Hochgebrge. Erdkunde 23: 205-215

Freitag,H. 1971a: Die natürliche Vegetation Afghanistans. Beitrage zur Flora und Vegetation Afghanistans I.

18

Ethnomedicinal Botany of the Eastern Himalaya

This paper investigates the wealth of medicinal plants used by the Apatani tribe of Arunachal Pradesh. Apatani have traditionally settled in seven villages in the Ziro valley of Lower Subansiri district of Arunachal Pradesh in the Eastern Himalayan region of India. The present study has resulted in the documentation of 158 medicinal plant species used by the Apatani group of villages.

These medicinal plant species were distributed across 73 families and 124 genera. Asteraceae was the most dominant family (19 species, 11 genera) of medicinal plants, followed by Zingiberaceae, Solanaceae, Lamiaceae and Araceae. For curing ailments, the use of aboveground plant parts was higher (80%) than the belowground plant parts in the Apatani group of villages.

Of the aboveground plant parts, leaf was used in the majority of cases (56 species), followed by fruit. Different belowground plant forms such as root, tuber, rhizome, bulb and pseudo-bulb were used by Apatani as a medicine. About 52 types of ailments were cured by using these 158 medicinal plant species. The results of this study are further discussed in the changing socio-economic contexts.

INTRODUCTION

Tribal communities are mainly the forest dwellers who have accumulated a rich knowledge on the uses of various forests and forest products over the centuries. India possesses a total of 427 tribal communities, of these more than 130 major tribal communities live in North East India, which is comprised of the 8 states Meghalaya, Mizoram, Manipur, Tripura, Sikkim, Assam, Nagaland and Arunachal Pradesh.

The major tribal communities of the North East India have been categorized into sub-tribes and if these sub-tribes are taken into account the total number of tribal groups reaches up to 300. In general, the tribes of North East India have been categorized into two broad ethnic communities, such as the Khasi and the Jaintia tribe of Meghalaya, who belong to 'Monkhemar' culture of Austoic dialect, and the rest of the tribal groups are basically Mongoloid, who belongs to Tibeto-Burman subfamily of Tibeto-Chinese group.

In the North East India, each state contains a number of tribal groups. Arunachal Pradesh is one of the states in North East India inhabited by 28 major tribes and 110 sub-tribes. Arunachal Pradesh is the 12th mega biodiversity region of the world. More than 545 species of orchids have been reported from the state, which is the highest number of orchid species known from any single state of India.

Such a rich biodiversity in the state has provided an initial advantage to its inhabitants for observing, and scrutinizing the rich flora and fauna for developing their own traditional knowledge. Most of the tribe economies have been historically engaged in subsistence agriculture or hunting and gathering. Over the years, they have developed a great deal of knowledge on the use of plants and plant products in curing various ailments.

A review of the literature reveals that many tribal areas and tribal communities in the eastern Himalayan region of India are either under explored or unexplored with regard to their floral wealth used in curing diseases.

The Apatani is one such little studied tribe of Arunachal Pradesh. Therefore, a need was felt to gather in-depth information on the plant species used by this tribal group and suggest that similar studies need to be carried out across the various groups of tribes for comparison as well as for documenting the knowledge which may be under threat due to the influence of modernization. The present paper thus aims to highlight and record in detail the traditional knowledge of the Apatani tribe on the use of medicinal plant species growing in and around their settlements.

Study Area: Apatani Group of Villages

Literally, the word Apatani is composed of two words-'Apa' and 'Tani'. According to the local language, 'Apa' means display of affection and 'Tani' stands for human race.

The Apatani, generally, speak in their own language which has no script. Traditionally, they had settled in seven villages (e.g. Hong, Hari, Billa, Dutta, Hija, Mudang-Tage, and Michi Bamin) those were organized in accordance with the traditional lines of the three forefathers called Nichi-Nitii, Tinii-Diibo-Dre-Hija, and Talyang-Hao.

These 7 villages are located in the Ziro valley of Lower Subansiri district in the central western part of Arunachal Pradesh in India between 26°55'-28°21' N and 92°40'-94°21' E. The Ziro valley (often called the Apatani valley) lies between the Panior and Kamla (Kuru) rivers at an altitude of 1524 to 2738 m a.m.s.l.

The Apatani group of villages is located at 2200 m elevation. The Apatani migrated to the present location from the Talle Valley located in south eastern region [7]. The pattern of Apatani villages is that of string settlements (village houses are in a straight line) and homes are made of bamboo and timber. The Apatani belong to the Tibeto-Mongoloid stock, and trace their descent from one legendary ancestor, the Abotani.

The Apatani believe in indigenous religion called as 'Donyi-Polo' and are patriarchal in social system. The traditional village council, which regulates and administers the community, consists of three bodies namely Akha Buliyang, Yapha Buliyang and Ajang Buliyang.

In each of these traditional institutions has one or two persons represent from each clan. Earlier, the Apatani had prominent tattoo marks on the face to distinguish themselves from other communities settled nearby. However, the practice of tattooing has been discouraged in the recent past and now is on the verge of extinction.

In 1991 census the population of Apatani was 22,526. The decadal (1991-2001) growth rate of the Apatani is 8.62%, which is much lower than that of the state (26.21%).

The Ziro valley has an area of 1058 km2 of which 43 km2 is under agriculture, and remaining under forests, plantations and settlements. It is bounded with the areas traditionally belonging to neighbouring Nishi tribe. The land holding size varies from 0.02 to 10.00 ha with over 93% holdings consisting of 0.026-3.00 ha.

The Ziro valley exhibits a humid sub-tropical to temperate type of climate with 108.1 cm rainfall and a temperature ranges from a maximum of 30.6°C to minimum of 1.1°C. The climatic, altitudinal and geomorphological variations have shaped the two major vegetation types in and around the study area-sub-tropical forests and temperate forests. Sub-tropical forests in the study area are represented by Castanopsis indica, Acer sp., Pinus wallichiana and Pinus roxburghii, whereas, the temperate forests are represented by Quercus glauca, Alnus nepalensis, Castanopsis indica, Pyrus sp., Prunus sp., Populus sp. and Acer sp. Many shrub species such as Berberis wallichiana, Viburnum foetidum, Prunus sp., Rubus sp., Spirea sp. and Symplocos sp. occur in the forested areas.

Table: Demographic profile of the Apatani in Ziro valley of Arunachal Pradesh

Year	Population		% to state
	Apatani	Arunachal Pradesh	
1961	10,793	3,36,588	3.21
1971	12,888	4,68,511	2.75
1981	16,580	6,31,839	2.62
1991	22,526	8,64,558	2.61
2001	24,650	10,91,117	2.26

Source: Census of India, Part IX-B, Government of India.

MEDICINAL PLANTS SURVEY

A literature survey was carried out for compilation of existing information on the medicinal plants used by Apatani villagers. In addition, field surveys in Apatani villages were undertaken during May and June 2005 to gather data on the indigenous uses of medicinal plant species by the Apatani. During the survey period, information was also gathered using semi-structured questionnaires on types of ailments cured by the traditional use of medicinal plants and plant parts used in curing different ailments. Cross-checking of data was made with the help of group discussions among different age classes of Apatani villagers that include both the genders of the society. The participant observation method was also employed to understand the methods and techniques adopted by the Apatani in curing diseases.

The surrounding forested area and agricultural land of the Apatani villages were also surveyed with local youths and knowledgeable elders for the identification of various medicinal plant species and their indigenous uses. Since there is lack of comprehensive records on floral diversity of North East Himalaya including Arunachal Pradesh, the plant specimens were identified through various floral inventories. The collected information was analyzed, and correlation was made between different genera and species of the medicinal plants in order to understand the pattern in medicinal plant uses and occurrences.

RESULTS AND DISCUSSION

The Apatani mainly subsist on agriculture and animal husbandry. Wet-rice cultivation is their most important agriculture practice. One of the Apatani proverbs reads "Tanii hii jebi danii", which means the Apatani depend on wet-rice cultivation. The Apatani have also developed a unique system of fish farming in their wet-rice croplands. They use available natural resources such as bamboo, cane, pine, Phragmites sp. and Castanopsis sp. in order to check the soil erosion, to conserve the soil fertility, to cultivate varieties of rice landraces, and to culture the fish in an integrated manner. Two species of bamboo

(Phyllostachys bambusoides and Dendrocalamus hamiltonii) are also cultivated in private lands by the Apatani for construction of houses and other domestic uses.

Bamboo shoots are also consumed by the Apatani as a vegetable. Apong, a locally prepared beer by fermenting rice, finger millet and barley, is an important beverage of the Apatani, which they prefer to consume with mutton. Domestic and semi-domestic cattle also play important role in maintaining the economic status of the Apatani. Possessing a large number of domestic animals is an indication of the prosperity of their respective owner. Mithun (Bos frontalis) is preferred mostly for the meat. In addition, pigs, cows, and multiple varieties of birds and fish are consumed by the Apatani. A number of wild edible fruits and vegetables are also collected by the Apatani from the nearby forested areas to supplement the domestic nutritional requirements.

Traditionally, the Apatani group of villages was not only familiar with the knowledge of medicinal plants but they were also expert traders and met their necessities in exchange of paddy, which was always in excess of their requirements. Earlier, they had no connection with the plains of Assam due to obstructions created by the Nishi who were earning a lot by acting as middlemen between the Apatani and the people residing in the plains. However, the Apatani had occupied a compact area in Ziro valley and were one of the self-sufficient tribes in North East India. Their immediate dependence on nature had developed knowledge which ultimately is reflected in their traditional culture, religion, local belief, folklore, taboos language and dialects. For many centuries, the Apatani had kept alive a self-managed system of folk medicine that was mainly based on herbal remedies. Their ingenuity still reflects their traditional management and sharing of natural resources in a way that there is optimum utilization of such resources. The Nishi are one of the neighbours of the Apatani who live at lower elevations and are the most populous tribe in the state. Over the past few decades, the interaction between the Apatani and the Nishi has increased many fold due to migration of Apatani people in search of better education in Itanagar, a capital of Arunachal Pradesh. The availability of motor roads and the invasion of modern civilization have also enhanced the day to day interaction and the exposure of the Apatani to the rest of the world. Such interaction has provided a possible sharing of traditional knowledge of the Apatani with their neighbouring community.

During the present course of investigations, a total of 158 medicinal plant species used by the Apatani group of villages were documented. These medicinal plant species were distributed across 73 families and 124 genera. In terms of number of medicinal plant species, Asteraceae was the most dominant family (19 species, 11 genera) of medicinal plants, followed by Zingiberaceae, Solanaceae, Lamiaceae, Araceae, and Verbanaceae. There was a significant positive correlation ($r = 0.92$, $p > 0.01$) between the number of genera and number of species used as medicine by the Apatani. The invention of maximum number of uses of Asteraceae by the Apatani tribe demonstrates the dominance of Asteraceae around the Apatani group of villages. Asteraceae is the most dominant family of medicinal plants across the North Eastern States of India.

Table: Dominant families of medicinal plants used by the Apatani in terms of number of species occupied

Family	Genera	Species
Asteraceae	11	19
Zingiberaceae	4	8
Solanaceae	2	7
Lamiaceae	5	5
Araceae	5	5
Verbenaceae	3	5
Rutaceae	3	5
Rosaceae	2	5
Urticaceae	4	4
Acanthaceae	4	4

J Ethnobiol Ethnomed. 2005; 1: 11.

Published online 2005 November 16. doi: 10.1186/1746-4269-1-11.

Table: Medicinal plant species, plant parts used and ailments cured by the Apatani of Ziro valley in Arunachal Pradesh

Sl No.	Species	Family	Part used	Uses
1	Acorus calamus L.	Araceae	Root	Cut, wounds, skin diseases, bone fracture
2	Ageratum conyzoides L.	Asteraceae	Leaf	Cut, wounds
3	Allium cepa L.	Liliaceae	Bulb	Eye pain
4	Allium hookeri Thwait.	Liliaceae	Bulb	Eruption of skin, cough, cold, wounds
5	Alocasia forniculata (Roxb.) Schott.	Araceae	Root	Crack of heels
6	Alstonia scholaris (L.) Br.	Apocynaceae	Leaf, bark	Headache, stomach disorder, menstrual disorder
7	Amomum aromaticum Roxb.	Zingiberaceae	Leaf, seed	Fever, abortion
8	Amorphophallus paeoniifolius (Dennst.) Nicolson	Araceae	Corn	Piles
9	Andrographis paniculata (Burm. f.) Wall. ex Nees	Acanthaceae	Leaf	Dysentery
10	Anisomeles indica (L.) O.K.	Lamiaceae	Shoot	Bodyache
11	Angiopteris evecta (Forst.) Hoffm.	Angiopteridaceae	Stem	Health tonic
12	Antidesma acidum Retz.	Euphorbiaceae	Leaf	Wounds
13	Argemone mexicana L.	Papaveraceae	Shoot	Skin diseases
14	Artemisia indica Willd.	Asteraceae	Leaf	Bodyache, asthma, skin diseases
15	Artemisia maritima L.	Asteraceae	Shoot	Blood purification
16	Artemisia nilagirica (Cl.) Pamp.	Asteraceae	Leaf	Cough, headache, sores
17	Asplenium nidus L.	Aspleniaceae	Leaf	Ulcer

18	Barleria prionitis L.	Acanthaceae	Leaf	Cough
19	Begonia roxburghii (Miq.) DC.	Begoniaceae	Leaf	Indigestion
20	Berberis wallichiana (Wall.) Brongn.	Berberidaceae	Fruit, root	Indigestion, bodyache
21	Bergenia ciliata (Haw.) Sternb.	Saxifragaceae	Root, leaf	Cut, wounds
22	Brassiopsis glomarulata (Bl.) Regel.	Araliaceae	Fruit	Cough
23	Buddleja asiatica Lour.	Buddlejaceae	Leaf	Inflammation
24	Callicarpa macrophylla Vahl	Verbenaceae	Leaf	Headache
25	Callicarpa vastita Roxb.	Verbenaceae	Leaf	Indigestion
26	Calotropis gigantea (L.) Br.	Asclepiadaceae	Root	Dog bite
27	Canarium resiniferum Brace ex King	Burseraceae	Fruit	Urinary complaints
28	Capparis spinosa Lam.	Capparaceae	Root	Rheumatic pain
29	Cardamine hirsuta L.	Brassicaceae	Leaf	Indigestion
30	Castanopsis tribuloides (Sm.) DC.	Fagaceae	Stem	Cough, goiter, indigestion
31	Centella asiatica L.	Apiaceae	Shoot	Constipation, gastritis, blood purification
32	Chenopodium ambrosioides L.	Chenopodidaceae	Leaf	Toothache
33	Christella parasitica (L.) Lev.	Thelypteridaceae	Fronds	Cut, wounds
34	Chromolaena odorata (L.) King & Robinson	Asteraceae	Leaf	Cut, wounds, headache, fever
35	Cirsium lapskyle Petral.	Asteraceae	Shoot	Indigestion
36	Cissampelos pareira L.	Menispermaceae	Tuber	Health tonic
37	Clerodendrum glandulosum Coleb. ex Wall.	Verbenaceae	Leaf	Blood pressure, fever, cough
38	Clerodendrum serratum (L.) Moonb	Verbenaceae	Leaf	Eye disorders
39	Coelogyne pectata Lindl.	Orchidaceae	Pseudobulb	Burns

40	Colocasia affinis Schott	Araceae	Leaf	Fever, respiratory disorder
41	Crassocephalum crepidioides (Benth.) Moore	Asteraceae	Leaf	Indigestion, headache, stomachache, cut, wounds
42	Crotolaria pallida Ait.	Fabaceae	Root	Bodyache
43	Croton roxburghii Balak	Euphorbiaceae	Fruit	Indigestion
44	Curcuma caesia Roxb.	Zingiberaceae	Rhizome	Cough, asthma
45	Curcuma aromatica Salisb.	Zingiberaceae	Whole plant	Blood purification
46	Curcuma zedoaria Rosc.	Zingiberaceae	Rhizome	Cold, cough
47	Cuscuta reflexa Roxb.	Cuscutaceae	Whole plant	Purgative
48	Cyathea gigantea (Wall. ex Hk. f.) Holt.	Cyatheaceae	Leaf	Bodyache
49	Cyathula prostrata (L.) Bl.	Amaranthaceae	Shoot	Appetizer, dysentery, skin diseases
50	Cymbidium aloifolium (L.) Sw.	Orchidaceae	Tuber	Wounds
51	Dendrocnide sinuta (Bl.) Chew.	Urticaceae	Leaf	Urogenital disorder, toothache, dysentery
52	Dicranopteris linearis (Burm. f.) Und.	Gleicheniaceae	Whole plant	Indigestion
53	Dicrocephala bicolor (Roth) Sch.	Asteraceae	Shoot	Digestive problems
54	Dillenia indica L.	Dilleniaceae	Furit	Stomachache
55	Dioscorea alata L.	Dioscoraceae	Tuber	Indigestion
56	Dioscorea bulbifera L.	Dioscoraceae	Tuber	Indigestion
57	Dioscorea hamiltonii Hk. f.	Dioscoraceae	Tuber	Dysentery
58	Diplazium esculentum (Retz.) Sw.	Athyriaceae	Fronds	Constipation
59	Ecbolium viride (Forsk) Alston	Meliaceae	Root	Rheumatism
60	Eclipta prostrata (L.) L.	Asteraceae	Shoot	Cut, wounds
61	Elaeagnus caudata Sch. ex Momiyama	Elaeagnaceae	Fruit	Health tonic
62	Elaeagnus pyriformis Hk. f.	Elaeagnaceae	Fruit	Constipation

63	Elatostema platyphyllum Wedd.	Urticaceae	Root	Vomiting
64	Elsholzia blanda (Benth.) Benth.	Lamiaceae	Leaf	Itching
65	Eluesine coracana (L.) Gaertn.	Poaceae	Grains	Stomach disorder, tonic, cold
66	Eupatorium odoratum L.	Asteraceae	Leaf	Wounds, cut
67	Erigeron bonariensis L.	Asteraceae	Leaf	Nose block
68	Eryngium foetidum L.	Apiaceae	Seed	Madness, headache
69	Ficus benjamina L.	Moraceae	Stem	Stomach disorder
70	Ficus hirta Vahl	Moraceae	Fruit	Wounds, cut
71	Gerbera pilosellioides (L.) Cass.	Asteraceae	Leaf	Rheumatic pain
72	Gloriosa superba L.	Liliaceae	Tuber	Killing lice in hairs
73	Gmelina arborea Roxb.	Verbenaceae	Leaf	Stomach disorder
74	Gynostemma pedata Bl.	Cucurbitaceae	Leaf	Throat ache
75	Gynura biscolor (Roxb. ex Willd.) DC.	Asteraceae	Leaf	Intestinal worms
76	Gynura nepalensis DC.	Asteraceae	Leaf	Indigestion
77	Hedychium coronarium Koen.	Zingiberaceae	Rhizome	Bodyache
78	Hedychium dekianum Rao & Verma	Zingiberaceae	Rhizome	Cut, wounds
79	Hedychium spicatum Buch.-Ham. ex Sm.	Zingiberaceae	Rhizome	Stomach disorder
80	Hibiscus rosa-sinensis L.	Malvaceae	Flower	Reproductive disorders
81	Houttuynia cordata Thunb.	Saururaceae	Shoot	Freshness, good sleep, heart disorders
82	Hyptis suaveolens (L.) Poit.	Lamiaceae	Leaf	Itching, cough, cold
83	Hypericum japonicum Thunb. ex Murr.	Hypericaceae	Stem	Cut, wounds
84	Impatiens latifolia L.	Balsaminaceae	Leaf	Headache, digestive disorder
85	Impatiens racemosa DC.	Balsaminaceae	Leaf	Digestive disorder
86	Indigofera tinctoria L.	Fabaceae	Root	Wound
87	Jasminum humile L.	Oleaceae	Root	Ringworm

88	Laginaria siceraria (Molina) Standl.	Cucurbitaceae	Fruit	Burns
89	Leonotis nepetifolia R. Br.	Lamiaceae	Seed	Burns
90	Lithocarpus dealbatus (Miq.) Rehder	Fagaceae	Fruit	Indigestion
91	Litsea cubeba (Lour.) Pers.	Lauraceae	Fruit	Cough, cold, hair tonic, indigestion, good sleep
92	Litsea salicifolia (Nees) Hk.f.	Lauraceae	Fruit	Bone fracture, stomach disorder
93	Lygodium scandens (L.) Sw.	Schizaeaceae	Leaf	Skin diseases
94	Mahonia napalensis DC.	Berberidaceae	Stem	Itching
95	Measa indica (Roxb.) DC.	Myrsinaceae	Fruit	Indigestion
96	Mikania micrantha Kunth.	Asteraceae	Leaf	Itching, skin diseases, headache
97	Miliusa roxburghiana (Wall. ex Griff.) Hk. f. & Th.	Annonaceae	Leaf	Headache
98	Molineria crassifolia Baker	Hypoxidaceae	Fruit	Diarrhoea
99	Molineria recurveta (Dryand) Hebbert.	Hypoxidaceae	Leaf	Bodyache
100	Mucuna pruriens (L.) DC.	Fabaceae	Stem	Eye disorder
101	Murraya koenigii (L.) Spr.	Rutaceae	Leaf	Stomach trouble
102	Musa paradissica L.	Musaceae	Fruit	Indigestion
103	Myrica esculenta Ham. ex D. Don.	Myricaceae	Fruit, bark	Indigestion, skin eruption
104	Myrsine semiserrata Wall.	Myrsinaceae	Seed	Skin diseases
105	Oenanthe javanica (Bl.) DC.	Apiaceae	Shoot	Indigestion
106	Oroxylum indicum (L.) Vent.	Bignoniaceae	Seed	Purgative, headache
107	Osbeckia stellata Buch.-Ham. ex D. Don	Melastomataceae	Leaf	Toothache
108	Oxalis corniculata L.	Oxalidaceae	Shoot	Appetizer, headache
109	Paedaria foetida L	Rubiaceae	Stem	Gastritis, diarrhea, stomach disorder
110	Passiflora foetida L.	Passifloraceae	Fruit	Respiratory disorder

111	Photinia integrifolia Lindl.	Rosaceae	Fruit	Indigestion
112	Perilla frutescens (L.) Britt.	Lamiaceae	Seed	Fever, headache
113	Physalis angulata L.	Solanaceae	Fruit	Gastric trouble
114	Physalis minima L.	Solanaceae	Fruit	Gastric trouble
115	Physalis peruviana L.	Solanaceae	Leaf	Pain in pregnancy
116	Picrorhiza kurrooa Benth.	Scrophulariaceae	Root	Cold, fever
117	Pinus roxburghii Sarg.	Pinaceae	Seed	Indigestion
118	Piper brachystachyum Wall.	Piperaceae	Seed	Cough
119	Piper trioicum Roxb.	Piperaceae	Root	Cough
120	Plantago major L.	Plantaginaceae	Leaf	Constipation
121	Plectranthus japonicus (Burm. f.) Koidz.	Acanthaceae	Leaf	Fever
122	Polygonum nepalense Meissn.	Polygonaceae	Leaf	Indigestion
123	Polygonum perfoliatum L.	Polygonaceae	Leaf	Indigestion
124	Portulaca oleracea L.	Portulacaceae	Stem, leaf	Appetizer
125	Pouzolzia hirta (Bl.) Hassk.	Urticaceae	Root	Constipation
126	Pterospermum acerifolium Willd.	Sterculiaceae	Flower	Earache
127	Rhus chinensis Miller	Anacardiaceae	Fruit	Blood dysentery
128	Rubia cordifolia L.	Rubiaceae	Shoot	Stomachache
129	Rubus calycinus Wall.	Rosaceae	Fruit	Stomach disorder
130	Rubus ellipticus Sm.	Rosaceae	Fruit	Indigestion
131	Rubus paniculatus Sm.	Rosaceae	Fruit	Stomach disorder
132	Rubus roseafolius Sm.	Rosaceae	Fruit	Indigestion
133	Rumex nepalensis Spr.	Polygonaceae	Leaf	Indigestion
134	Saurauria roxburghii Wall.	Saurauriaceae	Leaf	Constipation
135	Schefflera glomerata L.	Araliaceae	Fruit	Indigestion
136	Schizostachium capitatum	Poaceae	Shoot	Diarrhea, dysentery, stomach

	(Munro) Majumdar			disorder
137	Senna alata (L.) Roxb.	Caesalpiniaceae	Leaf	Skin diseases
138	Senna tora (L.) Roxb.	Ceasalpiniaceae	Leaf	Low blood pressure
139	Sphenomeris chinensis (L.) Maxon	Lindsaeceae	Fronds	Sprains
140	Solanum kurzii Brace ex Prain	Solanaceae	Fruit	Cough, worms infestation
141	Solanum myriacanthum Dunal	Solanaceae	Seeds	Toothache
142	Solanum nigrum L.	Solanaceae	Leaf	Liver tonic, indigestion
143	Solanum torvum Sm.	Solanaceae	Fruit	Cough, skin diseases
144	Sonchus asper (L.) Hill	Asteraceae	Shoot	Indigestion
145	Sonchus arvensis L.	Asteraceae	Shoot	Stomachache, gastritis
146	Spilanthus clava L.	Asteraceae	Leaf	Throat pain
147	Spilanthes paniculata DC.	Asteraceae	Leaf	Constipation
148	Stellaria media (L.) Vill.	Caryophyllaceae	Leaf	Itching
149	Stereospermum chelonoides (L. f.) DC.	Bignoniaceae	Leaf	Sprain
150	Strobilanthus helictus T. Anders.	Acanthaceae	Shoot	Indigestion
151	Terminalia chebula Retz.	Combretaceae	Fruit	Cough
152	Toddalia aculeata Pers.	Rutaceae	Fruit	Throat pain
153	Urtica dioica L.	Urticaceae	Leaf	Bone fracture
154	Vernonia cinerea (L.) Less	Asteraceae	Leaf	Indigestion
155	Zanthoxylum acanthopodium DC.	Rutaceae	Fruit	Dysentery
156	Zanthoxylum armatum DC.	Rutaceae	Fruit	Cold, cough, fever, appetizer
157	Zanthoxylum oxyphyllum Edgew.	Rutaceae	Fruit	Stomach disorder
158	Zingiber officinale Rosc.	Zingiberaceae	Rhizome	Cough

J Ethnobiol Ethnomed. 2005; 1: 11.

Published online 2005 November 16. doi: 10.1186/1746-4269-1-11.

Different parts of medicinal plant species were used by the Apatani as a medicine. For curing ailments, the use of aboveground plant parts was higher (80%) than the belowground plant parts. Of the aboveground plant parts, leaf was used in the majority of cases (56 species), followed by fruits. Different belowground plant forms such as root, tuber, rhizome, bulb and pseudo-bulb were also used by the Apatani as a source of curing ailments. The whole plant of 3 species [e.g. Curcuma aromatica Salisb., Cuscuta reflexa Roxb. and Dicranopteris linearis (Burm. f.) Und.] was used as medicine. These 158 medicinal plant species were used in curing about 52 types of ailments, of which the highest numbers of plant species (40 species) were used for the treatment of gastrointestinal disorders such as indigestion and constipation. About 19 medicinal plant species were used in curing cough and cold, and 15 medicinal plant species were used for healing cuts and wounds.

Table: Patterns in Apatani use of medicinal plant parts

Aboveground plant parts used	**Number of Species**	**Belowground plant parts used**	**Number of Species**
Whole shoot	15	Root	14
Leaf	56	Tuber	6
Fruit	31	Rhizome	6
Seed	10	Bulb	2
Stem	6	Pseudo-bulb	1
Fronds	4	Corn	1
Bark	2		
Flower	2		
Total	**126**	**Total**	**30**

J Ethnobiol Ethnomed. 2005; 1: 11.

Published online 2005 November 16. doi: 10.1186/1746-4269-1-11.

Previous studies carried out in North East India have reported 41 medicinal plant species used by the Apatani of Arunachal Pradesh. However, they had selected many North Eastern States and 12 different tribal communities for investigations. Based on their experiences, they had suggested the need of carrying out detailed investigations of each tribe. So far different authors have reported 1350 species of plants used in ethnomedicinal preparations, 665 species of food plants and 899 species for miscellaneous uses from the entire North East India. The present inventory of 158 medicinal plant species as used by the Apatani is one of its kinds in terms of the highest number of species recorded so far used by a single tribe of the North East India. This fact provides a strength to the statements of earlier researchers that North East India is still under-explored and certain areas in the district of Subansiri still remain unexplored.

Table: Major ailments cured by the Apatani in terms of using the plant species

Ailments	Number of plants used
Indigestion	40
Cough and cold	19
Cut and wounds	15
Headache	12
Stomach disorder	11
Skin diseases	11
Fever	8
Body-ache	6
Dysentery	6
Throat-ache	5

J Ethnobiol Ethnomed. 2005; 1: 11.

Published online 2005 November 16. doi: 10.1186/1746-4269-1-11.

Hence, a need for detailed investigations of ethnobotanical knowledge held by each tribal community in North East India is required before such valuable knowledge vanishes. In spite of the rich wealth of bio-resources and potential, development is far from meeting the expectations of local people in Arunachal Pradesh mainly in terms of existing health care facilities and herbal industries. Ethnomedicinal knowledge is also important from a humanitarian point of view in that in long run as this knowledge may help to identify important medicinal uses that can help in curing and healthcare around the world. Attempts should be made to share the benefits arising from such knowledge with its holders. The present inventory of medicinal plants used by the Apatani opens new avenues to scrutinize such a rich natural resource for further analysis in order to develop the potential of herbal medicine.

19

Design and Development of a Himalayan Studies Information System for India

The ever-increasing need for information, with its complexity and escalating costs; the enormous growth in publications, and the emergence of subject specialization have compelled librarians to share resources through information networks and systems. This paper describes the necessity of networking among the Himalayan Studies and Research Centers in India, allowing the sharing of information originating from the Himalayan Studies Information System (HIMIS). The paper also discusses in brief the definition of information systems, as well as the objectives and needs of a proposed HIMIS.

The recent advancements in the computer, communications, and networking technologies have brought about three paradigm shifts. There is the shift of information resources from print to electronic media, the shift in the role of information providers from passive to proactive, and the shift from manual to automated information delivery.

This has presented library and information professionals with a tremendous challenge, that of playing a proactive role not only in their routine activities (acquisition, processing, and dissemination), but also in the actual learning process of their clientele. Library and information professionals have to learn to scan, filter, interpret, analyze, repackage, and deliver information from a variety of sources in ways that are meaningful to their users.

Himalaya, the greatest physical feature of the earth, is not only an integral part of history and heritage, but it has also assumed the form of a social, cultural, and geo-political reality that cannot be ignored or underestimated. This mountain range makes an enormous contribution to our contemporary life, even as it influenced our history and mythology. Furthermore, this influence promises to extend even to the future.

The Himalayas have always remained a source of fascination and inspiration for people from all walks of life, and have been deemed by the peoples of the subcontinent to be the cradle of human civilization. The variety of cultures, terrains, forest physiographies, flora, and fauna of this region has lured the intelligentsia of the world since time immemorial. In recent years, however, the Himalayas have become the focus of attention of scientists and government alike. Efforts are underway for a better understanding of its highly complex environmental and ecological systems, and to bring about an all-around development of the region, which has remained backward throughout the centuries.

There has been a tremendous explosion of data and information in recent years, particularly in the field of Himalayan resources, with an increase in the number of research and development institutions at the national and international level. While most of these research institutions and universities possess excellent libraries and information centers, there is at present no information network by which coordination and sharing of resources could be effected for the mutual benefit of each of the existing libraries. Because there is little access to the right information at the right time, it has become difficult for one single organization to collect the data and information that are required by policy makers, administrators, and research scientists. The other scientific departments of the government of India have already started planning to begin information networking in their respective areas. Some of these projects are completed and others are in the process of implementation.

During the last decades, India has been active in setting up information systems and networks, and considerable progress has been achieved in this area. Since most of the information related to the Himalayas is scattered in different research-andstudies centers all over India, there is a need to develop a Himalayan Studies Information System (HIMIS). HIMIS will be a computer-communication network for linking various libraries and information centers of research and development (R&D) institutions, universities, and nongovernmental organizations (NGOs) working on the Himalayas. The system, therefore, has to take into account the specific information requirements of each development sector so far as its relevance to the Himalayas is concerned.

DEFINING INFORMATION SYSTEMS

The purpose of an information system is to provide accurate and relevant information to users at the right time and at the appropriate level of detail. This will help ensure that the corporate information resource is utilized fully.

Buckingham defines an information system as a system which assembles, stores, processes, and delivers information relevant to an organization (or to society), in such a way that the information is accessible and useful to those who wish to use it, including managers, staff, clients, and citizens. An information system is a human activity (social) system which may or may not involve the use of computer system.

Harrod's Librarians'Glossary defines information system as an organized procedure for collecting, processing, storing, and retrieving information to satisfy a variety of needs. According to Bowman, four different components can be identified:

(1) A store of useful information that has been accumulated over a period of time;

(2) a series of techniques used for adding material to and retrieving information from the store upon demand;

(3) a group of people who operate the system and are responsible for selecting information to be added, answering questions, organizing the store, and for implementing and modifying the techniques for both storage and retrieval; and

(4) the user. The ultimate test of any such system is the degree of satisfaction it gives the user who has specific information needs.

Setting Up HIMIS

The volume of Himalayan information plus the number of users and their various requirements have created a situation where it is almost impossible for any single library to provide information services singlehandedly. It is only through a network of all these information centers that some viable control of Himalayan information is feasible, not only at a local level, but also at the national and international level, to ensure effective use of information resources to the best advantage at a minimum cost. These days, information is being regarded as a national resource, and this awareness has led to computerbased information services such as indexing and abstracting at the national and international levels in the field of Himalayan studies.

Considering the importance of HIMIS, the government of India, through the agency of the National Information Systems in Science and Technology (NISSAT), should aid and support the proposed HIMIS generously. HIMIS is eminently suitable for several spheres of national activities, including planning and research. Reliable and timely information for decisionmaking becomes increasingly important for India, where a concept of social welfare has developed over the past three decades.

Many organizations have successfully developed their own information systems to plan, monitor, or control their research activities, and these have yielded increased research proficiency. The government should surely benefit from these methods. Apart from suggesting suitable solutions to the problems of planning, monitoring, allocation, control, and coordination of the departmental programs, one has to consider the special distribution of these programs. 10 The need to set up HIMIS has, therefore, to be considered in the context of the rapid development of Himalayan information as well as the increasing awareness of its relevance to societal development.

Objectives of HIMIS

HIMIS will be fully computerized so that an efficient system of storage and retrieval could be organized through networks linking all the Himalayanstudies centers with each other.

Users of the Proposed System

The proposed information system is planned to meet the needs of the specialists who are directly or indirectly concerned with Himalayan studies and research as a subject or as an activity. The following are the categories of those to whom the information would be supplied in a meaningful form within a reasonable time through HIMIS.

1. planners, policy makers, decision makers, administrators with respect to Himalayan development at government and nongovernment levels;
2. major institutions devoted to Himalayan study and research as a discipline;
3. international organizations such as the United Nations Educational, Scientific, and Cultural Organization (UNESCO) and the International Centre for Integrated Mountain Development (ICIMOD);
4. scientists engaged in the implementation and execution of plans and policies;
5. scientists and researchers engaged in Himalayan study and research;
6. teachers engaged in teaching about the Himalayas;
7. communicators who attempt to convey the information about development policies, plans, programs, and projects; and
8. NGOs working on projects about Himalayas.

Components of the Proposed HIMIS

For designing HIMIS, six essential components have been identified and proposed:

(1) National Resource Center on Himalayan Studies;

(2) library consortia;

(3) computerization of Himalayan institutes' libraries;

(4) information networking between Himalayan institutes;
(5) digitization of information material on Himalayas; and
(6) Himalayan information gateway.

National Resource Center on Himalayan Studies

As a part of the information system, a national-level resource center for Himalayan studies is also proposed on the pattern of other information centers in India, such as the National Information Center for Management Information (NICMAN), Ahmedabad, and the National Information Center for Food Science and Technology (NICFOS), Mysore, to name but two. These information centers have been established with the financial help of NISSAT, and at present are working as sectoral information centers of NISSAT. The planned objectives of the resource center are:

- to create a user-need-based information-technology (IT) resource center;
- to develop a strong collection of different types of information sources;
- to develop a user-friendly information-retrieval mechanism, such as an online facility for having access to international databases;
- to create an IT-based infrastructure;
- to develop a liaison with all Himalayan studies and research centers of India and other international centers for better information service through resource sharing and networking; and
- to provide bibliographies on selected topics on demand or even in advance of demand.

Himalayan-Studies Libraries Consortium

The concept of library consortia has been floating around for quite some time in India. Though it is the need of the hour, Indian libraries have yet to move in a definite direction in this regard. Strong resource-sharing activity among libraries, a prerequisite for the right attitude towards consortia activities, has not been as present in India as could be desired. Sudden influx of electronic information is forcing library consortia to materialize. Traditionally, the primary purpose of establishing a library consortium is to share physical resources amongst members. Access to resources is now considered more important than collection building, especially if the access is perpetual in nature. A library consortium helps libraries to get the benefit of wider access to electronic resources at an affordable cost and at the best terms of license.

A consortium with the collective strength of resources of the various institutions available to it is in a better position to address and resolve the problems of managing, organizing, and archiving electronic resources. The Indian National Digital Library in Science and Technology (INDEST) Consortium, which is set up by India's Ministry of Human Resource and Development, and UGC-Infonet, which is set up by the University Grant Commission of India are the best example of library consortia in India. Therefore, it is also proposed that a consortium of Himalayan institute's libraries may be formed to share the electronic resources of other libraries.

Computerization of Himalayan-Studies Institute's Libraries

Observance of an adherence to standard techniques, procedures, and methods is an essential prerequisite for the effective functioning of a network. Participating libraries will have to follow certain procedures and practices, without which the resources held by them cannot be effectively and meaningfully shared. In the context of library computerization, standardization is very necessary in such areas as classification, subject heading, and cataloging of various types of library materials; bibliographic description; and standard interchange of bibliographic data.

The Himalayan institutes have started the computerization of their libraries, beginning with creation of computerized databases of books, journals, reports, conference proceedings, annual reports, and monographs. But not all the housekeeping activities have been computerized. It is, therefore, suggested that every library should begin the computerization of each and every one of their activities. In India, libraries are generally using Dewey Decimal Classification (DDC) for classification, Anglo-American Cataloguing Rules (AACR) for cataloging rules, and Library of Congress (LC) for subject headings. Machine-Readable Cataloging (MARC) fomat is being used in the majority of libraries for creation of the database.

Himalayan Institute's Network

It is also proposed that there is a need for networking among the Himalayan Institute's libraries and information centers in the country for optimum resource sharing. Resource sharing and networking in libraries are powerful tools both for increasing productivity and enhancing services to meet the changing needs of library users. The proposed network ensures effective bibliographic control, document delivery, cooperative acquisition of serials and other literature in the field, and dissemination of relevant information. All the libraries and information centers of Himalayan-studies centers of India will be linked to the National Resource Center on Himalayan Studies. These libraries have been identified as regional centers of the proposed HIMIS. A network, in the first instance, envisaged a physical structure of links among the libraries and information centers established by means of computer and telecommunication links. Resource sharing is based on the concept that the collective strength and effectiveness of a group of libraries is greater than that of the sum of its individual members.

Digitization of Himalayan-Information Sources

Research publications are vital for any professional discipline, and it is crucial to preserve and provide access to them. Due to the amount of important information published in journals, conference proceedings, and reports, these efforts must be on a par with similar initiatives in other countries. Permanent preservation and enhanced access must be ensured vigorously now by the applications of new technology for digitizing and electronic access to valuable contents. Digitization provides unhindered access to information via computer and communication networks, justifying the need for using it for studying Himalayan literature. At present, very few copies of conference volumes, journals, and reports are published, and these are exclusively distributed to subscribers. The institutions involved rarely encourage readers to subscribe personally to such literature, thus placing it out of the reach of a large number of readers. The paper used for publishing these types of sources is of inferior quality, significantly reducing shelf life. In addition to providing increased and easy access to these publications, the most visible benefit of digitization is the fact that it preserves them.16 Some of the purposes of digitization, identified by different ongoing projects, are to:

- collect, store, and organize information and knowledge in digital form;
- promote economic and efficient delivery of information;
- leverage considerable investments in computing and communication infrastructures;
- strengthen communication and collaboration between research, government, and educational communities; and
- contribute for lifelong learning opportunities.

Keeping all of these points in mind, the digitization of Himalayan literature-particularly back volumes of journals, conference proceedings, annual reports, monographs, reports, and research papers published by Himalayan scientists in various journals, available in Himalayan studies centers of India-is very necessary. And it is one of the important and necessary aspects of the proposed HIMIS.

Himalayan-Studies Information and Subject Gateway

One of the major problems in accessing information from the Internet is that it is very difficult and time consuming to get reliable and relevant information in the shortest possible time. The effective and efficient way to provide easy access to quality information on the Internet is developing Subject Gateways in specific areas. "Subject gateways are online services and sites that provide searchable and browseable catalogues of Internetbased resources. Subject gateways will typically focus on a related set of academic subject areas."

To meet the information requirements of the scientific and academic communities in the digital era, various departments in India have developed or are still in the process of developing subject gateways in their respective areas. In recent years, there has been a tremendous explosion of data and information on the Internet, particularly in the field of Himalayan resources. As a result, it has become difficult for an individual-and also for an organization-to collect data and information. Thus, access to the right information at the right time has become very difficult.19 Since most of the information related to the Himalayas is scattered on the Web, it is necessary to develop a Himalayan-information subject gateway. This gateway will provide links to various libraries and information centers of R&D institutions, universities, and NGOs working in the Himalayan region. This gateway will be developed on the pattern of the Sayama Prasad Mookerjee Information Gateway of Social Science (SPMIGSS) developed by the Indian Council of Social Science Research (ICSSR). The system, therefore, has to take into account the specific information requirements of each development sector insofar as its relevance to the Himalayas is concerned.

Institutions Engaged in Himalayan Studies and Research

To reduce the quantum of information illiteracy, it is essential that information is readily available to an individual about the agencies that generate and publish Himalayan information-a huge task. The main hurdle has been the lack of appreciation of the role and importance of this type of institutional activity on a continuing basis. Bearing in mind the concern for setting up HIMIS, the first step is to identify the agencies and institutions that generate Himalayan information.

The information generated by these institutions may be contained in the form of files, computerized databases, reports, institutional publications, dissertations and theses, articles in journals, and conference and seminar papers. The information also is accumulated through state-of-the-art reports, serials, and yearbooks. India has a reasonably good institutional setup for Himalayan research.

CONCLUSION

All Himalayan studies and research centers have to assume the major responsibility for developing HIMIS. The government of India needs to be convinced of the usefulness and utility of such a system. It is necessary to emphasize that in the absence of such an information system, a large amount of research talent and resources will be wasted in duplicated efforts. It is hoped that the Himalayan institutions and scientists engaged in Himalayan studies and research will be able to impress upon the government of India the need for an early formulation and implementation of HIMIS. This information system will also supplement the resources and services of the participating libraries as "libraries acting together can more effectively satisfy user needs and thus meet the objectives at reduced costs." The success of the venture shall depend upon financial support, guidance, and encouragement received from government of India.

Bibliography

Aukland, L.: (1997). *The Effect of Selective Logging on Amphibian Diversity of Budongo Forest*, Uganda. B. A., Oxford University.

Babweteera, F.: (1998). *Influence of Gap-size and Age on the Diversity and Abundance of Climbers in Budongo Forest Reserve*, Uganda. M. Sc., Makerere University.

Bahati, J.: (1995). *Impact of Arboricidal Treatments on the Natural Regeneration of Species Composition in Budongo Forest*, Uganda. M. Sc., Makerere University.

Barrows, M.: (1996). *A Survey of the Intestinal Parasites of the Primates in Budongo Forest*, Uganda. Glasgow University.

Daily, G. C.: *Nature's Services: Social Dependence on Natural Ecosystem*, Island, Washington, DC, 1997.

Fairgrieve, C.: (1995). *The Comparative Ecology of Blue Monkeys (Cercopithecus mitis stuhlmanni) in Logged and Unlogged Forest, Budongo Forest Reserve*, Uganda, Edinburgh University.

Hills, C.: (1998). *An Analysis of Phylogeny and Gene Flow in a Population of Pan troglodytes schweinfuthii*. M. Sc., Oxford University.

Johnson, K.: (1993). *Local Uses of Budongo's Forest Products*. M. Sc., Oxford University.

Johnson, K.: (1996). *Hunting in the Budongo Forest*, Uganda. SWARA.

Johnson, K.: (1996). *Local attitudes towards the Budongo Forest*, Western Uganda. Indigenous Knowledge & Development Monitor.

Miller, P. L.: (1993). *Some dragonflies of the Budongo Forest*, Western Uganda. Opusc.

Mooney, H. A., Cushman, J. H., Medina, E., Sala, O. E. and Schulze, E. D.: *Functional Role of Biodiversity: A Global Perspective*, John Wiley, Chichster, UK, 1996.

Mork, K. & Solvang, R.: (1996). *Edge Effects on an Understorey Bird Community in Budongo Forest Reserve*, Uganda, Agricultural University of Norway.

N. K. Shah, S. D. Bhatt, and R. K. Pande: *Himalaya: Environment Resources and Development,* Almora, Shree Almora Book Depot, 1990.

Owiunji, I.: (1996). *The Long Term Effects of Forest Management on the Bird Community of Budongo Forest Reserve*, Uganda. M. Sc., Makerere University.

P. C. Bose: *"National Agricultural Research Information System,"* Delhi, Indian Library Association, 1991.

Reynolds, V. & Reynolds, F.: (1965). *Chimpanzees of the Budongo Forest*, New York, Rinehart and Winston.

Reynolds, V.: (1965). *Budongo: A Forest and its Chimpanzees*, London, Methuen.

S. P. Agrawal: *Handbook of Libraries, Archives and Information Centers in India*, New Delhi, Information Industry Pub., 1986.

Schulze, E. D. and Mooney, H. A., *Diversity and Ecosystem Function*, Springer-Verlag, Berlin, 1993.

Shekhar Pathak and Anup Sah: *Kumaon Himalaya,* Nainital: Kumaon Mandal Vikas, Nigam Ltd. by Gyanodaya Prakashan, 1993.

Shiel, D.: (1997). *The Ecology of Long-term Change in a Ugandan Rainforest*. D. Phil., Oxford University.

Singh, J. S. and Singh, S. P.: *Forests of Himalaya: Structure, Functioning and Impact of Man*, Gyanodaya Prakashan, Nainital, 1992.

Spini, L.: (1998). *The Frequency and Significance of Social Grooming in the Sonso Community of Chimpanzees at the Budongo Forest*, Uganda. M. Sc., Oxford University.

Wilson, E. O.: *The Diversity of Life*, Norton, New York, 1992.

Index

□□□